Delivering Essential

CONTENTS

PART III: WORKING BETTER, WORKING TOGETHER

5 **Joint Public–Private Initiatives and Developing-Country Health
Systems** 109
Annie Heaton

CONTRIBUTORS

Amir Attaran Associate Fellow, International Economics Programme, The Royal Institute of International Affairs; Associate Professor, Faculty of Law and Institute for Population Health, Ottawa.

Jim Attridge Visiting Fellow, Centre for Health Management, Imperial College London

Rifat Atun Director, Centre for Health Management, Imperial College London

Henk den Besten Director, International Dispensary Association, Amsterdam

Anne C. Conroy Special Assistant to the Vice President, Republic of Malawi

Joseph Gonzi International Dispensary Association, Amsterdam

Brigitte Granville Professor of International Economics and Economic Policy, Centre for Business Management, Queen Mary, University of London; formerly Head of International Economics Programme, The Royal Institute of International Affairs

Annie Heaton was Research Analyst for Save the Children UK between 1999 and 2003. She is now a freelance researcher.

Louisiana Lush Health Policy Unit, Department of Public Health and Policy, London School of Hygiene and Tropical Medicine

Justin C. Malewezi Vice President, Republic of Malawi

Bizwick Mwale Executive Director, National AIDS Commission, Republic of Malawi

Richard Pendame Secretary for Health, Republic of Malawi

Alexander S. Preker Chief Economist, Health, Nutrition and Population, World Bank, Washington, DC

Jeffrey L. Sturchio Vice President, External Affairs, Europe, Middle East and Africa, Merck & Co., Inc.

PREFACE AND ACKNOWLEDGMENTS

The theme of this book is given by Louisiana Lush: 'Medicines, along with healthcare providers, ... form the backbone of a health system, and access to these products is the key to maintaining good health and preventing premature death.' This volume attempts to provide a coherent overview of how to reinforce that backbone, without the distraction of ideology. At its heart is the practical question of how to get the best medicines consistently into the hands of all those in developing countries who need them.

The book is organized in three parts. Part I opens with a general survey by Louisiana Lush of why the poor lack access to essential medicines. The author discusses several tools that countries have to solve this problem, such as the development of an essential drugs list, clear treatment guidelines and the strengthening of health systems. As patients, especially the poorest ones, may find the cost of medicines prohibitive, this first chapter sets out a number of financing options, including public revenues, social health insurance, out-of-pocket spending and international financing through grants and loans. The responsibility to deliver medicines and to finance them appropriately lies with various bodies – national governments, international organizations, bilateral programmes and public–private partnerships – but the author concludes that their achievements so far have been mixed.

Alexander Preker in Chapter 2 makes a strong economic case for access to medicines. He stresses that in many low-income countries, health gaps lead to development traps. That is, improvements are needed in the standard of health in order to continue economic growth, but increased spending on health is often impossible owing to a lack of capacity to shift public expenditure towards the health sector. Raising health standards to allow for economic growth to continue is estimated to cost between $30 billion and $60 billion in countries with a per capita annual GDP of up to $7,000. A significant share of this expenditure would be used to pay for access to essential medicines. The author stresses that the most important source of increased health expenditure is economic growth. Donor support can be successful only at the margins, and if it favours countries that are committed to health spending.

Part II describes the divide between the needs of developing countries in search of essential medicines and the reality of medicines as a first-world commodity that reaches developing countries only with difficulty. In Chapter 3, Anne Conroy, Justin Malewezi, Bizwick Mwale and Richard Pendame highlight the frustrations of a small African country, Malawi, in responding to health crises. The authors illustrate from experience the challenges faced by developing countries in trying to mobilize sufficient resources to deliver a basic healthcare package and to scale up HIV/AIDS prevention, care and treatment. They present a picture of near total indifference on the part of international aid donors: even though Malawi is demonstrably a very poor and indebted country, and even though it has worked diligently to put forward a clear package of basic health needs and their costs, international aid donors have undermined its ambitions to do something meaningful about HIV/AIDS by making a series of swingeing cuts to the programme budgets it offered. The story is one of obstructionism rather than cooperation by the international organizations responsible for helping countries such as Malawi; and if it represents the typical experience of low-income countries, the prospect of mitigating crises such as HIV/AIDS is worse than bleak.

In Chapter 4, Jim Attridge and Rifat Atun expound upon the regulation and development of the pharmaceutical industry in emerging countries, which are important to ensure competitive access to essential medicines. They argue that developing countries have dual interests, determined by their public health and industrial policy objectives, which sometimes are at cross-purposes – intellectual property laws are an example. They propose a model which tries to balance the desire of emerging countries for the latest in pharmaceutical innovation with their ability to pay, given that newer medicines are generally priced higher than existing medicines because of their therapeutic advantages and because of the need to furnish an incentive for future R&D investment. The authors' general aim is to show that access to medicines and the existence of a sustainable pharmaceutical sector are mutually compatible objectives.

Part III contains four chapters on how the problem of access to medicines can be tackled by partnerships that, unlike in the past, include the private sector. Chapter 5, by Annie Heaton, discusses the recent proliferation of joint public–private initiatives (JPPIs) and outlines their key design characteristics and the nature of pharmaceutical companies' commitments to them. It stresses that JPPIs, to realize their full potential, must not be treated as one-off philanthropy or exceptionalism on the part of countries or companies but ought instead to be part of national health planning, with all that implies for 'staying the course' when it comes to the long-term shared goal of strengthening health systems.

In Chapter 6, Jeffrey L. Sturchio explains the Accelerating Access Initiative (AAI) for HIV/AIDS. Five companies, joined later by two others, responded to calls from UN organizations for a new public–private partnership that would expand the global response to AIDS. Although, as the author emphasizes, no specific criteria have been established for evaluating the 'success' of the AAI, its existence has acted as a catalyst for activities outside its framework. Moreover, the lessons learned, or the hypotheses supported, as a result of the AAI have contributed significantly to the shape, tenor and thrust of critical initiatives that have arisen since its founding. The AAI experience provides essential guidance about what may and may not work in countering the HIV/AIDS epidemic.

In Chapter 7, Henk den Besten and Joseph Gonzi tell the unique story of the International Dispensary Association (IDA), which is the world's largest non-profit distributor of essential medicines to developing countries. The IDA's core business model is based on sourcing generic medical products on a large-scale competitive basis; performing an independent quality assurance and quality control assessment of each product and supplier, using its own staff and laboratory facilities; and filling individual orders received from buyers in developing countries from its stock in Amsterdam. The value added for buyers is that they can purchase products of known quality, in a reliable supply chain, for little more than would be the case if they were to undertake the sourcing themselves.

In Chapter 8, Amir Attaran goes back to the question of understanding patents and out-licensing in the procurement of anti-retroviral medicines. He argues that the concern that patents impede access to medicines is answerable through a combination of careful investigation of patent status and prices with judicious steps to introduce remedies such as patent waivers and out-licensing where constraints demonstrably exist. The author calls for a consensus among international organizations in order to encourage progress in out-licensing.

The book ends with a general survey by Amir Attaran and Brigitte Granville of the major issues involved in delivering essential medicines. This final chapter summarizes the main steps that have been advocated. Drawing freely on the content of the volume, Chapter 9 proposes some broad recommendations that should guide policy.

We are grateful to Merck & Co., Inc. for its generous financial support for this publication. We warmly thank Joann Fong for her patience and assistance throughout this project, Kim Mitchell for his excellent copy-editing, and Matthew Link for designing another superb cover; and special thanks to Margaret May for so beautifully delivering another book on essential medicines after its long and difficult gestation.

A.A.
B.G.

GLOSSARY, ACRONYMS AND ABBREVIATIONS

AAI	Accelerating Access Initiative (for HIV/AIDS)
AIDS	Acquired immunodeficiency syndrome
API	Active pharmaceutical ingredient
ART	Anti-retroviral therapy
ARV	Anti-retroviral
CABS	Common Approach to Budgetary Support (IMF)
CARICOM	Caribbean Community
CEA	Cost-effectiveness analysis
CEE	Central and eastern Europe
CHAM	Christian Health Association of Malawi
COMISCA	Council of Health Ministries of Central America
DALY	Disability-adjusted life-year
DOTS	Directly Observed Therapy Strategy: a WHO-recommended tuberculosis control strategy
DTCA	Direct-to-consumer advertising
EBM	Evidence-based medicine
EC	European Commission
ECOWAS	Economic Community of West African States
EDL	WHO Model List of Essential Drugs (formerly Essential Drugs List)
EHP	Essential Healthcare Package
EMEA	European Medicines Evaluation Agency
FAO	Food and Agriculture Organization
FDA	Food and Drug Administration (US)
FDI	Foreign direct investment
GATT	General Agreement on Tariffs and Trade
GCP	Good clinical practice
GDP	Gross domestic product
GDP	Good distribution practice

GFATM	Global Fund to Fight AIDS, TB and Malaria
GIRP	Groupement Internationale de la Répartition Pharmaceutique Européene
GLC	Green Light Committee: A Working Group on DOTS- Plus
GLP	Good laboratory practice
GMP	Good manufacturing practice
GNI	Gross national income
GNP	Gross national product
HE	Health expenditure
HIV	Human immunodeficiency virus
HIPC	Heavily Indebted Poor Countries
HSSP	Health Sector Strategic Plan
ICG	WHO International Coordinating Group on vaccine provision for epidemic meningitis control
ICH	International Conference on Harmonization (April 1999) 'to eliminate and ensure quicker access to safe, effective and good quality new pharmaceutical products'
ICRC	International Committee of the Red Cross
ICT	Information and communication technology
IDA	International Dispensary Association
IFPMA	International Federation of Pharmaceutical Manufacturers Association
IFPW	International Federation of Pharmaceutical Wholesalers
IMF	International Monetary Fund
IMR-	Infant mortality rate
IP	Intellectual property. The concept includes patents, copyright, trade marks and geographical denominations.
IUATLD	International Union against Tuberculosis and Lung Disease
JPPIs	Joint public–private initiatives
LDCs	Least-developed Countries. UN classification based on income, health and education standards, and economic vulnerability.
MDR-TB	Multi-drug-resistant tuberculosis
MDGs	Millennium Development Goals. The UN General Assembly incorporated these goals in the Millennium Declaration in September 2000, while setting new targets for reducing the proportion of people suffering from hunger, increasing access to improved water sources, improving the lives of slum dwellers, and reversing the spread of HIV/AIDS, malaria, tuberculosis and other major diseases.
MNCs	Multinational companies
MPRSP	Malawi Poverty Reduction Strategy Paper
MTEF	Medium-term Expenditure Framework

MSF	Médecins Sans Frontières
NGO	Non-governmental organization
NHS	National Health Service (UK)
NICE	National Institute of Clinical Excellence (UK)
NRM	National Resistance Movement
NTP	National Tuberculosis (Control) Programme
OECD	Organization for Economic Cooperation and Development
OFT	Office of Fair Trading
OTC	Over-the-counter
PAHO	Pan-American Health Organization
PEAP	Poverty Eradication Action Plan
PI	Protease inhibitor (see Appendix 6.1 for details)
PMTCT	Prevention of mother-to-child transmission
PPP	Purchasing power parity
PSRPs	Poverty Reduction Strategy Papers
QA/QC	Quality assurance and quality control
QALY	Quality-adjusted life-year
R&D	Research and development
SADC	Southern African Development Community
SHI	Social health insurance
SME	Small and medium-sized enterprises
SOPs	Standard operating procedures
STI	Sexually transmitted infections
SWAp	Sector-wide approach
TASO	The AIDS Support Organization (Uganda)
TQA	Testing and quality assurance
TQM	Total quality management
TRIPS	WTO Agreement on Trade-Related Aspects of Intellectual Property Rights, agreed at the end of the Uruguay Round of trade talks in 1994
UNAIDS	Joint United Nations Programme on HIV/AIDS
UNDP	United Nations Development Programme
UNFPA	United Nations Fund for Population Activities
UNGASS	UN General Assembly Special Session on HIV/AIDS
UNICEF	United Nations Children's Fund
UNMHCP	Uganda National Minimum Health Care Package
USAID	US Agency for International Development
UWESO	Uganda Women's Effort to Save Orphans
WHO	World Health Organization
WIPO	World Intellectual Property Organization
WTO	World Trade Organization
YLS	Years of life saved

PART I
INTRODUCTION AND OVERVIEW

1 WHY DO THE POOR LACK ACCESS TO ESSENTIAL MEDICINES?

Louisiana Lush

INTRODUCTION

Since the discovery of aspirin in the late nineteenth century and the widespread advances in chemical science in the middle of the past century, drugs have been used routinely to cure disease, alleviate pain and prevent illness. For infectious diseases, antibiotics, antimalarials and antituberculosis drugs are among the most potent chemical compounds ever invented. Drugs for chronic conditions – cardiovascular diseases and others – have also transformed the face of modern health care. Medicines, along with healthcare providers, therefore form the backbone of a health system, and access to these products is the key to maintaining good health and preventing premature death.

Nevertheless, despite these scientific and technological advances, many people do not have access to pharmaceuticals (see Figure 1.1); they continue to fall ill or to die from easily preventable or treatable disease. The poor are more likely than the rich to fall ill, to have inadequate access to care and to receive substandard care when they do access it, sometimes with fatal consequences. This inequality holds both within and across nations, according to a wide range of social, economic and cultural criteria, and varying access to essential medicines plays an important role in explaining differences in health outcomes.

'Essential medicines' is a term coined by the World Health Organization (WHO). It is defined as those drugs that satisfy the healthcare needs of the majority of the population and that should therefore be available at all times, in adequate amounts and appropriate dosage forms and at a price that individuals and the community can afford (WHO, 2000b). In 1977, the WHO responded to calls for better access to pharmaceuticals by publishing a list of 208 such drugs – the Essential Drugs List – which all countries should prioritize in their national drug system. The list included generic as well as in-patent pharmaceuticals, and in 2001, when the most recent list was published with 325 drugs, 12 anti-retroviral medicines for the prevention and treatment of the HIV disease were added (WHO, 2001b).

Figure 1.1: Access to essential drugs around the world

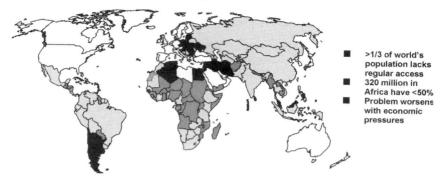

Percentage of populations and number of countries with regular access to essential drugs:

□ 1 = <50%   (43)
□ 2 = 50-80%   (64)
■ 3 = 80-95%   (30)
□ 4 = >95%   (41)
■ 5 = no data available (1)

Source: http://www.who.int/medicines/library/pptpres/generics/7

The importance of the essential medicines concept lies in its ability to address the problems of access to drugs through systems to regulate their quality, rational use and sustainable financing. The goal is to narrow the gap between the potential impact of drugs on disease and the reality that for many of the world's poor, they remain unavailable, unaffordable, unsafe or improperly used. By implementing systems to manage the supply of drugs, health managers can ensure regular updates of new therapies, high drug quality and research into new products.

ACCESS TO MEDICINES: THE CONTEXT

To date, despite decades of international action, over one-third of the world's population lacks adequate access to drugs (see Figure 1.1) (WHO, 2000c). In Africa and Southeast Asia, improved diagnosis and treatment of illness could save an estimated four million lives each year (WHO, 2000c). (See Figure 1.2 for the number of deaths from diseases in developing countries in 1990.) Two-thirds of deaths in Africa and Southeast Asia among children and young adults are due to seven diseases, for which cheap and effective prevention and treatment exist (WHO, 1999). These children are dying because drugs that they need are not being made available to them. The impact of improving access to essential medicines on death rates at all ages is potentially vast.

Figure 1.2: Developing-country deaths from infectious and parasitic, and non-communicable diseases (millions, 1990)

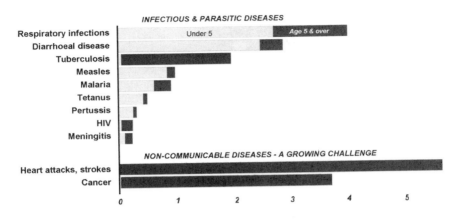

Source: http://www.who.int/medicines/library/pptpres/generics/4

Access to essential medicines can be examined in terms of how individuals or households exercise demand for drugs, including financial, geographical and socio-cultural variations. A considerable body of literature provides empirical evidence on such demand-side explanations for inequalities of access to health care, including differences in behaviour in seeking such care, ability to pay for drugs and willingness to comply with treatment. Studies from Nepal, Pakistan, Bolivia and the United States show that in both high- and low-income countries, although the poor are more likely to fall ill than the rich, they are less likely to seek help and less able to pay for it (Holloway et al., 2002; Elliott et al., 2001; Perry, 2000; Khan et al., 2000). Furthermore, particularly for diseases such as HIV/AIDS and tuberculosis, significant socio-economic differentials have been found in patients' willingness to adhere to treatment over longer periods of time (Friedland and Williams, 1999; Khan et al., 2000).

The economic impact of poor access is also substantial. In developed countries, typically less than one-fifth of total health expenditure is private spending on drugs, as shown in Figure 1.3. In the poorest countries, by contrast, this proportion can be up to two-thirds – with between 50 and 90 per cent of drugs being paid for out of pocket (WHO, 2001a). The impact of drug purchasing on households has been found to be large, especially among the poor: a major illness can seriously deplete household finances. Illness has been found to be a significant factor in explaining why poor households remain trapped in poverty, as it pushes them further into debt and dependency and

Figure 1.3: Private spending on drugs as percentage of total spending, developed and developing countries

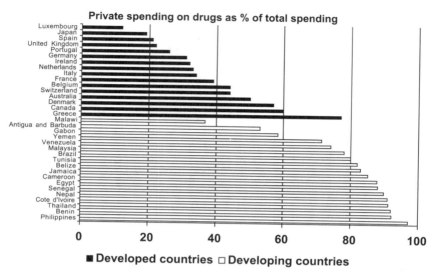

Source: http://www.who.int/medicines/library/pptpres/generics/6

reduces their capacity to save. Health systems of poor countries, where pharmaceuticals represent the largest public expenditure on health after personnel costs, also face a heavy burden in payment for medicines.

In order to understand the relationship between health systems and access to medicines, an alternative, more pragmatic, supply-side approach must be taken. For example, the WHO conceptualizes access to essential medicines through a framework that incorporates drug prices, sustainable financing mechanisms, rational selection and use, and a reliable health and supply system. Using this framework, it addresses the following objectives: to update drug selections regularly so as to reflect new therapeutic options and needs; to ensure drug quality and safety; and to develop new and better drugs for emerging diseases and changing resistance patterns. The next section examines these different supply-side elements of access.

HOW CAN ACCESS BE IMPROVED?

Appropriate selection and use

According to the WHO, up to three-quarters of antibiotics are prescribed inappropriately, even in advanced health facilities, and only half the patients who receive the right medicine take it correctly. Partly as a result, antimicrobial resistance is widespread for major diseases, including tuberculosis, diarrhoea, pneumonia, malaria and gonorrhoea. One of the main reasons for poor-quality prescribing is a lack of systems to provide clear guidelines to providers about what are the most cost-effective treatments for different conditions. In 2000, according to the WHO, only one country in six had adequate mechanisms in place to regulate drug prescription (Ratanawijitrasin and Wondemagegnehu, 2000).

To reduce the inappropriate prescription of drugs, the main policy recommendation is to develop an essential drugs list. This process involves defining what drugs are most needed according to the prevalence of diseases in a country, purchasing medicines through international competitive tendering and ensuring that once purchased, they are used as intended. In Chad, the introduction of a national drug policy along these lines between 1995 and 2001 led to an increase in the population with access to essential medicines from 46 to 60 per cent (WHO, 2000a). Although seemingly rational and with clear benefit for public health, this has proved to be a surprisingly controversial effort around the world, principally because it is seen to interfere with pharmaceutical companies' 'right' to market products directly to health providers and patients. In Bangladesh, for example, when the government tried to introduce an essential drugs list in 1982, it came under heavy political pressure to prevent the bill going through from the American embassy, itself acting to protect the interests of the US pharmaceutical industry (Chowdhury and Chetley, 1996). In South Africa in 1997, a new medicines bill that aimed to rationalize drug licensing and prescription came under criticism from the US government and from the American pharmaceutical industry, which eventually took the South African government to court (Bombach, 2001).

The essential drugs list policy process also includes the development of clear treatment guidelines, especially where healthcare delivery will be primarily by nurses through a primary healthcare system. These providers need to be trained and supported in the effective use of essential medicines. They also need to be able to promote rational use by their customers or patients. This approach too has drawn criticism, particularly from US actors, for limiting the choice available to patients because in America, unlike in the European Union, pharmaceutical companies are permitted to market direct to patients. Nevertheless, the goal remains to prescribe drugs that represent the best balance of quality, safety, efficacy and cost in circumstances in which many people are illiterate or poorly educated.

Strengthening health systems

Reliable health and drug supply systems are a prerequisite for the adequate delivery of drugs. In many poor countries, however, the health system is extremely weak, underfunded and oversubscribed. Over the past 20 years, considerable effort has gone into reforming health sectors in order to develop systems that can deliver health services in a more efficient and equitable way. Nevertheless, large gaps remain between what is supposed to be provided and what exists on the ground. Furthermore, little evaluation of the impact of different essential medicines policies has taken place, so that the understanding of what can actually improve access for the poor is weak (Ratanawijitrasin et al., 2001).

Recent policy developments intended to improve access to essential medicines include establishing essential drugs programmes, improving the supply of drugs, creating cost-sharing mechanisms and devising new regulatory measures (Ratanawijitrasin et al., 2001). In most low-income countries, a central drug purchasing authority has been set up through which drugs enter the country and are distributed into the public-sector health facility network. Private providers may or may not also receive their drugs through this system. Increasingly, and often under the guidance of international organizations such as the World Bank, these authorities have been encouraged to use international tendering processes for procuring drugs (World Bank, 2000). In terms of access, in theory these bodies should improve the efficiency with which medicines on the essential drugs list come into a country's health system and the international tendering process should promote competition and lower prices. In reality, they remain inefficient and sometimes corrupt, so that weak central procurement systems are a major factor in poor access to essential medicines.

Once in a country, drugs are intended to pass down to health service outlets by way of district health management offices, which order them according to local needs. However, like the central purchasing mechanism, these systems suffer from poor management capacity all down the line. As a result, for some priority diseases, such as tuberculosis or sexually transmitted diseases, separate distribution systems may be established in which a national programme purchases the drugs independently, outside the central purchasing system, and then distributes them directly to district officers for special delivery to facilities (Lush et al., 1999; Cairncross et al., 1997).

Often these separate distribution systems associated with priority diseases are linked to drug donation programmes. Donors themselves prioritize disease areas, such as family planning, HIV/AIDS or tuberculosis, and in their desire to see their initiatives implemented as efficiently as possible they may prefer to provide drugs, training and other investments through separate, dedicated systems. Sometimes known as vertical programmes, these separate management systems can improve access to drugs for a particular problem. However, they can also interfere with the development of a more integrated and rational approach to healthcare management in which the government takes the lead and develops services according to its own priorities (Mayhew et al., 2000).

Sustainable financing mechanisms

In many poor countries, a wide range of financing mechanisms is required in order to pay for drugs and to improve access to them. In most of these countries, some combination of the following will exist, managed with greater or less efficiency: public revenues, social health insurance, out-of-pocket spending, and international financing through grants and loans. Cost-sharing for medicines is now a common feature of health systems of many countries, both rich and poor. However, even where most financing is in the private sector, it is necessary for the government to maintain some kind of control over how the money is spent, in order to focus on efficiency of expenditure and equity of access.

Traditionally, governments in developing countries provided central funding for essential medicine procurement for free delivery in public health facilities. During the past 30 years, however, as a result of structural adjustment policies and concerns over the balance of payments, the health system has had to cut costs through introducing user fees and increasing patients' payment for drugs. A review of the introduction of user fees in poor countries found they reduced access to medicine, especially where governments did not explicitly formulate a policy on exemptions for the poor (Russell and Gilson, 1997). In one region of Ghana where a decentralized, facility-based fee system was established along with a policy on exemptions for the poor, wide variations in prices were found and exemptions were generally ignored (Nyonator and Kutzin, 1999). In the United States, a study found that after the introduction of cost-sharing for medicines, the use of essential drugs decreased by 9–14 per cent among deprived groups and that this raised the number of serious illnesses among them (Tamblyn et al., 2001). User fees may also be unofficial, typically cash payments for services received or for drugs and other commodities. In Bangladesh, where such fees are widespread in a context of new market reforms, a study found that they distorted human resource development and reduced health clinic efficiency, thereby diminishing patient satisfaction and ability to pay (Killingsworth et al., 1999).

To appreciate why the poor lack access to essential medicines, it is also important to understand that contrary to expectation, much of the health care the poor receive, especially their medicines, is provided by the private sector. The principal difference between high- and low-income countries is that in the latter, health care is largely financed privately, whereas in the former there is a predominance of social insurance schemes (WHO, 2001a). In sub-Saharan Africa, a mere eight per cent of the population is covered by a social insurance scheme. The most common private finance mechanism in poor countries is out-of-pocket spending, rather than pre-paid insurance. In Burkina Faso, around 70 per cent of health spending is out of pocket, equating to $3–5.40 per person each year (Sauerborn et al., 1995). In Kenya, a study found that 70 per cent of mothers used shop-bought medicines first in treating childhood fevers and that only 49 per cent ever went to a clinic (Molyneux et al., 1999). Developing ways to use market mechanisms for improving the supply of drugs without having too great an impact on their price and hence accessibility is therefore a priority (Hanson et al., 2001). Another mechanism for supporting the poor is community drug funds, which are often established with financial support from international aid agencies. Research on these funds in Honduras showed that they can increase access to care by promoting the rational use of medicines and community participation in the financing and oversight of primary healthcare activities. However, they also have the problems of sustainability beyond the time of subsidy and insufficient management capacity (Fielder and Wight, 2000).

Drug development and pricing

Given the dependence on out-of-pocket payment for drugs, the price of pharmaceutical products will clearly have a dramatic effect on access. Prices can vary hugely, both within and between countries. A study of ethambutol 100 mg (a generic drug used to treat tuberculosis) found a 95-fold difference in price between the private sector in the United States and the tender price in Zimbabwe (Laing and McGoldrick, 2001).

In low-income countries, affordable prices for drugs are dependent on a wide range of factors. First, there must be transparent price information for the relevant consumer, whether the healthcare provider or the patients themselves. Often, this information is not available, but it can facilitate much more rational prescribing. Second, for both generic and in-patent drugs, competition can make a significant difference to the price. It should be encouraged, whether drugs are purchased centrally, through an international tendering process, or at private pharmacies. Drugs in patent can still be open to competition where different chemicals or formulations exist for the same purpose. Third, national tariffs and taxes on pharmaceutical products often represent a large proportion of the over-the-counter price. Such tariffs are therefore significant barriers to improved access to essential medicines and are the responsibility of national governments. Information about the impact on access of poor-country governments' drug price regulation is limited. One study, in the Lao People's Democratic

Republic, found that trade-offs had to be made between quality of pharmaceutical services (and their price) and geographical equity of access (Stenson et al., 1997).

In addition to these national-level factors, international law and regulation, particularly under the auspices of the World Trade Organization's (WTO) Agreement on Trade-Related Aspects of Intellectual Property (TRIPS), have been accused of hindering the poor's access to medicines. Prior to TRIPS, there were no international minimum standards for pharmaceutical intellectual property protection: a wide range of regulatory frameworks existed in different countries; and patents were for restricted times and often for processes rather than products. Many have suggested that the requirement for poor countries to comply with the WTO's strict intellectual property rules will raise prices and deny access to medicines. However, the evidence also suggests that there is a weak correlation between the existence of a patent in a country and the availability of a drug. One study found that anti-retrovirals were not under patent in many countries in Africa but were still not available, suggesting that patents are not the principal reason for lack of access (Attaran and Gillespie-White, 2001).

In the future, regulating when and how the conditions for compulsory licensing can be used and establishing parallel importing mechanisms will be important ways to improve access to drugs by the poor (WHO, 2002). Much debate continues today on how to price drugs so as to reflect countries' ability to pay and thereby ensure that price does not remain a barrier to access to drugs. Differential pricing, alternatively known as equity or preferential pricing, is one means of reducing the cost of medicines. The bulk purchase of commodities, economies of scale in manufacturing and product uniformity, each coordinated at the international level, have also been shown to reduce prices to between one and five per cent of rich-country market levels (WHO, 2001a). However, serious questions remain over which health problems and products should be priorities for differential pricing, which countries should benefit, how to regulate pricing, and how to finance, purchase and distribute differentially priced drugs efficiently. Above all, how to prevent diversion away from intended countries and populations, and how to prevent rich-country governments from demanding the same prices are ongoing conundrums for international advocates of this type of scheme.

Besides reducing prices paid by consumers, it is also important for the international community to ensure that ways are found to stimulate the development of drugs and vaccines for neglected (or orphan) diseases, such as trypanosomiasis and leishmaniasis, for which there is almost no demand in high-income countries and therefore little market (Schieppati et al., 2001). Here, inefficient access relates to other problems, such as fluctuating production and a lack of field-based drug research, as well as to the factors discussed above (Pecoul et al., 1999). Incentives to private companies to develop drugs based on subsequent profit will clearly not work in these areas, and it is likely that the only way to improve access to medicines for neglected diseases is through enhanced cooperation between public-sector funds and private-sector drug development capacity (Vandersmissen, 2001). However, experiences with the medicine praziquantel for schistosomiasis show that the discovery of a new drug also needs to be supplemented by explicit action to ensure that it reaches poor people in poor countries (Reich and Govindaraj, 1998).

ENABLING ACCESS: WHOSE RESPONSIBILITY?

Responsibility for enabling improvements in access to medicines for the poor lies with a wide range of organizations and institutions. For rich countries, this responsibility lies squarely with national governments, but the situation is much more complex for poor countries, where the vast majority of the world's poor live. Here, national governments, international organizations, rich-country aid programmes and pharmaceutical companies have played various parts in enhancing (and, unfortunately, sometimes reducing) access to medicines. Furthermore, international treaties clearly support a theoretical role for international organizations in increasing such access. Understanding the roles these bodies have played in reality is crucial to understanding why the poor do not have adequate access.

National governments

The national governments of poor countries have the leading role in providing access to medicines in order to promote public health as a social good (Over, 1999). To improve the efficiency of provision, many governments have enacted major healthcare reforms, including separating policy-making from healthcare provision functions, privatizing elements of the health system and decentralizing decisions and finances to local levels (Reich, 1995; Mwabu, 1995; McPake, 2002; Mills, 1998). Nevertheless, service provision remains highly inequitable – as in developed countries, richer, more urban and educated population groups have much higher levels of health care than those in rural areas with little education and low income. Many reasons exist for these persisting inequities; they have been discussed above. However, the political system in many poor countries also prevents governments from taking rational decisions over resource allocation (Walt and Gilson, 1994). Healthcare spending is often a low priority, for example relative to defence or law and order, and health budgets tend to be one of the first items cut in conditions of fiscal constraint such as under International Monetary Fund (IMF) stabilization packages. Although there have been changes in the attitude of international financial institutions towards protecting pro-poor programmes, these institutions' incentives to governments do not always promote public health. For instance, maintaining government revenue from tariffs on pharmaceutical products – as encouraged by stabilization packages – may take precedence over ensuring the cheapest over-the-counter price for medicines.

Decisions about the allocation of resources and how to implement health programmes are rarely taken in the rational, mechanistic way that international agencies like to portray them (Walt et al., 2004). Pharmaceutical policy is no different from other policies and has long been seen to be the result of multiple competing agendas and a balancing act by governments under pressure to serve the poor on the one hand, and to respond to private corporations, physicians and pharmacists on the other (Reich, 1995). Policy change is therefore incremental, determined by the interests of the various individuals and organizations involved, at both the national level and the peripheral parts of the health system, and the context in which they work. As a result, the picture of healthcare provision in poor countries is an extremely complex one, with multiple actors (instead of one government health system) and unreliable communication between them.

International organizations

To this complex scene must be added a large number of international organizations involved in health care for the poor (Buse and Walt, 1997; Mayhew et al., 2004, forthcoming). International organizations involved range from the WHO, through various UN agencies, to the World Bank, each with different goals and agendas, and frequently not very coherent in their approach (Buse and Walt, 1997; Mayhew et al., 2004, forthcoming). The WHO has the longest involvement with essential medicines and has a well-established programme based in Geneva. Its technical contribution to disseminating information and advocating a more rational use of drugs has been significant but its funds for assisting governments are limited. The WHO's moral authority in many low-income countries remains high and its guidelines for prescribing for a number of diseases also promote the rational use of drugs. Most recently, it included anti-retrovirals on its international essential drugs list, and it is at the forefront of initiatives to increase access to these medicines for the poor.

Since the late 1980s, the World Bank has taken a more prominent role than the WHO in providing large-scale financial assistance for health through loans and credits. Its projects for health-sector development, as well as for specific disease issues (for example, tuberculosis or sexually transmitted infections), have often included assistance with procuring drugs. Such initiatives have proved controversial, usually because they impose the rigours of international competitive tendering on existing ad hoc and potentially anti-competitive purchasing mechanisms. Furthermore, the World Bank's association with structural adjust-ment programmes, under which it has frequently advocated the introduction of user fees and the increased privatization of health care in low-income countries, has attracted considerable criticism. Substantial evidence exists now that such interventions have reduced attendance at public-sector health services, particu-larly by the poor (McPake, 2002). More recent policy in the health sector from the World Bank takes a more explicit approach towards ways of dealing with the problems of the poor, but this has yet to filter through significantly to country loans (Owoh, 1996).

The activities of other organizations impinge indirectly on health. For example, the IMF imposes strict fiscal restraint regimes, which constrain the ability of governments to implement public-sector programmes. At the global level, the WTO's regulation of international trade has recently had a major impact on the availability of essential medicines. These organizations rarely take public health concerns into account in their decision-making and do not coordinate well with existing global public health initiatives, but they can have a substantial impact on availability (Lush, 2001).

Bilateral aid programmes

Many of the world's richest countries have aid programmes through which they channel money to poor countries for health care, either directly (bilaterally) or through international organizations (multilaterally), including UN agencies, the European Commission and various new funds (see below). Although this aid has made substantial contributions to increasing access to medicines, it could go much further. Very few countries' aid programmes have ever met the commitment to contribute 0.7 per cent of GDP to aid made in 1992 at the Rio de Janeiro United Nations Earth Summit. Many aid projects place restrictions on the kind of activity that can be undertaken and prioritize specific diseases over others. These may enhance access to medicines for particular problems, notably HIV/AIDS, tuberculosis, malaria, immunizations and family planning, but they can also undermine efforts to make drug purchasing and distribution systems more efficient. Furthermore, although most rich countries have enacted some sort of pharmaceutical price control policy in order to balance their own economic and public health goals (Jacobzone, 2000), some governments have been instrumental in preventing developing countries from doing the same (for example Bangladesh – see Chowdhury and Chetley, 1996).

The large number and wide range of international and bilateral aid programmes in the health sector pose the risk that managing the process of receiving aid may distract national health officials from their real job of improving access to health care. In response, coordination mechanisms have sometimes been introduced, including Sector-Wide Approaches (SWAps) and Poverty Reduction Strategy Papers (PRSPs) (Buse and Walt, 1997). Within areas such as HIV/AIDS, the UN has also tried to coordinate country-level initiatives. Coordination efforts have often foundered, however, owing to the diversity of donors' objectives, priorities and styles of working. As a result, in many of the poorest countries, substantial time is taken up with applying for and monitoring donor financial assistance, with detrimental effects on the timely establishment of adequate systems of their own. The balance between the positive and the negative impacts of aid on access to medicines is therefore a delicate one.

Public–private partnerships and the pharmaceutical industry

In addition to this confusing picture of organizations involved in health care in poor countries, a number of new initiatives have recently started up, under the general name of 'public–private partnerships' (Widdus, 2001; Walt and Buse, 2000). These initiatives are usually established in order to foster cooperation between a public-sector body (an aid programme or a government) and a private company (often a pharmaceutical company), thereby combining public funds with corporate expertise or commodities. Although all are interested in enhancing access to medicines or vaccines for the poor, they vary enormously in objectives, governance and impact. These partnerships can be divided into those involved in new drug research and development, such as Medicines for Malaria, and those actually distributing drugs to countries through donation programmes, for example the Mectizan Donation Programme. As they are usually established at the global level, the extent to which recipient-country governments are involved in their decision-making and priority-setting can be extremely limited. Furthermore, independent evaluations of their impact on access to medicines, especially for the poor, are rare.

The pharmaceutical industry in particular has recently been far more involved in addressing the problems of access to drugs, owing to pressure from a number of activist organizations worldwide (Oxfam, 2001; VSO, 2000). Currently, especially when there is a patent, the lack of product competition means essentially that drug companies can set whatever price a market will bear. Social contracts between industry and society to offer profit incentives for companies to conduct research and development of new pharmaceuticals have been questioned more and more. In particular, the extraordinary profitability of the research-based pharmaceutical sector, alongside a rising awareness of the international failure to meet the needs of the poor, especially for HIV/AIDS treatment, has focused media and popular attention on this issue (Lush, 2001). This is especially a problem for drugs for tropical diseases, which do not affect rich countries. Only 13 of the 1,233 new drugs which reached the market between 1975 and 1997 were approved for tropical diseases (Pecoul et al., 1999).

As a result, rich-country governments have come under pressure to modify their regulatory frameworks for the pharmaceutical research and manufacturing industries in order to ensure that wealthy states' needs do not override those of the poor (Commission on Intellectual Property Rights, 2002; Cullet, 2002). At the same time, debate has raged over intellectual property rules and patenting processes. There has been consensus in some areas – such as waiving licences for certain key infectious disease medicines – but dissent remains in others, including the circumstances under which generic copies of branded medicines may be traded. In general, it is now agreed by most governments that for certain health problems (notably HIV/AIDS, tuberculosis and malaria), cheap drugs have to be made available to poor countries. How best to achieve this and, in particular, how to minimize the political repercussions in rich countries remain open questions. In addition, the introduction of more systematic ways of ensuring that poor countries receive cheap drugs for all their health problems remains hotly contested by some governments (Oh, 2003).

CONCLUSION: WHY IMPROVE ACCESS FOR THE POOR?

This chapter has examined some of the reasons why the poor do not have adequate access to essential medicines and demonstrated ways in which governments, international organizations and private pharmaceutical companies might contribute to improving their access. Many individuals and bodies have a part to play, each with their own interests and ways of working. One important question framing the interests of these organizations is whether increasing the poor's access to medicine should be a priority at all and, if so, why. Two possible justifications have been widely used: first, a justice argument, that inequality in access to essential medicines is unfair and inequitable, and should therefore be reduced; second, a public good argument of economic externalities, that by denying the poor access to medicines their productivity is reduced, to the detriment of society at large (Woodward, 2000).

All too frequently, these two arguments have been juxtaposed and presented as mutually exclusive. This is mistaken – both justice and economic productivity can be served through increasing the poor's access to drugs. The distinction between *inequalities* in access to health and *inequity* is contentious, but it is summarized here as follows. Inequality in health is unfair, rather than simply a fact of life, when poor health is itself a result of the unjust distribution of the determinants of health (for example, financial resources or education). The social conditions that lead to marked inequalities in health are detrimental to everyone, for example through the spread of infectious disease or the occurrence of violence and crime. Despite harmful social conditions, inequalities in health are often avoidable through the programmes of governments determined to improve the public condition. Those inequalities are amenable to public intervention, and government programmes' impact on inequalities ought to be a principal consideration in policy-making. Finally, public health programmes that reduce inequality in health can also be cost-effective, therefore meeting the requirements of both justice and economic rationale. Such programmes include vaccination campaigns and the provision of access to drugs that cure infectious diseases. Recently, it has been argued persuasively that better health contributes substantially to economic development (Commission on Macroeconomics and Health, 2001).

It is therefore difficult to argue that access to essential medicines should not be a priority for the world's decision-makers: equity and economic justifications are both strong. But so far achievements have been mixed and debates antagonistic. At the international level, despite several years of negotiation in the media spotlight, it is not yet clear how international treaties will be used by national governments to balance the intellectual property requirements of corporations with the public health needs of the poor. Communication between different networks – public health professionals and intellectual property lawyers – remains fraught with philosophical and linguistic barriers. Political imperatives in rich countries inhibit generosity towards poor countries. In middle-income countries, often with the starkest inequalities in access to health care, balancing the needs of emerging pharmaceutical sectors with those of the poor is extremely complex. Inevitably, the voices of the more powerful corporations are heard more loudly than those of the poor.

The fact remains, however, that even if prices are reduced to rock-bottom levels, access for the poor will probably remain hampered by the parlous state of the health systems they depend on. In Chad, total expenditure per head on medicines for 2001 was $0.12 (WHO, 2000a). The cost of a year's package of essential medicines has been put at $12 per head by the World Bank. A year's supply of highly active anti-retroviral therapy has been estimated to cost between $450 and $3,500 (Schwartlander et al., 2001). The gap between current and required expenditure appears large but could be filled relatively easily on a global scale – and efforts such as those of the Global Fund for HIV/ AIDS, Tuberculosis and Malaria are trying to do so (Brugha and Walt, 2001). Nevertheless, the Global Fund's coffers are insufficiently resourced. Governments and the aid agencies that support them have a long way to go in order to make a realistic claim that they are fulfilling their duty to provide access to essential medicines for the poor.

REFERENCES

Attaran, A. and L. Gillespie-White (2001), 'Do patents for antiretroviral drugs constrain access to AIDS treatment in Africa?', *Journal of the American Medical Association*, 286: 1886–92.

Bombach, K. M. (2001), 'Can South Africa fight Aids? Reconciling the South African Medicines and Related Substances Act with the Trips Agreement', *Boston University International Law Journal*, 19: 273–306.

Brugha, R. and G. Walt (2001), 'A global health fund: a leap of faith?', *British Medical Journal*, 323: 152–4.

Buse, K. and G. Walt (1997), 'An unruly melange? Coordinating external resources to the health sector: a review', *Social Science and Medicine*, 45: 449–63.

Cairncross, S., H. Peries and F. Cutts (1997), 'Vertical health programmes', *The Lancet*, 350: S20–S21.

Chowdhury, Z. and A. Chetley (1996), 'Essential drugs in Bangladesh: the ups and downs of a policy', *The Ecologist*, 26: 27–34.

Commission on Intellectual Property Rights (2002), *Integrating Intellectual Property Rights and Development Policy* (London: Commission on Intellectual Property Rights).

Commission on Macroeconomics and Health (2001), *Macroeconomics and Health: Investing in Health for Economic Development* (Geneva: World Health Organization).

Cullet, P. (2002), unpublished manuscript, London.

Elliott, B. A., M. K. Beattie and S. E. Kaitfors (2001), 'Health needs of people living below poverty level', *Family Medicine*, 33: 361–6.

Fielder, J. L. and J. B. Wight (2000), 'Financing healthcare at the local level: the community and drug funds of Honduras', *International Journal of Health Planning Management*, 15: 319–40.

Friedland, G. H. and A. Williams (1999), 'Attaining higher goals in HIV treatment: the central importance of adherence', *AIDS*, 13: S61–S72.

Hanson, K., L. Kumaranayake and I. Thomas (2001), 'Ends versus means: the role of markets in expanding access to contraceptives', *Health Policy and Planning*, 16: 125–36.

Holloway, K. G., Bharat R. Gautam, Trudy Harpham and Ann Taket (2002), 'The influence of user fees and patient demand on prescribers in rural Nepal', *Social Science and Medicine*, 54: 905–18.

Jacobzone, S. (2000), *Pharmaceutical Policies in OECD Countries: Reconciling Social and Industrial Goals* (Paris: Organization for Economic Cooperation and Development).

Khan, A., J. Walley, J. Newell and N. Imdad (2000), 'Tuberculosis in Pakistan: social–cultural constraints and opportunities in treatment', *Social Science and Medicine*, 50: 247–54.

Killingsworth, J. R., N. Hossain, Y. Hedrick-Wong, S. D. Thomas, A. Rahman and T. Begum (1999), 'Unofficial fees in Bangladesh: price, equity and institutional issues', *Health Policy and Planning*, 14: 152–63.

Laing, R. O. and K. McGoldrick (2001), *Tuberculosis Drug Issues: Prices, Fixed Dose Combination Products and Second Line Drugs* (Boston, MA: Boston University School of Public Health).

Lush, L. (2001), 'Editorial: International effort for anti-retrovirals: a storm in a teacup?', *Tropical Medicine and International Health*, 6: 491–5.

Lush, L., J. Cleland, G. Walt and S. Mayhew (1999), 'Defining integrated reproductive health: myth and ideology', *Bulletin of the World Health Organization*, 77: 771–7.

Mayhew, S., L. Lush, J. Cleland and G. Walt (2000), 'Implementing the integration of component services for reproductive health', *Studies in Family Planning*, 31: 151–62.

Mayhew, S., G. Walt, L. Lush and J. Cleland (2004, forthcoming), 'Donor involvement in reproductive health: saying one thing and doing another?', *International Journal of Health Services*.

McPake, B. (2002), 'The globalisation of health sector reform policies: is "lesson drawing" part of the process?', in K. Lee, K. Buse and S. Fustukian (eds), *Health Policy in a Globalising World* (Cambridge: Cambridge University Press).

Mills, A. (1998), 'Health policy reforms and their impact on the practice of tropical medicine,' *British Medical Bulletin*, 54: 503–13.

Molyneux, C. S., V. Mung'Ala-Odera, T. Harpham and R. W. Snow (1999), 'Material responses to childhood fevers: a comparison of rural and urban residents in coastal Kenya', *Tropical Medicine and International Health*, 4: 836–45.

Mwabu, G. (1995), 'Healthcare reform in Kenya: a review of the process', *Health Policy*, 32: 245–55.

Nyonator, F. and J. Kutzin (1999), 'Health for some? The effects of user fees in the Volta Region of Ghana', *Health Policy and Planning*, 14: 329–41.

Oh, C. (2003), *Don't Waste Our Time: Developing Countries Criticise Attempts to Limit Scope of Diseases in Paragraph 6 Negotiations* (Geneva: Third World Network).

Over, M. (1999), 'The public interest in a private disease: an economic perspective on the government role in STD and HIV control', in K. Holmes, P. F. Sparling, P. Mardh, S. M. Lemon, W. E. Stamm, P. Piot and J. N. Wasserheit, *Sexually Transmitted Diseases* (London: McGraw-Hill).

Owoh, K. (1996), 'Fragmenting healthcare: the World Bank prescription for Africa', *Social Transformation and Humane Governance*, 21: 211–35.

Oxfam (2001), *Dare to Lead: Public Health and Company Wealth*, Oxfam Briefing Paper on GlaxoSmithKline (Oxford: Oxfam).

Pecoul, B., P. Chirca, P. Trouiller and J. Pinel (1999), 'Access to essential drugs in poor countries: a lost battle', *Journal of the American Medical Association*, 281: 361–7.

Perry, B. and W. Gesler (2000), 'Physical access to primary healthcare in Andean Bolivia', *Social Science and Medicine*, 50: 1177–88.

Ratanawijitrasin, S., S. B. Soumerai and K. Weerasuriya (2001), 'Do national medicine drug policies and essential drug programs improve drug use? A review of experiences in developing countries', *Social Science and Medicine*, 53: 831–44.

Ratanawijitrasin, S. and E. Wondemagegnehu (2000), *Multi Country Study on Effective Drug Regulation* (Geneva: World Health Organization).

Reich, M. R. (1995), 'The politics of health sector reform in developing countries: three cases of pharmaceutical policy', in P. Berman (ed.), *Health Sector Reform in Developing Countries* (Boston, MA: Harvard University Press), pp. 59–99.

Reich, M. R. and R. Govindaraj (1998), 'Dilemmas in drug development for tropical diseases. Experiences with praziquantel', *Health Policy*, 44: 1–18.

Russell, S. and L. Gilson (1997), 'User fee policies to promote health services access for the poor: a wolf in sheep's clothing?', *International Journal of Health Services*, 27: 359–79.

Sauerborn, R., A. Nougtara, M. Borcher, M. Hien, J. Benzler, E. Koob et al. (1995), 'The economic costs of illness for rural households in Burkina Faso', *Tropical Medicine and Parasitology*, 46: 54–60.

Schieppati, A., G. Remuzzi and G. Silvio (2001), 'Modulating the profit motive to meet needs of the less-developed world', *The Lancet*, 358: 1638–41.

Schwartlander, B., J. Stover, N. Walker et al. (2001), 'Resource needs for HIV/AIDS', *Science Express*, 21 June; also in *Science*, 292 (5526): 2434–6, 29 June.

Stenson, B., G. Tomson and L. Syhakhang (1997), 'Pharmaceutical regulation in context: the case of Lao People's Democratic Republic', *Health Policy and Planning*, 12: 329–40.

Tamblyn, R., R. Laprise, J. A. Hanley, M. Abrahamowicz, S. Scott, N. Mayo et al. (2001), 'Adverse events associated with prescription drug cost-sharing among poor and elderly persons', *Journal of the American Medical Association*, 285: 421–9.

Vandersmissen, W. (2001), 'WHO expectation and industry goals', *Vaccine,* 19: 1611–15.

VSO (2000), *Drug Deals: Medicines, Development and HIV/AIDS* (London: Voluntary Service Overseas).

Walt, G. and K. Buse (2000), 'Editorial: Partnership and fragmentation in international health: threat or opportunity?', *Tropical Medicine & International Health,* 5: 467.

Walt, G. and L. Gilson (1994), 'Reforming the health sector in developing countries: the central role of policy analysis', *Health Policy and Planning,* 9: 353–70.

Walt, G., L. Lush and J. Ogden (2004), 'International organisations in transfer of infectious diseases: iterative loops of adoption, adaptation, and marketing', *Governance* 17(2): 189–210.

WHO (1999), *Report on Infectious Diseases: Removing Obstacles to Health Development* (Geneva: World Health Organization).

WHO (2000a), *Highlights of the Year 2000 in Essential Drugs and Medicines Policy* (Geneva: World Health Organization).

WHO (2000b), *The Use of Essential Drugs* (Geneva: World Health Organization).

WHO (2000c), *The World Health Report 2000 Health Systems: Improving Performance* (Geneva: World Health Organization).

WHO (2001a), *More Equitable Pricing for Essential Drugs: What Do We Mean and What Are the Issues?* (Geneva: World Health Organization).

WHO (2001b), *WHO Model List of Essential Medicines: The 12th Model List of Essential Medicines* (Geneva: World Health Organization).

WHO (2002), *Network for Monitoring the Impact of Globalization and Trips on Access to Medicines* (Bangkok: World Health Organization).

Widdus, R. (2001), 'Public-private partnerships for health: their main targets, their diversity, and their future directions', *Bulletin of the World Health Organizations,* 79: 713–20.

Woodward, A. K., (2000), 'Why reduce health inequalities?', *Journal of Epidemiological Community Health,* 54: 923–9.

World Bank (2000), *Technical Note: Procurement of Health Sector Goods* (Washington, DC: World Bank).

2 FROM HEALTH TO WEALTH AND BACK TO HEALTH

Alexander S. Preker

INTRODUCTION

Health, wealth, spending on health care, and poverty alleviation are closely related (Jamison, Bloom and Ruger, 1998; Pan American Health Organization, 2001; Horton, 2002; Wagstaff, 2002b). Good health, nutrition and reproduction policies and effective health services are critical links in the chain of factors that enable countries to break out of the vicious circle of poverty, high fertility, poor health and low economic growth (World Bank, 2000b) and replace it with a virtuous circle of greater productivity, low fertility, better health and rising incomes (World Bank, 1993 and 1997a; World Health Organization, 2000).

But for people on low incomes, there is not enough money to go round. As a result, health services (preventive and curative) and other health-enhancing policies (education, nutrition, reproductive health, infrastructure, hygiene and sanitation systems) are often under-funded. This leads to high morbidity and mortality from conditions that are preventable or curable even in many low-income countries. The resulting reduction in labour productivity curtails economic growth and development. Health gaps lead to development traps. Often, improvements are needed in health status in order to continue economic growth. But increased spending on health may be impossible owing to lack of both binding fiscal constraints and political will. Economic growth translates into more spending on health, even if the share of health spending in GDP remains constant. Other sources of revenue to fill the health gap would include shifting some public spending from other sectors towards health. The private sector is another source of potential revenues; and there has been much discussion during recent years about increasing international aid (public and private).

The Millennium Development Goals (MDGs) have become a set of quantitative targets for development policy in terms of poverty reduction and improvements in health, education, gender equality, the environment and other aspects of human development.[1] Progress since 1990 in achieving the health-related MDGs has, however, been uneven across countries and regions, as it has been in achieving all individual goals themselves (Preker, Langenbrunner and Suzuki, 2001; Devarajan, Miller and Swanson, 2002).

This chapter explores linkages between health, economic growth, spending on health care and poverty. According to this analysis, many low-income countries are caught in a development trap where more health expenditure is needed to reach health targets that will ensure continued economic development. But such money is often not available owing to binding fiscal constraints on the public budget available to the health sector.

CONFRONTING THE DEVELOPMENT DILEMMA

This section explores the complex relationship between health, wealth, spending on health care, and poverty alleviation and its implications for development policies in low- and middle-income countries (see Figure 2.1).

Figure 2.1: Links between health, wealth and other determinants of good health

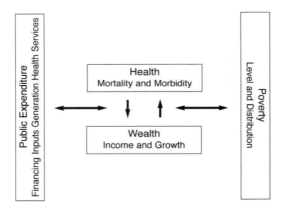

From health to wealth

Although the topic has been hotly debated since Adam Smith's *Wealth of Nations*, the determinants of economic growth and prosperity are still not fully understood (Landes, 1998; Easterly, 2001). Why have some countries in Latin America and

---

[1] The proposal to develop such a set of goals was first made by the Ministers of Development from the OECD Development Assistance Committee (DAC) in 1995 (OECD, 1996). The General Assembly of the United Nations incorporated these goals in the Millennium Declaration in September 2000, while setting new targets for reducing the proportion of people suffering from hunger, increasing access to improved water sources, improving the lives of slum dwellers, and reversing the spread of HIV/AIDS, malaria, tuberculosis and other major diseases (United Nations, 2000 and 2001).

the East Asia and Pacific region gone through rapid economic growth and development in the past decade, while others in sub-Saharan Africa, South Asia and the Central Asian republics have stagnated or experienced negative growth, leaving a large part of their population in poverty? What role do globalization and international aid play in all of this (Dollar and Collier, 2001)?

Overall, the number of people in the world living in absolute poverty (defined as having an income of less than $1 a day) has fallen by an estimated 200 million since 1980 (World Bank, 2000b).

The factors contributing to economic growth and prosperity include policies and institutions that foster good governance, private-sector investment, trade liberalization, natural resource conservation, basic education and health. Good health too is now recognized as an important contributor to economic growth and development (Barro, 1991; Jamison, Bloom and Ruger, 1998; Strauss, 1998; Bhargava, Jamison et al., 2001; Pan American Health Organization, 2001; Wagstaff, 2002b). And poor health is seen as an important dimension not only of poverty but also of poor economic performance (Gwatkin, Guillot and Heiveline, 1999; Gwatkin, 2000a; World Bank, 2000b; Wagstaff, 2002d).

The following provides examples of evidence on ways in which good health contributes to improved growth and development:

- Nutrition links to labour productivity and growth (Strauss, 1986; Behrman, 1993; McGuire, 1996; Ramachandran, 1997; Haddad and Bouis, 1999; Horton, 1999; Horton and Ross, 2000; Rogers, 2002);
- Fertility and population dynamics links to growth (Kelley and Schmidt, 1995; Bloom and Williamson, 1998; Eastwood and Lipton, 1999);
- Child health (Schweinhart, Barnes and Weikart, 1993; Karoly, Greenwood et al., 1998; Van der Gaag and Tan, 1998; Heckman, 1999; Belli and Appaix, 2002) and youth health links to growth (Knowles and Behrman, 2003);
- Healthy workers' ability to work harder and longer (Pan American Health Organization, 2001);.

The following points provide examples of evidence on ways in which poor health and unhealthy habits reduce economic growth and development (Hammoudi and Sachs, 1999):

- HIV/AIDS links to labour productivity and growth (Over, 1992; Kambou, Devarajan and Over, 1993; Ainsworth and Over, 1994; Bloom and Mahal, 1995; World Bank, 1999; Africa Development Forum, 2000; Bloom and Canning, 2000; Bell, Devarajan and Gersbach, 2003);
- Malaria links to labour productivity and growth (Cowper, 1987; Chima, Goodman and Mills, 2003);
- TB links to labour productivity, growth and household incomes (Ramachandran, 1997; Needham, Godfrey-Faussett and Foster, 1998; Kamolratanakul,

Sawert et al., 1999; Rajeswari, Balasubramanian et al., 1999; Ahlburg, 2000; Jack, 2001);
- The economic burden on households of tobacco (Jha and Chaloupka, 2000);
- Disability, earnings loss, unemployment and taxation (Cook, Judice and Hazelwood, 1996; Boden and Galizzi 1999);
- The high cost of treating diseases and the needed healthcare systems (World Bank, 1993 and 1997a; World Health Organization, 2000; Izumi, Tsuji et al., 2001).

Good health contributes to the general quality of life as well as to productivity. Many diseases are not fatal, but they are disabling. Some 200 million people throughout the world – 90 per cent of them in sub-Saharan Africa – are infected with the parasitic schistosome worm, one billion people suffer from anaemia and there are 300,000–500,000 new cases of malaria each year. Chronic fatigue and other symptoms mean the economic burdens of these illnesses for the patient include loss of income, and out-of-pocket expenditure. And the economic burden for the country includes low productivity and the direct costs of treatment.

The relationship between health and wealth is non-linear (see Figure 2.2). Substantial improvements in health can occur even at low-income levels, but this does not necessarily lead to growth or good development policies in other spheres of the economy. Nonetheless, poor health can be an important constraint on development as national income rises.

As income rises, good health contributes increasingly to human capital and is essential to economic growth. For example, a single treatment of children in the West Indies for whipworm dramatically improved school learning and subsequent workforce participation and productivity. Labour productivity has been shown to increase with better iron and calorie intake in Indonesia and Kenya. Similarly, there is evidence that reduced fertility rates and declining youth dependency ratios can have a positive impact on economic growth, if associated with domestic savings and investment in human capital. Ultimately, however, a biological threshold is reached in life expectancy and other health-related indicators. Yet economic growth and development may continue even after reaching this plateau in health, nutrition and population outcomes.

... And back to health

The relationship between income, health spending and health outcomes in developing countries is now well established (World Bank, 1993; Pritchett and Summers 1996; World Bank, 1997a; World Health Organization, 2000;

Figure 2.2: The impact of health on wealth (GDP/capita)

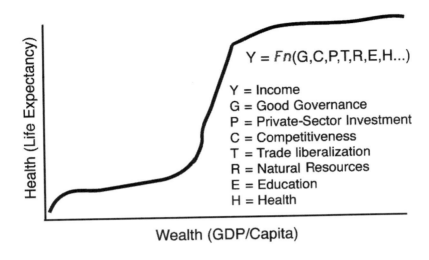

Subramanian, Belli and Kawachi, 2002). Richer countries do better across a wide rage of health indicators. As a result of complex synergies among income levels and expenditure on education, better housing, clean water, sanitation systems, infrastructure and health services, people all over the world live almost 25 years longer today than they did at similar income levels in 1900. This relationship between income and health is robust even when more refined statistical techniques are used to eliminate the possible endogenous effects of health on income itself (Case, 2001).

The relationship between wealth and health is, as noted, non-linear (see Figure 2.3). Substantial investment may be needed in extrasectoral programmes and basic infrastructure before a critical threshold is reached at which health gains are observed at low-income levels. But then, small increases in economic growth may result in even greater improvement in health outcomes.

Ultimately, everyone dies. There is a biological limit to improvements in health and life expectancy, and further economic growth may occur without parallel improvements in broad indicators of health status such as life expectancy.[2] In some countries, health may even deteriorate at the upper end owing to chronic illnesses related to unhealthy lifestyles and excess consumption of unhealthy food, tobacco and alcohol.

[2] Such broad indicators of health status may, however, underestimate a continued improvement in the quality of health such as mobility, relief from pain, and emotional wellbeing.

Figure 2.3 The impact of wealth (GDP/capita) on health

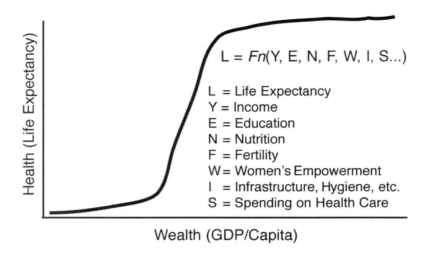

The relationship between economic growth and better health is as valid for maternal and child mortality as it is for the major disease challenges facing low-income countries. Child mortality decreases as income rises, a relationship sometimes used as a performance indicator for a country's overall development policy (Wang, Jamison et al., 1999). Malnutrition and other indicators of poor health also decrease with rising income (Alderman, Appleton et al., 2000). Extrasectoral programmes are important to this relationship because they often improve the effectiveness of specific health programmes, especially at very low income levels. For example, investment in roads allows pregnant mothers to get to delivery services on time and enables vaccines to arrive at health centres without the cold chain being broken (Wagstaff, 2002c). Also, basic education enables mothers to make informed health choices (World Bank, 1993).

Health spending can be good for health and economic growth

There is a robust, although modest, correlation between spending on health care and health outcomes in low- and middle-income countries (Filmer and Pritchet, 1999; Wagstaff, 2002a).[3] Such studies from developing countries refute earlier research by the Organization for Economic Cooperation and Development (OECD) that questioned the contribution of health services to improvements in health status relative to other measures such as sanitation, income and

---

[3] Other outcome measures such as birth rate and population composition (e.g. proportion of the population under 15 years) are not significantly associated with health spending; see Gbesemete and Gerdtham (1992).

education (Illich, 1976; McKeown, 1979; Newhouse and Friedlander, 1980).

There is much more evidence on the impact of health spending on specific interventions and health outcomes (Evans, 1990; Murray, Evans et al., 2000). Early work using such techniques in developing countries looked mainly at the cost-effectiveness of specific interventions (Barnum, 1986), disease control programmes (Barnum, Tarantola et al., 1980), and investment projects (Barnum, 1987; Prescott and de Ferranti, 1985; Mills, 1985a and 1985b;). This type of work exploded following publication of the *World Development Report 1993: Investing in Health* (World Bank, 1993) and subsequent extensive work in this area by the World Bank (Jamison, Mosley et al., 1993), and the World Health Organization (Murray, 1996). There are now many interventions that, if implemented well, would have a large impact on reducing the burden of disease, especially among the poor (Gwatkin and Heuveline, 1997; World Bank, 1997a; Claeson, Mawji et al., 2000). Musgrove provides a decision tree for rational use of public spending in the health sector (Musgrove, 1999).

Several challenges have emerged to the use of cost-effectiveness analysis (CEA), especially as a basis for priority setting or allocative efficiency within a given budget envelope or to undertake bottom-up costing to estimate marginal extra dollars spent on the health sector (Williams, 1997; Filmer, Hammer et al., 2000 and 2002; Jack, 2000). Proponents of CEA defend their position with equal vigour (Musgrove, 2000a and 2000b; Rivlin, 2000). Analysts and decision-makers correctly note that resource allocation decisions affecting the entire health sector must also take into account social concerns for the sick, reductions in social inequities in health, the wellbeing of future generations, the insurance effect (spreading the cost of infrequent but expensive care across population groups) and the political economy of the middle classes who pay taxes (Hauck, Smith et al., 2002).

In most settings, the cost and time required to evaluate the large set of interventions needed before CEA can be used to identify opportunities to enhance allocative efficiency may be prohibitive. The difficulties of generalizing context-specific CEA studies have been institutionalized by the proliferation of national and subnational guidelines for CEA practice, all using slightly different methods. Finally, additional confounding factors include poor quality of data; confusion between marginal, average and shared costs; competing risks and synergies; failure to include non-monetary costs such as time and lost income; and miscalculation of discount rates (Hammer, 1996; Peabody, 1999)

Despite such scepticism, there is a good understanding today of the extra-sectoral synergies that are needed to achieve positive health outcomes (Wagstaff, 2002c) and of the role that preventive and curative health services play in this story (World Bank, 1993; van Doorslaer, Wagstaff et al., 2000; World Health Organization, 2000; Wagstaff, 2002d). Simply stated, many countries could get a bigger bang for their buck if they ensured that health spending was targeted at specific interventions known to improve outcomes, and if patients used health services that provide such care when they became ill instead of wasting scarce resources on ineffective interventions.

... Especially if targeted to the poor

Low- and middle-income countries spend about $280 billion a year on health care, 11 per cent of the $2.6 trillion spent worldwide on health care in 2000. Yet their populations still shoulder about 90 per cent of the global burden of disease. More than 1.3 billion of the world's poor still do not have access to effective and affordable drugs, surgeries, and other interventions they could afford even on low incomes (World Bank, 2002d).

There exist large differences in the proportion of national GDP spent on health – from less than 1 per cent in some countries to 15 per cent in the United States. Per capita health expenditures (public and private) vary almost 1,000–fold among countries – from around $3 to $5 per capita per year in some low-income countries such as Mali to $3,600 in the United States (the ratio would be 1:225 using PPP-adjusted dollars). Sub-Saharan Africa and South Asia are the hardest hit in terms of both current spending and the dismal prospects for increased spending as a result of economic growth (World Bank, 2002d). Moreover, a large part of the population in some of the world's poorest countries

Figure 2.4: Low-income countries have less pooling of revenues

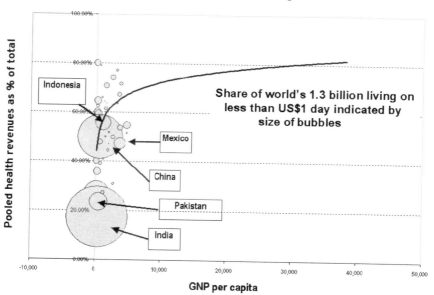

also do not benefit from insurance protection against the cost of illness (see Figure 2.4). Scarce public resources are often spent disproportionately on the rich (Castro-Leal, Dayton et al., 1999 and 2000; Gwatkin, 2001). Extensive work has been done recently on ways that governments can target health programmes more effectively to the poor (Gwatkin and Heuveline, 1997; Claeson and Waldman, 2000; Gwatkin, 2000b).

HEALTH GAPS AND DEVELOPMENT TRAPS

When the charts from the health-wealth and wealth-health functions (Figure 2.5) are combined, it becomes apparent that many countries will confront a serious health-wealth trap during their development. At low-income levels, poor health may become a significant obstacle to economic growth and development. For example, malnutrition, high fertility rates, infectious and other diseases (malaria, TB, schistosomiasis, river blindness, HIV/AIDs, anaemia) and chronic conditions (cerebro- and cardiovascular disease, depression, diabetes, physical disability) are often associated with low labour market participation and productivity of the workforce. Likewise a number of health problems are known to impair early childhood development (malnutrition, anaemia, parasitic infections). This often leads to impaired learning and reduced labour market participation and productivity of the future workforce. Reaching equilibrium point A (see Figure 2.5) many low- and middle-income countries must make significant investments in health care. But such investments cost money, money either not available at all at that income level or not allocated to the health sector. Hence the development trap that confronts such countries.

Figure 2.5: Health gaps and development traps

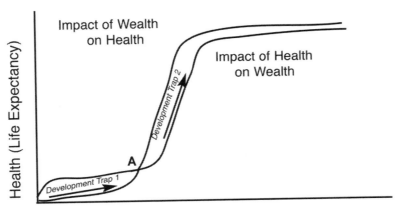

Costing the expenditure shortfall

Various attempts have been made to estimate the expenditure shortfall in achieving good health in low-income countries. Using bottom-up and marginal benefit costing, a team of researchers working for Working Group 5 of the Macroeconomic Commission on Health suggested that developing countries would need an additional $25 billion to $50 billion a year (0.5 to 1.0 per cent of their GDP) to scale up health systems to implement priority health programmes targeting several major communicable diseases (TB, malaria, and HIV/AIDS), child health and maternal/reproductive health (Kumaranayake, Kurowski et al., 2001; World Health Organization, 2001; World Health Organization, 2002b).

Three costing scenarios were used for the analysis, reflecting different assumptions (the baseline year for the estimates was 2002):

- *Scenario 2007A* estimated the cost of expanding the lower levels of the district health system during the next five years.
- *Scenario 2007B* estimated the cost of rapidly scaling up priority programmes even if this required substantial investments at every level of the health service delivery system during the next five years.
- *Scenario 2015* estimated the cost of expanding the existing health system to implement the priority programmes needed to achieve the MDG targets.

Table 2.1 summarizes the key findings from this research. A more detailed breakdown of costs per disease category and regions of the world is provided in the background paper (Kumaranayake, Kurowski et al., 2001).

The analysis focused on poor countries, defined as countries with a GNP of $1,200 or less in 1999 dollars, making the estimates roughly comparable to the $1,000 cut-off estimates from the production frontier analysis. All costs were marginal (i.e., additional costs) needed over and above current expenditures. Three types of costs were considered: capital investment in infrastructure, incremental recurrent costs, and management and administrative costs.

Table 2.1: Annual incremental cost of scaling up priority programmes

	2007A	2007B	2015
Total ($ billion)	11–14	23–9	40–52
Per capita ($)	3–3	5–7	8–11
Per cent of GNP	0.3–0.4	0.6–0.8	0.8–1.0

Production frontier analysis of the expenditure shortfall

Using production frontier analysis, another team of researchers working for Working Group 3 of Working Group 5 of the Macroeconomic Commission on Health came up with an estimate of the same order of magnitude (Preker, Langenbrunner et al., 2001). To establish a production frontier relative to health spending and the MDGs, two assumptions were made. First, the maximum level of total resources for health care that a country can potentially mobilize is likely to be less than or equal to the current highest spender at similar income levels.

Although there is some variation within income bands, the income versus health spending elasticity is well documented in the literature (Schieber and Maeda, 1997). Countries already spending much more than the best performers in outcomes at similar income levels may still benefit from additional spending (based on spending/outcome elasticities), but there is probably also considerable room to improving the efficiency of their spending, since other countries, with fewer resources, do much better.

An exponential regression on a double log scale was used to construct the production frontier using the health expenditure (total and public) per GDP per capita data points for the high performers under each of the selected health indicators. Given the small size of the resulting data set for the production frontier countries, the application of more refined statistical techniques such as stochastic analysis was not relevant. Once the production frontier was established, the gap could be calculated between the target health expenditure corresponding to the best performers and the observed health expenditure for any country, adjusting for the population size.

Figures 2.6 and 2.7 provide an example of the expenditure gap using the absolute level of spending in countries that performed the best on mortality for children under five years of age compared with the expenditure for the production frontier countries. Figure 2.6 shows the production frontier trend lines for total expenditure on health care, using best performance on mortality for children under five years of age, maternal mortality, life expectancy, adult male mortality, adult female mortality, TB prevalence and HIV/AIDs prevalence. Figure 2.7 shows the production frontier trend lines for public expenditure on health care using best performance on various health outcomes. Both the countries used to determine the frontier (large circles) and non-frontier countries (small circles) are indicated on each graph.

Figures 2.6 and 2.7 illustrate the expenditure gap that would have to be filled in the case of six countries (these countries were used as case-study examples on scaling up for the September 2002 Development Committee Report (World Bank, 2002a). The total and public expenditure gap for countries with a per capita income of less than $7,000 was estimated by summing the gap for each of

Table 2.2: Total health expenditure needed to achieve frontier expenditure levels, for countries with GDP<$7,000 per capita ($m)

Frontiers are the best 20 per cent of performers in:

GDP per capita	Number of countries	Child mortality, aged < 5 years (1990–2000)	HIV prevalence (1999)	TB incidence (1999)	Life expectancy (1997)	Adult male mortality (1997)	Adult female mortality (1997)	Maternal mortality (1995)
0–300	22	345	505	1,137	1,356	1,133	654	916
300–1000	47	1,947	3,462	10,875	14,670	11,731	3,992	5,134
1000–3000	40	1,472	3,891	4,475	4,322	5,110	2,905	2,562
3000–7000	26	28,488	60,986	20,958	13,882	25,731	29,728	15,003
Total:	135	32,252	68,844	37,445	34,230	43,705	37,279	23,616

Table 2.3: Public health expenditure needed to achieve frontier expenditure levels, for countries with GDP<$7,000 per capita ($m)

Frontiers are the best 20 per cent of performers in:

GDP per capita	Number of countries	Child mortality, aged < 5 years (1990–2000)	HIV prevalence (1999)	TB incidence (1999)	Life expectancy (1997)	Adult male mortality (1997)	Adult female mortality (1997)	Maternal mortality (1995)
0–300	22	154	407	1,079	241	725	186	337
300–1000	47	4,606	14,211	26,414	6,125	19,537	5,478	9,954
1000–3000	40	675	3,901	3,617	823	2,613	972	1,547
3000–7000	26	47,864	86,565	19,280	28,657	21,859	51,968	40,807
Total:	135	53,299	105,083	50,390	35,846	44,734	58,603	52,644

Figure 2.6 Expenditure frontier and six countries: GDP per capita and total health expenditure

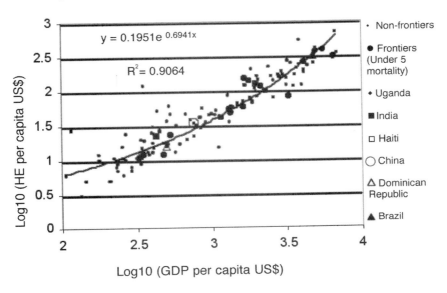

Figure 2.7 Expenditure frontier and six countries: GDP per capita and public health expenditure

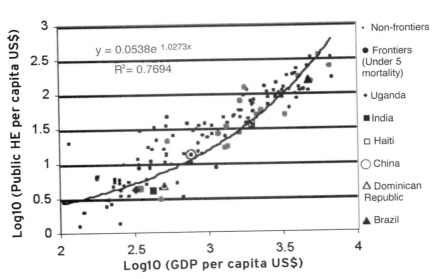

the individual countries within several income bands (see Tables 2.2 and 2.3).[4] Countries spending more than the expenditure frontier were assigned a value of zero even though they might still benefit from additional spending in terms of reaching the target outcome indicator.

Country gap = Y–y, where Y = ce^{bx} (if Y > y) and gap = 0 where Y < y

where c and b are constants; e is the base of the natural logarithm; y is observed log10(HE per capita $) of all countries; Y is the estimated log10 (HE per capita $) from frontiers; x is observed log10 (GDP per capita $) of frontiers.

The use of production frontiers to estimate the cost of scaling up provided the following insights:

- For the 135 countries where GDP per capita is less than $7,000, between $25 billion and $70 billion of additional spending would be needed to bring the low spenders up to the level of the high performers, depending on the outcome indicator used to establish the frontier.
- The best performers on health outcome are not always the highest spenders. Both India and China, where the largest share of the world's poor live, already spend more in terms of total expenditure on health than the frontier spending in the best performing countries.
- The best performers are not evenly distributed across income groups. The best performers for HIV prevalence rates are seen across all GDP levels, while the best performers for tuberculosis are seen only at higher GDP levels of log10 (GDP per capita > 2.9) or GDP per capita > $900). Other health outcomes start having best performers around the GDP levels of log10 (GDP per capita < 2.7) or GDP per capita < $500, for example in Armenia, Azerbaijan, Georgia.

The use of production frontiers indicates the constraints that developing countries face in scaling up spending to accelerate progress towards the MDGs. Since the limit is not the sky and since developing countries have to live within realistic budget constraints, this analysis points to a need for significant targeting and selectivity in additional spending. One way to reduce the total gap in needed spending would be to target specific income groups where the needs might be deemed the greatest. For example:

---

[4] Exponential regressions on a log scale were used both for health expenditure and GDP, after observing patterns of relative fit for simple linear regressions, power regressions, polynomial regressions, as well as in ordinary scale both for health expenditure and GDP. Log scale for both GDP and health expenditure was used as converting them into log scale gave a higher R-squared than the one in ordinary scale. Exponential regressions were chosen because the fitted line showed higher R-squared (0.91) than R-squared of power regression line (0.87) and polynomial regression line (0.83), and also because the exponential regressions gave a higher intercept than simple linear regressions, where the values of R-squared of these two regressions were almost the same (0.91). The exponential regression line was also established by controlling for levels of female primary education, but this did not produce a significantly different result.

- For the 22 countries where GDP per capita is less than $300, between $350 million and $1.4 billion of additional spending would be needed to bring the low spenders up to the level of the high performers, depending on the outcome indicator used to establish the frontier. For public expenditure on health, the additional amount would be $150 million to $1 billion.
- For the 47 countries where GDP per capita is $300 to $1,000, between $2 billion and $15 billion of additional spending would be needed to bring the low spenders up to the level of the high performers, depending on the outcome indicator used to establish the frontier. For public expenditure on health, the additional amount would be between $5 billion and $26 billion.
- For the 40 countries where GDP per capita is $1,000 to $3,000, between $1.5 billion and $5 billion of additional spending would be needed to bring the low spenders up to the level of the high performers, depending on the outcome indicator used to establish the frontier. For public expenditure on health, the additional amount would be between $700 million and $4 billion.
- For the 26 countries where GDP per capita is $3,000 to $7,000, between $14 billion and $61 billion of additional spending would be needed to bring the low spenders up to the level of the high performers, depending on the outcome indicator used to establish the frontier. For public expenditure on health, the additional amount would be between $19 billion and $87 billion.

The use of production frontiers for this type of analysis has several significant constraints. The results do not provide any insights into the potential impact of additional spending. The lagging countries could spend up to and even beyond the efficiency frontier without improving health outcomes. Although the frontier approach sheds some light on the limits of spending, it does not inform policy-makers about the contents of those reforms. To understand the policy contents and implementation issues other tools of investigation are needed.

CONCLUSION

This chapter has shown that the level of additional spending needed might be much more than the $25 billion to $50 billion estimated by the research done for the Macroeconomic Commission on Health (World Health Organization, 2002a, 2002b and 2002c). A significant share of this additional spending would be on essential medicines.

The additional funding could come from growth in national income (which would be automatically translated into higher health spending), a shift of some public spending towards the health sector, increased private consumption of effective care, increased international aid (public and private) and direct foreign investment in the health sector of developing countries.

To achieve this and other development goals, many authors have recently emphasized the need for a more balanced role of the state and the private sector (Stern and Stiglitz, 1997; Stern, 2002). This is equally true in the health sector (Preker and Harding, 2000). The transition economies of the former socialist bloc have had to make a wrenching shift from state-led central planning to cope with the failure of state-led development strategies (Preker and Feachem, 1996; World Bank, 1996). The lesson from these and other countries' experiences has been that states that try to do too much cannot deliver on their promises and are often driven by the self-serving interests of bureaucrats (World Bank, 1995 and 2000a). In the language of some authors, governments would do better to focus on steering (policy-making and coordination), while leaving the rowing (production of most inputs and services) to non-governmental and private providers (Osborne and Gaebler, 1993).

Development also requires an effective state, one that encourages and complements the activities of private businesses and individuals (World Bank, 1997b). The evidence is growing that government failure, poor governance, corruption and a negative investment climate contribute significantly to economic stagnation and poverty. Building the institutions that foster an appropriate engagement of the state, that facilitate private-sector investment, and that allow participation of the poor, is therefore essential to any successful development policy relating to the economy in general (World Bank, 2002c) and more specifically in the health sector (Harding and Preker, 2003). Unfortunately, in many of the worst-performing countries, the additional resources needed outstrip potential sources of revenues, both domestic and international. Donor aid is unlikely to be a solution by itself but it may be important at the margin if it is well targeted to the poor and contributes to systemic reforms.

This suggests that any analysis should not ignore the problem of governments' inability to allocate resources and deliver services effectively, especially in the case of access to essential medicines. Indeed, donor support for such inputs should tie in with government performance in terms of overall resource allocation priorities and outcomes.

REFERENCES

African Development Forum (2000), *HIV/AIDS and Economic Development in Sub-Sahara Africa* (Addis Ababa: African Development Forum).

Ahlburg, D.A. (2000), *The Economic Impacts of Tuberculosis: Stop TB Ministerial Conference Background Note* (Geneva: WHO/CDS/STB).

Ainsworth, M. and M.A. Over (1994). 'The economic impact of AIDS on Africa', in M. Essek, S. Mboup and P. J. Kanki (eds), *AIDS in Africa* (New York: Raven).

Alderman, H., H. Appleton, L. Haddad, L. Song and Y. Yohannes (2000), *Reducing Child Malnutrition: How Far Does Income Growth Take Us?* (Washington, DC: World Bank).

Barnum, H.N. (1986), 'Cost savings from alternative treatments for tuberculosis', *ocial Science and Medicine*, 23(9): 847–50.

Barnum, H. (1987), 'Evaluating healthy days of life gained from health projects', *Social Science and Medicine*, 24(10): 833–41.

Barnum, H.N., D. Tarantola and I.F. Setiady (1980), 'Cost-effectiveness of an immunization programme in Indonesia', *Bulletin of the World Health Organization*, 58(3): 499–503.

Barro, R.J. (1991), 'Economic growth in a cross-section of countries', *Quarterly Journal of Economics*, 106(2): 407–43.

Behrman, J.R. (1993), 'The economic rationale for investing in nutrition in developing countries, *World Development*, 21(11): 1749–57.

Bell, C., S. Devarajan and H. Gersbach (2003), *The Long-run Economic Costs of AIDS: Theory and an Application to South Africa*, Policy Research Working Paper No. 3152 (Washington, DC: World Bank), June.

Belli, P. and O. Appaix (2003), *The Economic Benefits of Investing in Child Health*, HNP (Health, Nutrition and Population) Discussion Paper (Washington: World Bank), May.

Bhargava, A., D.T. Jamison, L.J. Lau and C.J.L. Murray (2001), 'Modeling the effects of health on economic growth', *Journal of Health Economics*, 20(3): 423–40.

Bloom, D. and J. Williamson (1998), 'Demographic transitions and economic miracles in emerging Asia, *World Bank Economic Review*, 12(3): 41955.

Bloom, D.E. and D. Canning, 18 February (2000), 'Public health: the health and wealth of nations', *Science*, 287(5456): 1207–09.

Bloom, D.E. and A.S. Mahal (1995), *Does the AIDS Epidemic Really Threaten Economic Growth?* (Cambridge, MA: NBER).

Boden, L.I. and M. Galizzi (1999), 'Economic consequences of workplace injuries and illnesses: lost earnings and benefit adequacy', *American Journal of Industrial Medicine*, 36(5): 487–503.

Case, A. (2001), *Does Money Protect Health Status? Evidence from South African Pensions* (Princeton, NJ: Woodrow Wilson School, Princeton University).

Castro-Leal, F., J. Dayton, L. Demery and K. Mehra (1999), 'Public social spending in Africa: do the poor benefit?', *World Bank Research Observer*, 14(1): 49–72.

Castro-Leal, F., J. Dayton, L. Demery and K. Mehra (2000), 'Public spending on health care in Africa: do the poor benefit?', *Bulletin of the World Health Organization*, 78(1): 66–74.

Chima, R.I., C.A. Goodman and A. Mills (2003), 'The economic impact of malaria in Africa: a critical review of the evidence, *Health Policy*, 63(1): 17–36.

Claeson, M., T. Mawji and C. Walker (2000), *Investing in the Best Buys: A Review of the Health, Nutrition, and Population Portfolio, FY199399* (Washington, DC: World Bank).

Claeson, M. and R.J. Waldman (2000), 'The evolution of child health programmes in developing countries: from targeting diseases to targeting people', *Bulletin of the World Health Organization*, 78(10): 1234–45.

Cook, E.D., A.K. Judice and A.C. Hazelwood (1996), 'The Americans with Disabilities Act: prescription for tax relief', *Health Finance Management* Supplement: 10–16.

Cowper, L.T. (1987), 'Future role of the Agency for International Development in world-wide malaria control programs', *Journal of the America Mosquito Control Association*, 3(3): 489–93.

Devarajan, S., M.J. Miller and E.V. Swanson (2002), *Goals for Development: History, Prospects and Costs* (Washington, DC: World Bank).

Dollar, D. and P. Collier (2001), *Globalization, Growth, and Poverty: Building an Inclusive World Economy* (Oxford: Oxford University Press).

Easterly, W. (2001), *The Elusive Quest for Growth: Economists' Adventures and Misadventures in the Tropics* (Cambridge, MA: MIT Press).

Eastwood, R. and M. Lipton (1999), 'The impact of changes in human fertility on poverty', *Journal of Development Studies*, 36(1): 1–30.

Evans, D.B. (1990), 'What is cost-effectiveness analysis?' *Medical Journal of Australia*, 153 Suppl: S7–9.

Filmer, D. and L. Pritchet (1999), The impact of public spending on health: does money matter?', *Social Science and Medicine*, 49(10): 1309–23.

Filmer, D., J. Hammer and L. Pritchet (2000), 'Weak links in the chain: a diagnosis of health policy in poor countries', *World Bank Observer,* 15(2): 199–224.

Filmer, D., J. Hammer and L. Pritchet (2002), 'Weak links in the chain: a prescription for health policy in poor countries', *World Bank Observer,* 17(1): 47–66.

Gbesemete, K.P. and U.G. Gerdtham (1992), 'Determinants of healthcare expenditure in Africa: a cross-sectional study', *World Development,* 20(2): 30–38.

Gwatkin, D. (2000a), 'Health inequalities and the health of the poor: What do we know? What can we do?', *Bulletin of the World Health Organization,* 78(1): 3–17.

Gwatkin, D.R. (2000b), 'Health inequalities and the health of the poor: what do we know? What can we do?', *Bulletin of the World Health Organization,* 78(1): 3–18.

Gwatkin, D. (2001), 'Poverty and inequalities in health within developing countries: filling the information gap', in D. Leon and G. Walt, *Poverty, Inequality, and Health: An International Perspective* (Oxford: Oxford University Press) pp. 217–46.

Gwatkin, D.R., M. Guillot and P. Heuveline (1999), 'The burden of disease among the global poor', *The Lancet,* 354(9178): 586–9.

Gwatkin, D.R. and P. Heuveline (1997), 'Improving the health of the world's poor', *British Medical Journal,* 315(7107): 497–8.

Haddad, L. and H.E. Bouis (1999), 'The impact of nutritional status on agricultural productivity: Wage evidence from the Philippines', *Oxford Bulletin of Economics and Statistics,* 53(1): 45–68.

Hammer, J. (1996), *Economic Analysis for Health Projects, World Bank: Washington, 1996* (Washington, DC: World Bank).

Hammoudi, A. and J. Sachs (1999), *Economic Consequences of Health Status: A Review of the Evidence* (Cambridge, MA: Center for International Development, Harvard University).

Harding, A. and A.S. Preker (eds) (2003), *Private Participation in Health Service,* Health, Nutrition, and Population Series (Washington, DC: World Bank).

Hauck, K., P.C. Smith and M. Goddard (2002), *Priority Setting for Health* (Washington, DC: World Bank).

Heckman, J.J. (1999), *Policies to Foster Human Capital.* NBER Working Paper Series No. 7288 (Cambridge, MA.: National Bureau of Economic Research).

Horton, J. (1999), 'Opportunities for investments in nutrition in low-income Asia', *Asian Development Review,*17(1): 246–73.

Horton, R. (2002), 'The health (and wealth) of nations', *The Lancet,* 359(9311): 993–4.

Horton, S. and J. Ross (2000), *The Economics of Iron Deficiency* (Toronto: University of Toronto).

Illich, I. (1976), *Limits to Medicine, Medical Nemesis: The Expropriation of Health* (Harmondsworth: Penguin).

Izumi, Y., I. Tsuji, T. Ohkubo, A. Kuwahara, Y. Nishino and S. Hisamichi (2001), 'Impact of smoking habit on medical care use and its costs: a prospective observation of National Health Insurance beneficiaries in Japan', *International Journal of Epidemiology,* 30(3): 616–21; discussion 622–3.

Jack, W. (2000), 'Public spending on health care: how are different criteria related? A second opinion', *Health Policy,* 53(1): 6–17.

Jack ,W. (2001), 'The public economics of TB control', *Health Policy,* 57(2): 79–96.

Jamison D.T., D.E. Bloom and J.P. Ruger (1998), *Health, Health Policy, and Economic Outcomes* (Los Angeles: UCLA Center for Pacific Rim Studies).

Jamison, D.T., W.H. Mosley, A. Measham and J.L. Bobadilla (eds) (1993), *Disease Control Priorities in Developing Countries* (Washington, DC: World Bank).

Jha, P. and F.J. Chaloupka (2000), 'The economics of global tobacco control', *British Medical Journal,* 321(7257): 358–61.

Kambou, G., S. Devarajan and M. Over (1993), 'The economic effects of the AIDS epidemic in sub-Saharan Africa: a general equilibrium analysis', *Review of Economic Development,* 1(1): 37–62.

Kamolratanakul, P., H. Sawert, S. Kongsin, S. Lertmaharit, J. Sriwongsa, S. Na-Songkhla, S.

Wangmane, S. Jittimanee and V. Payanandana (1999), 'Economic impact of tuberculosis at the household level', *International Journal of Tuberculosis and Lung Disease*, 3(7): 596–602.

Karoly L.A., P.W. Greenwood, S.S. Everingham, J. Hoube, M.R. Kilburn, C.P. Rydell, M. Sanders and J. Chiesa (eds) (1998), *Investing in Our Children: What We Know and Don't Know About the Cost and Benefits of Early Childhood Interventions* (Santa Monica, CA: Rand).

Kelley, A. and R. Schmidt (1995), 'Aggregate population and economic growth correlations: the role of the components of demographic change', *Demography* 32(4): 543–55.

Knowles, J.C. and J.R. Behrman (2003), *Assessing the Economic Benefit of Investing in Youth in Developing Countries*, HNP Discussion Paper (Washington, DC: World Bank), March.

Kumaranayake, L., C. Kurowski and L. Conteh (2001), *Costs of Scaling-up Priority Health Interventions in Low and Selected Middle Income Countries: Methodology and Estimates* (Geneva: WHO).

Landes, D.S. (1998), *The Wealth and Poverty of Nations: Why Some Are So Rich and Some So Poor* (New York: W.W. Norton).

McGuire, J. (1996), *The Payoff from Improving Nutrition* (Washington, DC: World Bank).

McKeown, T. (1979), *The Role of Medicine: Dream, Mirage or Nemesis?* (Oxford: Basil Blackwell).

Mills, A. (1985a), 'Economic evaluation of health programmes: application of the principles in developing countries', *World Health Statistics Quarterly*, 38(4): 368–82.

Mills, A. (1985b), 'Survey and examples of economic evaluation of health programmes in developing countries', *World Health Stat Q* 38(4): 402–31.

Murray, C.J.L. (1996), *Global Burden of Disease: A Comprehensive Assessment of Mortality and Disability from Diseases, Injuries, and Risk Factors in 1990 and Projected to 2020* (Cambridge, MA: Harvard University Press).

Murray, C.J.L., D.B. Evans, A. Acharya and R.M.P.M. Baltussen (2000), 'Development of WHO guidelines on generalized cost-effectiveness analysis', *Health Economics*, 9(3): 235–51.

Musgrove, P. (1999), 'Public spending on health care: how are different criteria related?' *Health Policy*, 47(3): 207–23.

Musgrove, P. (2000a), 'Cost-effectiveness as a criterion for public spending on health: a reply to William Jack's second opinion', *Health Policy*, 54(3): 229–33.

Musgrove, P. (2000b), 'A critical review of a critical review: the methodology of the 1993 World Development Report, Investing in Health', *Health Policy and Planning*, 15(1): 110–15.

Needham, D.M., P. Godfrey-Faussett and S.D. Foster (1998), 'Barriers to tuberculosis control in urban Zambia: the economic impact and burden on patients prior to diagnosis', *International Journal of Tuberculosis and Lung Disease*, 2(10): 811–17.

Newhouse, J.P. and L.J. Friedlander (1980), 'The relationship between medical resources and measures of health: some additional evidence', *Journal of Human Resources*, 15(2): 200–18.

OECD (1996), *Shaping the 21st Century: The Contribution of Development Co-operation* (Paris: OECD).

Osborne, D. and T. Gaebler (1993), *Reinventing Government* (New York: Plume).

Over, M.A. (1992), *The Macroeconomic Impact of AIDS in Sub-Saharan Africa* (Washington, DC: World Bank).

Pan American Health Organization (2001), *Investment in Health: Social and Economic Returns*, Scientific and Technical Publication No. 582 (Washington, DC: Pan American Health Organization).

Peabody, J. (ed.) (1999), *Policy and Health: Implications for Development in Asia* (Cambridge: Cambridge University Press).

Preker, A.S. and R.G.A. Feachem (1996), *Market Mechanisms and the Health Sector in Central and Eastern Europe*, Technical Paper Series No. 293 (Washington, DC: World Bank),

June.

Preker, A.S. and A. Harding (2000), *The Economics of Public and Private Roles in Health Care: Insights from Institutional Economics and Organizational Theory*, HNP Discussion Paper (Washington, DC: World Bank), June.

Preker, A.S., J. Langenbrunner and E. Suzuki (2001), *The Global Expenditure Gap: Securing Financial Protection and Access to Health Care for the Poor* (Geneva: World Health Organization).

Prescott, N. and D. de Ferranti (1985), 'The analysis and assessment of health programs', *Social Science and Medicine*, 20(12): 1235–40.

Pritchett, L. and L.H. Summers (1996), 'Wealthier is healthier', *Journal of Human Resources*, 31(4): 841–68.

Rajeswari, R., R. Balasubramanian, M. Muniyandi, S. Geetharamani, X. Thresa and P. Venkatesan (1999), 'Socio-economic impact of tuberculosis on patients and family in India', *International Journal of Tuberculosis and Lung Disease*, 3(10): 869–77.

Ramachandran, R. (1997), *Economic Impacts of Tuberculosis on Patients and Family* (Chennai: Tuberculosis Research Centre, Indian Council of Medical Research).

Rivlin, M.M. (2000), 'Why the fair innings argument is not persuasive', *BMC Medical Ethics*, 1(1): 1.

Rogers, B. (2002), *Health and Economic Consequences of Malnutrition, Background Paper, UNICEF* (New York: UNICEF and Washington, DC: Health, Nutrition and Population Unit, World Bank). Available at *http://www1.worldbank.org/hnp/Preface_Combating.asp*

Schieber, G. and A. Maeda (eds) (1997), *A Curmudgeon's Guide to Health Financing* (Washington, DC: World Bank).

Schweinhart, L.J., H. Barnes and D. Weikart (1993), *Significant Benefits: The High/Scope Perry Preschool Study Through Age 27* (Ypsilanti, MI: High Scope Press).

Stern, N. (2002), *A Stategy for Development* (Washington, DC: World Bank).

Stern, N. and J. Stiglitz (1997), *A Framework for a Development Strategy in a Market Economy: Objectives, Scope, Institutions and Instruments*, European Bank for Reconstruction and Development, Working Paper No. 20: 1–27.

Strauss, J. (1986), 'Does nutrition raise farm productivity?', *Journal of Political Economy*, 94: 297–320.

Strauss, J. (1998), 'Health, nutrition, and economic development', *Journal of Economic Literature*, 36(2): 766–817.

Subramanian, S.V., P. Belli and I. Kawachi (2002), 'The macroeconomic determinants of health', *Annu Rev Public Health*, 23: 287–302.

United Nations (2000), *A Better World for All: Progress Toward the International Development Goals* (New York: United Nations).

United Nations (2001), *Road Map Towards the Implementation of the United Nations Millennium Declaration* (New York: United Nations).

Van Der Gaag, J. and J.-P. Tan (1998), *The Benefits of Early Child Development Programs: An Economic Analysis* (Washington, DC: World Bank).

Van Doorslaer, E., A. Wagstaff, H. Van Der Burg, T. Christianser, D. De Graeve, I. Duchesne, U.G. Gerdtham, M. Gerfin, J. Geurts, L. Gross, U. Hakkinen, J. John, J. Klavus, R.E. Leu, B. Nolan, O. O'Donnell, C. Propper, F. Puffer, M. Schellhorn, G. Sundberg and O. Winkelhake (2000), 'Equity in the delivery of health care in Europe and the US', *J Health Econ*, 19(5): 553–83.

Wagstaff, A. (2002a), *Economic Growth and Government Health Spending: How Far Will They Take us Towards the Health MDGs* (Washington, DC: World Bank).

Wagstaff, A. (2002b), 'Health Spending and Aid as Escape Routes from the Vicious Circle of Poverty and Health', Development Research Group and Human Development Network, World Bank/School of Social Sciences, University of Sussex, mimeo, September. Available at *http://www.fosba.org/images/adamwagstaff.pps* (Washington, DC: World Bank).

Wagstaff, A. (2002c), *Intersectoral Synergies and the Health MDGs: Preliminary Cross-Country*

Findings, Collaboration and Policy Simulations (Washington, DC).

Wagstaff, A. (2002d), 'Poverty and health sector inequalities', *Bulletin of the World Health Organization*, 80(2): 97–05.

Wang, J., D.T. Jamison, E. Bos, A.S. Preker and J. Peabody (1999), *Measuring Country Performance on Health: Selected Indicators for 115 Countries* (Washington, DC: World Bank).

Williams, M. (1997), 'Rationing health care. Can a fair innings ever be fair?', *British Medical Journal*, 314(7079): 514.

World Bank (1993), *World Development Report 1993: Investing in Health* (New York: Oxford University Press).

World Bank (1995), *Bureaucrats in Business: The Economics and Politics of Government Ownership* (Washington, DC: World Bank).

World Bank (1996), *World Development Report 1996: From Plan to Market* (Oxford: Oxford University Press).

World Bank (1997a), *Sector Strategy for HNP* (Washington, DC: World Bank).

World Bank (1997b), *World Development Report 1997: The State in a Changing World* (Oxford, Oxford University Press).

World Bank (1999), *Confronting AIDS: Public Priorities in a Global Epidemic*, rev. edn (Washington, DC: World Bank).

World Bank (2000a), *Reforming Public Institutions and Strengthening Governance: A World Bank Strategy* (Washington, DC: World Bank).

World Bank (2000b), *World Development Report 2000/2001: Attacking Poverty* (Oxford/New York: Oxford University Press).

World Bank (2002a), *Development Effectiveness and Scaling Up: Lessons and Challenges from Case Studies* (Washington, DC: World Bank).

World Bank (2002b), *Global Economic Prospects and the Developing Countries 2003* (Washington, DC: World Bank).

World Bank (2002c), *World Development Report 2002: Building Institutions for Markets* (Oxford: Oxford University Press).

World Bank (2002d), *World Development Indicators* (Washington, DC: World Bank).

World Health Organization (2000), *Health Systems: Measuring Performance* (Geneva: WHO).

World Health Organization (2001), *Macroeconomics and Health: Investing in Health for Economic Development* (Geneva: WHO).

World Health Organization (2002a), *Development Assistance and Health* (Geneva: WHO).

World Health Organization (2002b), *Improving Health Outcomes of the Poor* (Geneva: WHO).

World Health Organization (2002c), *Mobilisation of Domestic Resources for Health* (Geneva: WHO).

PART II
PUBLIC-SECTOR RESPONSES

3 RESPONDING TO HEALTH CRISES: THE FRUSTRATONS OF A SMALL AFRICAN COUNTRY

Anne C. Conroy, Justin C. Malewezi, Bizwick Mwale and Richard Pendame

INTRODUCTION

A recent article in *Science*, 'Malawi: A Suitable Case for Treatment', argues that 'one country's efforts to secure help in tackling its HIV/AIDS epidemic indicates the gulf between needs and the resources available to meet them' (Cohen, 2002). This chapter tells that story. It illustrates the challenges faced by developing countries in trying to mobilize sufficient resources to improve health indicators and to scale up HIV prevention, care and treatment.

The first section of the chapter provides the context and outlines Malawi's poverty and economic development, its health indicators, the HIV/AIDS crisis, the pandemic's economic impact and the relationship between it and the current food crisis in the country.

The second section outlines Malawi's national health policy, the government's commitment to the health sector and the design of the Essential Healthcare Package (EHP), which will be implemented within the context of a sector-wide approach (SWAp). It addresses the issue of reforms to drug procurement and distribution, identified as key reforms that underpin implementation of the EHP and the Global Fund to Fight HIV/AIDS, Tuberculosis and Malaria – a UN fund to buy medicine for developing countries. It also outlines the essential elements of the National Strategic Framework for HIV/AIDS Prevention and Care. This provides the guiding policy for all interventions in the area of HIV/AIDS.

The third section sketches the main constraints upon responding to the health and HIV/AIDS crisis: the government budget, financial allocations to the health sector, limited human resources and the inability of the poor to pay for health services.

The final section outlines the process of Malawi's application to the Global Fund. Following the Durban HIV/AIDS conference in July 2000, the Malawi government recognized that promoting access to anti-retroviral therapy was crucial for the country's economic survival. It also recognized the need for comprehensive investment in human resources development, health services infrastructure and laboratory and diagnostic facilities. In the words of Jon Cohen, 'Malawi's experience of putting together a plan to deal with its mounting HIV/AIDS disaster symbolizes the difficulties that poor countries and international organizations face in confronting the epidemic with inadequate funds and limited health services' (Cohen, 2002).

CONTEXT

Poverty and economic development

Malawi is one of the poorest countries in the world, with a population of 11.24 million and an estimated per capita annual income of $170. The recent Malawi Poverty Reduction Strategy Paper states that poverty there is widespread, deep and severe. The most recent poverty analysis suggests that 65.3 per cent of its population are poor, that 29 per cent of the population live in extreme poverty and that poverty is most severe in the rural areas. Income inequality is exceptionally high.

Malawi's human development indicators are very poor: the adult literacy rate is 56 per cent (72 per cent for men and 42 per cent for women). Up to 70 per cent of rural women can neither read nor write. Secondary school enrolment is low: only 22 per cent of boys and 12 per cent of girls. Socioeconomic trends for Malawi remain unfavourable compared to other countries in southern Africa. The UN's 2003 *Human Development Report* ranked Malawi 162nd of 174 countries.

The economy depends on smallholder agriculture, which accounts for 33 per cent of gross domestic product (GDP) and provides a livelihood for 85 per cent of the population. Land pressure is severe, and a typical landholding is less than one hectare. The continuous cropping of the same land has led to a decline in soil fertility and to environmental degradation. Malawi is a landlocked country. It has limited export opportunities and is over-dependent on tobacco as an export crop. Tobacco sales accounted for approximately 60 per cent of its export revenue in 2001, with tea, sugar and cotton accounting for 9.1 per cent, 9.0 per cent and 1.2 per cent respectively. The prospects for economic diversification are limited and transport costs for exports are very high.

The economic growth rate has consistently been below the 6 per cent level that is required to make an appreciable impact on poverty. It averaged 2.6 per cent between 1997 and 2000, and there was negative growth (−1.5 per cent) in 2001–2 owing to the food crisis. This indicates that economic growth has barely kept pace with population growth. On 27 February 2002, the government of Malawi declared a state of disaster, indicating that the country was facing a catastrophic situation with up to 78 per cent of farm families without food. In

May the Food and Agriculture Organization stated: 'Poor harvests in 2001, low maize stocks, rapidly increasing food prices, late rains and devastating floods in several districts have contributed to the food crisis' (FAO–WFP, 2002). The World Food Programme estimated that 3.2 million people were seriously affected by the food crisis in early 2002. Experts at the United Nations currently anticipate that the emergency in Malawi may last for several more years. Chronic poverty and food insecurity persist.

Poverty reduction is the central policy objective of the government of Malawi. However, its ability to reduce poverty is limited by a poor macroeconomic performance and low levels of domestic savings and investment. Gross fixed investment has fallen from about 14 per cent of GDP in the early 1990s to only 10 per cent of GDP in 2001. Since 1995, inflation and interest rates have been high and volatile. On average, the National Consumer Price Index has grown by an average of 34 per cent per annum since 1995. Moreover, real interest rates have been at around 20 per cent, discouraging private-sector investment.

Malawi's economy is also highly indebted: there are high levels of internal and external debt and of debt service obligations. Internal debt was estimated at MK40 billion (around $400 million) at the end of 2002 and external debt was estimated at $2.6 billion in 2003. The external debt-to-GDP ratio was 146 per cent in 2000. The present level of domestic debt is unsustainable, with interest payments on Treasury Bills accounting for 100 per cent of domestic revenues in 2003. The voted government budget in 2002–3 was MK43 billion ($537 million), or $50.51 per capita at July 2002 exchange rates. External debt-service obligations average around $70 million, even with interim debt relief under the Heavily Indebted Poor Countries (HIPC) Initiative.

Once debt-service obligations are met, the Malawi government is left with around $34 per capita to promote economic development and reduce poverty. This figure, set against the conditions summarized in Box 3.1, encapsulates Malawi's impossible condition.

Health indicators

Malawi has very poor health indicators. According to the 2000 Demographic and Health Survey, life expectancy is 39 years, the infant mortality rate is 183 per 1,000 and the under-five mortality rate is 247 per 1,000 (DHS, 2000). Vaccination coverage rates show a decline, from 82 per cent to 70 per cent, over the past decade, which suggests a rise in morbidity and a decline in the use of health facilities. The maternal mortality rate has doubled over the past decade, from 620 per 100,000 live births to 1,120 per 100,000 live births (DHS, 1990 and 2000). The statistics for 2000 indicate only a modest decline in fertility rates, from 6.7 to 6.3, and no appreciable decline in fertility rates for women

---

Box 3.1: Malawi's principal challenges

- Poor literacy in the population (56%).
- Over-dependence on commodities as exports (tobacco is 60% of export revenue).
- An economic growth rate (−1.5% in 2002) that recently has been consistently lower than the rate of population growth.
- Ubiquitous food insecurity with up to one-third of the population in need of humanitarian assistance; 50% of children are stunted owing to chronic malnutrition.
- An onerous debt burden, even after interim debt cancellation (debt is 150% of GDP).
- Massive increases in HIV/AIDS, malaria, tuberculosis and most other infectious diseases (accounting for at least 70% of hospital admissions).
- An orphan crisis that will devastate the country. An estimated 650,000 children have been orphaned, 45% owing to HIV/AIDS, out of a population of 11.24 million.
- A small government budget, inadequate to meet human needs ($34 per Malawian).

---

under 30, reflecting the low socio-economic status of women (DHS, 2001). Levels of child malnutrition are unacceptably high: nearly half of children under five are malnourished and stunted in growth.

Statistics indicate that 70 per cent of in-patient deaths are due to pneumonia, tuberculosis, malaria, anaemia, nutritional deficiencies and HIV/AIDS. Most of the adult deaths are associated with HIV infection, but the majority of patients do not know that they are HIV-infected.

The HIV/AIDS pandemic is also fuelling an increase in tuberculosis. Annual notified TB cases have increased from just over 7,500 in 1987 to nearly 25,000 in 1999. The strong link between HIV/AIDS and TB means that TB cases must be identified early and that HIV care and support must be integrated in the national TB control programme. This involves providing quality voluntary counselling and screening and testing patients for opportunistic diseases associated with HIV infection.

Malaria is also a major public health problem in Malawi. It accounts for 40 per cent of hospital admissions, and children under five are most at risk. Malaria results in 18 per cent of all hospital deaths and is also the leading cause of out-patient visits. It is estimated that there are six million cases of adult malaria and 9.7 million cases of child malaria per annum. The number of cases may be under-recorded, as many people treat themselves at home and do not visit a health facility.

The HIV/AIDs crisis

Malawi has a high HIV/AIDS prevalence. The National AIDS Commission (NAC) estimates that at the end of 2003, 14.4 per cent of the population aged 15–49 were living with HIV/AIDS (with a range of between 12 and 17 per cent). Malawi's HIV/AIDS prevalence is the eighth highest in the world. There are an estimated 110,000 new infections every year. AIDS is the leading cause of death among adults, with 80,000 AIDS-related deaths in 2003 and a total of 710,000 deaths since the beginning of the pandemic.

The implications of the pandemic are very serious:

- Nearly 650,000 children under the age of 18 are orphans, 45 per cent owing to HIV/AIDS.
- The death rate for adults has tripled since 1990.
- The number of cases of tuberculosis is three times as high as it would have been in the absence of the AIDS pandemic.

The estimates also indicate that the need for expanded services is enormous:

- 170,000 people are currently in need of anti-retroviral (ARV) treatment.
- Hundreds of thousands more need access to voluntary counselling and testing to determine their HIV status.
- 650,000 orphans and vulnerable children need support.
- About 500,000 pregnant women need good antenatal care including HIV counselling and testing. About 80,000 need ARV treatment to prevent vertical transmission.

The primary mode of HIV transmission in Malawi remains through unprotected heterosexual sex; more women are infected than men. Approximately 8 per cent of transmission is believed to occur from mother to child: the annual total of HIV-positive births is more than 20,000, or about 4.3 per cent of total births. Transmission risks owing to unsafe blood transfusions, inadequate observation of universal precautions and men having sex with men are unknown but thought to be negligible (2 per cent or less) (Ministry of Health and Population, 2003).

A recent World Bank study of HIV/AIDS in Africa concluded that its effects are much more pervasive than the 0.3–1.5 per cent diminution in the economic growth rate that has been forecast (Bell et al., 2003). Figures such as these do not include the broader effects of the disease on families, communities and enterprises – what happens when all the adults in a country are dead and nobody is left to raise the young and teach them skills? Economic growth will be retarded, as the pandemic erodes savings and leads to a decline in investment by both government and private individuals. But this is the least of it. A look at the food crisis explains how the situation is more complex.

The relationship between HIV/AIDS and the food crisis in Malawi

The HIV/AIDS pandemic is a major cause of the current food crisis in Malawi and throughout southern Africa. HIV/AIDS has a devastating impact at the household, community and national levels. It has eroded coping mechanisms to the point where individuals, families and communities can no longer absorb the shocks to agricultural production.

Research in Malawi has demonstrated the devastating impact of HIV/AIDS on smallholder agriculture. The pandemic has eroded smallholders' ability to deal with transitory and chronic food insecurity, which is exacerbated by deepening poverty, a loss of labour and an inability to invest in technology in order to increase productivity. When HIV/AIDS strikes a household, the family has to invest in health care and, ultimately, funerals, while women's work ceases to be productive because they must increasingly look after the sick. Children are often forced out of school so as to contribute labour to the household. Even when children contribute to agricultural labour, the impact of HIV/AIDS on agricultural production is devastating. Land is taken out of cultivation, husbandry practices are delayed, the cropping pattern shifts away from labour-intensive high-value crops and the household cannot afford to invest in productivity-enhancing factors such as improved seed and fertilizer. As a result, agricultural productivity declines, income and food security decrease and the household falls into a vicious cycle of poverty from which it cannot recover (Care International Malawi, 2002).

There are probably biological linkages too between HIV/AIDS and the food crisis. Poor nutrition and poor health weaken the immune system and quite possibly increase vulnerability to HIV infection and accelerate progress to full-blown HIV/AIDS (Stillwaggon, 2001). Assuming that malnutrition advances the pathogenicity of HIV, as it does for other diseases, a vicious cycle is set up: HIV/AIDS deaths create food insecurity; food insecurity causes malnutrition; and malnutrition accelerates HIV infection and future HIV/AIDS deaths.

The food crisis itself has increased high-risk sexual behaviour as traditional coping mechanisms have eroded and people have turned to transactional sex for survival. Data from the Ministry of Health and Population (MoHP) and from the World Health Organization in Malawi have demonstrated that the number of sexually transmitted infections increased by 31 per cent in the first six months of the food crisis, while the number of teenage pregnancies increased by 93 per cent. There was also a significant increase in abortions and complications of pregnancy. This increased maternal mortality. The World Health Organization concluded that 'without prompt attention to sexual and reproductive health needs within the context of the humanitarian response, the impact of the food crisis will extend beyond the duration of the current food shortage by increasing the burden of ill health, particularly in the area of maternal and newborn health,

HIV transmission and HIV/AIDS deaths' (World Health Organization and Ministry of Health and Population, 2002).

HEALTH AND HIV/AIDS POLICY

National health policy

The Malawi government is committed to promoting access to health services as stipulated in the Constitution, and it has increased annual expenditure on health from an average of 6–9 per cent of voted expenditure in the 1990s to 12–15 per cent in 2001.

Formal health services in Malawi are provided by four main agencies: the Ministry of Health and Population, which has overall responsibility for health services (60 per cent); the Christian Health Association of Malawi (CHAM), which accounts for 37 per cent; and the Ministry of Local Government and the private sector, which account for the balance.

The most recent national health plan has identified the major health challenges as high child mortality and morbidity, high maternal mortality and morbidity, and assorted mortality and morbidity owing to infectious diseases, including but not limited to HIV/AIDS, tuberculosis and malaria.

A number of important initiatives have been taken to support implementation of the National Health Plan. This involves giving greater autonomy to some health units, such as the tertiary care hospitals and the Central Medical Stores (CMS). It also means decentralizing functions to the districts. But the single most important change has been to set priorities and to define a national Essential Healthcare Package.

The design and implementation of the EHP is the core strategy for improving the health status of Malawians. The EHP addresses the following conditions: malaria, acute respiratory infections, conditions that are preventable by immunization, acute diarrhoeal disease, nutrition conditions, maternal pregnancy conditions, sexually transmitted infections (STI) (including HIV/AIDS and opportunistic diseases associated with HIV/AIDS), tuberculosis, eye and ear infections, schistosomiasis and injuries.

The EHP is intended to provide a basis for a shared vision of the health sector in terms of public and donor finance, and a sector-wide approach is seen as the mechanism for sectoral planning. The two strategies are intended to improve the equity and efficiency of resource allocation. There is also an expectation that the EHP and SWAp will serve to mobilize additional resources for an agreed programme of work.

Reforms to drug procurement and distribution

Another key element of health-sector reform concerns the management of the Central Medical Stores. As the principal source of pharmaceuticals for the public and the charitable and mission health facilities, the CMS and its 'supply chain system' are of obvious importance. At present, the supply chain shows various weaknesses, resulting in an erratic supply of medicines and medical supplies (Ministry of Health and Population, 2002). In order to address these concerns, the CMS was turned into an autonomous trust in July 2003. This has required it to be capitalized, initially at $15 million, for which the source of finance is not apparent (Ministry of Health and Population, 2002). There is also a need for additional technical assistance to improve the operational effectiveness of the CMS Trust.

The National Strategic Framework for HIV/AIDS Prevention and Care

There is a very strong political commitment to fight HIV/AIDS in Malawi. The President, Dr Bakili Muluzi, launched the National Strategic Framework for HIV/AIDS Prevention and Care in October 1999. All ministers and politicians include messages on HIV prevention and care at political meetings and there is cross-party commitment to this at all levels. The National HIV/AIDS Commission reports to the Office of the President and to the cabinet in order to ensure multi-sectoral coordination and to promote a broad response to the challenges posed by the pandemic.

HIV/AIDS issues are prioritized in Malawi's Poverty Reduction Strategy Paper, which is the guiding document for all the government's relations with the international financial institutions. The general goal of the National Strategic Framework is to reduce the incidence of HIV/AIDS and other STIs and to improve the quality of life for those infected and affected by HIV/AIDS. Its major purposes are:

1. Promoting and intensifying comprehensive community-based responses;
2. Ensuring that gender concerns are addressed in all interventions;
3. Promoting the greater involvement of people living with HIV/AIDS;
4. Intensifying activities for young people, who account for 50 per cent of new infections;
5. Integrating prevention and care as the only meaningful way of responding to the pandemic.

CONSTRAINTS ON RESPONDING TO THE HEALTH AND
HIV/AIDS CRISIS

The government budget and health financing

As noted above, the total voted government budget for 2002–3 was MK43.1 billion ($537 million).[1] Tax revenue was estimated at MK27 billion ($337 million) and grants at MK16 billion ($200 million). Balance-of-payments support was the largest component of donor grants at MK9.3 billion ($116.3); project aid was MK3.6 billion ($45 million); and HIPC grants were MK3.4 billion ($42.5 million). Balance-of-payments support and HIPC debt relief were suspended at the end of 2001 because the government was off-track with the IMF programme. The IMF went to its board in September 2003 to approve a new IMF programme; this has resulted in the resumption of some of the balance-of-payments support that was withheld by the CABS (Common Approach to Budgetary Support) donors. While this support was suspended, the Bretton Woods institutions approved two credit facilities totalling nearly $70 million to meet Malawi's emergency requirements arising from the food crisis. Government expenditure has increased substantially during this crisis, leading to an increase in domestic debt and the need for parliament to approve a supplementary budget of MK9 billion ($112 million) towards the end of the financial year.

The budget for the Ministry of Health and Population for the 2002–3 fiscal year was MK4.46 billion ($55.8 million), or 12.4 per cent of total voted recurrent and capital funding. This compares with a figure of MK5.3 billion, or 15.1 per cent of voted expenditure, in the 2001–2 fiscal year. HIPC financing in the health sector focuses on the key areas of drugs, health-worker training and primary health care.

The cost of providing the EHP has been estimated at $22 per capita (Ministry of Health and Population, 2004). However, recent analysis by the SWAp partners concludes that this is an underestimate, particularly if the government is to deliver ARV therapy for HIV/AIDS and to improve the quality of supervisory services and the availability of care from primary to tertiary levels. The current budgetary allocation for health, at $5–6 per capita, is already below that required to meet the EHP's requirements, to say nothing of these added priorities. The national health accounts estimated that total per capita expenditure on health in 1999 was around $12.4, or about double the public expenditure, with private or out-of-pocket expenditure contributing the balance. Total health financing is estimated at $66 million per annum, including $10 million outside the budget (e.g. via NGOs). The Ministry of Health and Population

[1] The exchange rate was $1 = MK80 in July 2002. The value of the Malawi Kwacha had depreciated to a rate of $1 = MK106 in September 2003.

has estimated that there is a financing gap of $156 million per annum between needs and resources for implementation of even the most rudimentary EHP – almost three times the total health budget. The Ministry of Health needs around $1.5 billion over the next six years to implement the EHP in full. However, it has scaled down the scope of the programme of work to reflect real absorptive capacity and has reduced its financial requirement to $735 million over six years: an additional $89 million in the first year and $322 million over the next three years (Ministry of Health and Population, 2004). Even with planned increases in funding for health from Malawi's donor partners, health services are likely to remain under-funded for the medium term and this will continue to have an adverse impact on health indicators.

The human resources constraint

Malawi's financial limits are exacerbated by the fact that human resources are also scarce. There are only 85 trained physicians in the Ministry of Health and Population and probably fewer than 200 physicians in the country – one for every 45,000 citizens. The MoHP has 381 clinical officers, who are the backbone of health-service delivery. There are also severe shortages in nursing and paramedical staff. Only 10 per cent of health professionals in the MoHP and CHAM are defined as highly skilled, and 65 per cent of staff have minimal training. It is almost impossible to find trained health staff to fill positions, and between 30 per cent and 50 per cent of the available positions are vacant. This is especially a problem in rural areas.

There are high levels of attrition for healthcare workers, made worse by death in their ranks caused by HIV/AIDS. A recent report commissioned by the Malawi Institute of Management suggests that deaths account for between one and two per cent of the total workforce each year (Malawi Institute of Management, 2003). Another problem is that qualified staff emigrate elsewhere in Africa or abroad, attracted by better pay. And as over one-third of graduates of the health training institutions are required to replace the attrition of personnel each year, it is very difficult to increase staffing levels rapidly in the short term.

The Malawi government is implementing a six-year emergency training programme focusing on training nurses, clinical officers and medical assistants, and technical personnel, including pharmacy, laboratory and environmental health assistants. This programme is funded from the recurrent budget and the HIPC resources that were temporarily suspended. All teaching institutions are currently operating at full capacity, which is possible only by paying foreign salaries so as to attract additional tutors. Also, the Dutch and Norwegian governments, with support from the WHO, are providing assistance to the College of Medicine in order to increase the number of physicians.

The MoHP is concerned that increasing training without making health-sector salaries more competitive will do little to ameliorate the current situation. Without salary support, the extra training will just prepare highly skilled Malawians to emigrate to Britain, Canada, South Africa and elsewhere, worsening the problem noted above. Almost daily, the newspapers in Lilongwe carry advertisements from recruiting companies which arrange visas for Malawian healthcare professionals to emigrate to those destinations, where the pay is vastly superior. The MoHP is attempting to respond by establishing a health services commission, and draft legislation is under way, but no meaningful effort to retain health personnel is possible without significant additional resources. Additional investment in human resources and health services infrastructure is a prerequisite for successful implementation of the EHP and all programmes for HIV/AIDS prevention and care.

The inability of the poor to pay for health services

One option for increasing the level of finance for the health service is to charge user fees and to expand health insurance schemes. However, this would be onerous for patients, and even the 'free' care now available from the public system is costly, as recent research data from the national health accounts demonstrate. Overall, 26 per cent of all finances in the health sector are out-of-pocket expenditure; and among the ultra-poor, health care accounts for between 7.4 and 10 per cent of annual consumption. As a case in point, the cost to patients of obtaining a TB diagnosis in urban Lilongwe averages MK972 ($13) in out-of-pocket expenses (and up to 22 days out of work while accessing a diagnosis). For well-to-do patients, this amounts to 124 per cent of total monthly income; for the poor this rises to 248 per cent of income or 584 per cent of income after food expenses (Kemp, 2002). Patients are forced to cope by missing meals or taking loans and selling assets, all of which reduce their economic security and further endanger their health. Thus, even so-called 'free' care such as Malawi now offers actually conceals enormous hidden burdens for the poorest citizens.

Recent evidence concerning the use of social health insurance (SHI) schemes also gives cause for caution about introducing them in very poor environments. According to a study financed by the UK Department for International Development (DFID) on health insurance in sub-Saharan Africa, experience from low-income countries indicates that SHI schemes fail to achieve equity of access or expanded healthcare coverage – both key objectives of the Malawi Poverty Reduction Strategy Paper.

None of this is to deny that there are circumstances in which payment for health services is appropriate. Although the government aims to provide the

EHP for free, the National Health Plan states that 'services over and above the EHP will be provided, but accompanied by fee schedules and other mechanisms that will make it possible to share or recover costs completely' (Ministry of Health and Population, 1999). This allows for strategic cost-sharing initiatives outside EHP provision (Ministry of Health and Population, 2002). Nevertheless, and considering the general poverty of Malawi's citizens, there is very limited scope for invoking user fees or for creating health insurance schemes to provide for health services, in particular the provision of essential drugs such as anti-retrovirals for HIV/AIDS, that lie outside the EHP. Financial support simply must come from outside.

MOBILIZING ADDITIONAL RESOURCES FOR HEALTH CARE: MALAWI'S APPLICATION TO THE GLOBAL FUND

The theme of the July 2000 Durban HIV/AIDS conference was 'Breaking the Silence', and the emphasis was on the need for people infected with HIV to live positively. Recognizing that the operative words of this concept were 'to live positively', the Malawian government established a technical working group in October 2000 to address the issue of how to expand access to ARVs. An international meeting was held with the largest possible participation, including the Ministry of Health and Population, the National HIV/AIDS Commission, CHAM, the College of Medicine, people living with HIV/AIDS, UN institutions, Search for a Cure, the US Center for Disease Control, the Institute of Human Virology and others.

The Vice President of Malawi opened the conference, noting that:

> Promoting access to anti-retroviral drugs is a further component of the strategy to support people living with HIV/AIDS. ARVs lower the viral load and thus contribute to preventing transmission of the virus. People are also more willing to undergo voluntary counselling and testing and to disclose their HIV status if there is a possibility of getting treatment. Promoting access to ARVs keeps patients alive longer and thus delays the time when children become orphans. (Malewezi, 2000)

The Vice President also noted that providing greater access to HIV/AIDS treatment remains an enormously complex issue with numerous obstacles. Financing is the key need, and among other obstacles are a lack of human resources and inadequate diagnostic, laboratory and treatment facilities. Actually to provide access to ARV treatment would in fact require reinvigorating the whole health system.

The technical working group formalized in October 2000 set to work domestically first. Then in June 2001, it travelled to Harvard University and the

UN General Assembly. Advice was taken from experts at every opportunity. It was decided to prepare a proposal for the newly announced Global Fund to Fight HIV/AIDS, Tuberculosis and Malaria, which would soon be accepting applications.

Malawi's first proposal, prepared in August 2001, in anticipation of the Global Fund, was ambitious. It set the goal of reducing HIV-related illnesses and deaths so that HIV/AIDS would no longer pose a threat to economic growth, political stability and democracy itself. Among the principal measures were intensifying prevention efforts, expanding voluntary HIV counselling and testing, improving the overall health delivery system, treating opportunistic infections in a comprehensive manner, expanding access to ARV therapy for all eligible patients and providing nutritional support for people living with HIV/AIDS and for other vulnerable households.

The programme was also expensive: it called for a budget of $1.62 billion over seven years. Of this, $218 million was for human resources development, taking in the full implementation of the MoHP Human Resources Plan and salary increases for health workers, to retain them in service. A substantial proportion of the budget was intended to develop capacity in the health sector. The programme also provided $47 million to upgrade laboratory infrastructure in the national reference laboratories and in hospitals and districts around the country. Another $350 million was earmarked to support implementation of the EHP (at the time, this was estimated at $12 per capita). Support for improving management of the control of medicines and finances and for better performance auditing was estimated to require another $49 million. But the largest share by far, $854 million, was set aside for the services themselves: support for community home-based care ($14 million), nutritional supplementation for HIV/AIDS patients, care givers and their dependent children and households ($110 million), the treatment of opportunistic infections ($313 million) and the provision of anti-retroviral therapy ($417 million).

This first proposal attracted considerable controversy. The budget of $1.6 billion over seven years was greeted not only with scepticism but also with scorn. Nevertheless, Malawi's estimate was not altogether out of line with international rhetoric at the time. The Global Fund did estimate that $10 billion was needed annually to address HIV/AIDS, tuberculosis and malaria globally. In seeking $229 million per annum for its HIV/AIDS needs, Malawi sought little more than two per cent of the total amount that the Global Fund and its many supporters agreed was needed.

The donors received Malawi's draft and immediately expressed concern that there was too much emphasis on care and treatment, and that this would divert attention from the focus on prevention in the National Strategic Framework. They questioned the investment in training and human resources development envisaged in the proposal, noting that it would be difficult to retain trained staff in the health sector without increasing salaries, and to increase health-sector salaries in isolation from the rest of the public-sector reform programme. They were also concerned that the proposal was not fully integrated into the EHP in the context of the SWAp process, and that the programme would be implemented in a vertical manner.

The donor community noted, in a letter to the National HIV/AIDS Commission in August 2001, that

> while the proposed programme may accurately reflect the true need and the costs associated with meeting that full need [to contain HIV/AIDS], there was need to consider a scaled-back Plan B incorporating more prioritization, cost-effectiveness analysis, and less ambitious capacity and financial requirements.

Donor priorities were focused on the development of the EHP and the SWAp, for which there was significant technical assistance and consultancy support. The overlaps between the EHP and the Global Fund proposal in the areas of treatment of opportunistic infections, voluntary counselling and testing and community home-based care were acknowledged but the potential for resources from the Global Fund to close the financing gap for implementation of the EHP was apparently not recognized.

The Malawi team then decided to redefine and narrow its task, concentrating specifically on scaling up ARVs in resource-poor settings. With funding from the Liverpool School of Tropical Medicine, the Malawi delegation held consultations with experts from the Liverpool School, the HIV Unit of the World Health Organization and Harvard University in early September 2001. It was decided that Malawi would scale down its proposal to an amount of less than $500 million over five years.

Upon returning to Malawi the team worked towards that objective. By the end of December 2001 the group had prepared a comprehensive five-year proposal for all three Global Fund diseases (HIV/AIDS, tuberculosis and malaria). The total budget was $557 million, and it envisioned expanding access to HIV/AIDS treatment, reaching 100,000 patients over five years. Like its costlier predecessor, the proposal emphasized a comprehensive attack on the disease, including $210 million for the management of opportunistic infections and $136 million for ARV therapy. It too pressed for significant support for health systems development, notably training to develop human resources, the establishment of laboratories needed to manage ARV therapy, improving the ability of the pharmacy system to handle a large volume of essential medicines, and so on.

The Global Fund finally called for proposals in mid-January 2002, expecting submissions in early March. The application format was complex, and significant work was required in order to translate the existing proposal into it. After this reworking, Malawi's proposal shrank again – from originally $1.62 billion over seven years to $557 million over five years and now to $442 million over five years. It was a nearly 75 per cent reduction of the proposal that the donors had agreed 'accurately reflects the true need and the costs' of Malawi's health system. What was left was no longer sufficient to meet the needs of the EHP, but it did envisage providing access to ARVs to 100,000 patients and also significant support for home-based care and the management of opportunistic infections.

This was still too much, and in the week before the Global Fund application deadline the government was informed that the Global Fund would countenance proposals only up to a maximum of $2 per capita. That would cap its disbursement to Malawi at about $22 million annually. The government was also told explicitly that countries which were ambitious in developing comprehensive proposals would be discriminated against and that proposals 'over $300 million would be thrown in the bin'. Acting in accordance with these criteria, its Country Coordinating Mechanism refused to sign Malawi's proposal of $442 million – without that signature, the proposal would be dead on arrival. Malawi was explicitly instructed to reduce its proposal's specification for ARV provision and community home-based care and on no account to exceed an overall budget of $300 million.

The proposal was redrafted over an exhausting 48 hours. The number of patients scheduled to receive ARVs was reduced to 40,000, the community home-based care component was slashed and the component on malaria treatment was removed completely. The revised proposal, for $306 million, was endorsed by the Country Coordinating Mechanism. Table 3.1 gives a comparison of that proposal with the earlier ones (excluding the initial $1.6 billion proposal).

The Global Fund responded on 21 May 2002. It had deferred approval of funding for the first two years of the HIV element of the proposal and had decided to fast-track the approval process on certain conditions. It noted that the proposal was 'comprehensive and technically sound', but complained that 'the volume of resources appears to be very large and it is not clear that absorptive capacity exists to effectively use the amounts requested'. The Fund observed that 'a large proportion of the budget is devoted to human resources development [and] payment of salaries or salary supplementation', and asked that Malawi, 'explain how this will improve outcomes'. Most discouragingly, it again insisted that 'the budget amounts for all components should be revised downwards' and in particular that 'the amounts allocated for management, monitoring and evaluation must be significantly reduced'.

This was difficult 'advice' to follow, especially as there was a broad consensus that investment in human resource development and in retaining qualified staff

Table 3.1: Malawi's proposals ($000) to the Global Fund for aid to its health programme

Elements of proposal	First proposal	Revised proposal	Approved proposal
Voluntary counselling and testing	15,630.8	15,630.4	11,648.2
Prevention of mother-to-child transmission	19,796.9	19,814.5	4,287.6
Community home-based care	123,444.8	43,061.3	21,413.9
Management of opportunistic illnesses and ARVs	202,050.9	160,828.9	124,646.0
Malaria treatment	37,182.0	22,136.5	0.0
Systems strengthening and cross-cutting	30,322.2	31,031.5	22,385.5
Management and institutional support	13,540.5	13,744.1	11,757.2
Total requested	441,968.1	306,247.2	196,138.4

Source: Government of Malawi, Draft Proposal and Submissions to the Global Fund.

was essential to implementing the proposal to the Global Fund. There was also agreement that there was little or no scope to reduce the budget for management, monitoring and evaluation, as they were crucial for meeting the Fund's stringent fiduciary reporting requirements. However, there were few opportunities to discuss the matter with its staff, and the 'advice' was followed against the government's better judgment.

The budget was cut yet again. What had started as a plan to provide universal ARV coverage to all patients who needed it now aimed to treat only 25,000 patients over five years. The allocation for treating opportunistic infections was also cut, based on the optimistic assumption that once the EHP and SWAp processes were completed, additional resources would be mobilized for implementation. The budget for community and home-based care was halved. The salary support for the Malawi College of Medicine was removed, despite the knowledge that salary support was what had made it possible to retain tutors. Some money for technical assistance and for improving financial management of the National HIV/AIDS Commission was retained, as was technical assistance for drug procurement and monitoring in the Central Medical Stores.

After all these cuts, the revised proposal, for $196 million, was approved by the Global Fund at its September 2002 board meeting. No more than 12 per cent of the original funding request had survived. The ultimate irony was that Malawi was excluded from President Bush's $15 billion initiative to scale up prevention and treatment of HIV/AIDS. It met all the conditions outlined by the Bush administration but was excluded on the basis that its needs were met fully by the Global Fund grant and that there was no capacity to absorb additional funds. In reality, by August 2003 Malawi had received only $340,000 from the Global Fund. The original vision of 'reducing the burden of HIV-related illness and death so that HIV/AIDS no longer poses a threat to economic development' remains unattainable, as does equity in the provision of health care. Malawi has to choose who lives and who dies.

It is a tragic paradox that although the international community recognizes the need to scale up resources for HIV prevention, care and treatment, it is not prepared to finance it. Stephen Lewis has noted the 'grotesque obscenity' whereby the rich world spends close to a trillion dollars on defence and agricultural subsidies while Africa has slightly less than one billion dollars to spend on HIV/AIDS (Lewis, 2003). Until the international community changes its priorities, people will continue to suffer and die in their millions. This is not just; it is obscene. The international community should live up to the commitments made in the Millennium Development Goals.

CONCLUSION AND RECOMMENDATIONS

This chapter has demonstrated that Malawi, like most of southern Africa, faces a number of interlocking crises: poverty, indebtedness, macroeconomic instability, poor health, HIV/AIDS and chronic hunger and food insecurity – a 'perfect storm' that undermines prospects for recovery, much less development. Both the Malawi government and the international community face multiple constraints in trying to address this unprecedented confluence of negative forces. Here there is common ground.

What is lacking is a commitment to provide sufficient resources to translate agreed goals into reality. In July 2002 the World Health Organization announced a new target: three million people in the developing countries should have access to ARVs by 2005. This represents a ten-fold increase over the current position, but the target has been set at a time when the Global Fund is seriously underfunded: it faces a $4.6 billion shortfall in 2004. Stephen Lewis has noted that if these funds are not provided 'there will be no excuses left, no rationalization to hide behind, no murky standards to justify indifference – there will only be the mass graves of the betrayed' (Lewis, 2004).

The Global Fund is in a Catch-22 situation, in that it will receive additional resources from international donors only when it demonstrates results. Countries implementing programmes under the Global Fund also face a Catch-22. In the case of Malawi, we have had to systematically reduce investment in human resources and the health services infrastructure that are prerequisite for a rapid scaling-up of treatment.

This very cautious approach to scaling up will not work. The international community has to take some risks and believe governments when they cost investment programmes realistically. Many of the health systems of developing countries coping with HIV/AIDS pandemics are on the verge of collapse. They require substantial investment in infrastructure and human resources in order to increase interventions in prevention and care. We are not going to make a significant impact on the HIV/AIDS pandemic at the incremental rate that is now favoured. As Richard Feachem has noted, 'The current situation requires a substantial front-loaded capital investment to scale up existing efforts' (Feachem, 2002).

The most recent statistics on the HIV/AIDS pandemic demonstrate that 42 million people are infected; and in 2002, five million people became infected and 3.1 million died. The most recent predictions from the US National Intelligence Council is that without a massive global response, the prevalence of HIV/AIDS in China, Ethiopia, India, Nigeria and Russia could be three times higher than predicted, resulting in the infection worldwide of 100 million (Nullis, 2002). However, the international community has failed to provide sufficient money for the Global Fund. As a result, Malawi and other countries cannot scale up interventions in prevention and treatment and deal adequately with the devastation HIV/AIDS wreaks on the lives of the poor.

We know what needs to be done: the WHO's Commission on Macro-economics and Health has outlined a new strategy for investing in health for economic development:

> Timely and bold action could save at least 8 million lives each year by the end of the decade, expanding the life spans, productivity and economic wellbeing of the poor. Such an effort would require two important initiatives: a significant scaling up of resources currently spent in the health sector by poor countries and donors alike and tackling the non-financial obstacles that have limited the capacity of poor countries to deliver health services. (World Health Organization, 2001)

In conclusion we urge that the following actions be taken:

1. Deeper and more significant debt relief.
2. The international community to increase level of aid to 0.7 per cent of each state's GDP in accordance with international agreements.
3. The recommendations of the WHO's Commission on Macroeconomics and Health to be implemented in full.

These actions are required in order to promote economic development, reduce poverty and save lives. The alternative is cataclysm.

REFERENCES

Bell, Clive, Shantayanan Devarajan and Hans Gersbach (2003), *The Long-run Economic Costs of AIDS: Theory and an Application to South Africa*, Policy Research Working Paper No. 3152 (Washington DC: The World Bank), June.

Care International Malawi (2002), *Impact of HIV/AIDS on Agricultural Productivity and Rural Livelihoods in the Central Region of Malawi*, January.

Cohen, Jon (2002), 'Malawi: a Suitable Case for Treatment', *Science*, 297 (August).

DHS (various years), *Malawi Demographic and Health Survey* (Zomba, Malawi: National Statistical Office), see *www.nso.malawi.net/data_on_line/demography*.

FAO–WFP (2002), Crop and Food Supply Mission to Malawi, 29 May.

Feachem, Richard (2002), 'The Global Fund to Fight AIDS, Tuberculosis and Malaria Says: "Additional $2 Billion Needed Next Year to Fund AIDS, Tuberculosis and Malaria Programme"', Global Fund press release, 11 October.

Kemp, Julia (2002), Unpublished Discussion Paper for TB Equity Programme, Lilongwe; personal communication to authors.

Lewis, Stephen (2001), Luncheon Speech on HIV/AIDS and the Next Wave Countries, Centre for Strategic and International Studies, Washington, DC, October.

Lewis, Stephen (2003), 'The Politics of Resource Allocation', Panel Discussion on Resource Mobilization', 13th International Conference on AIDS and STIs in Africa (ICASA), Nairobi, 21–26 September.

Lewis, Stephen (2004), Notes for a Press Briefing, United Nations, New York, 3 March.

Malawi Institute of Management (2003) *HIV/AIDS and Attrition: Assessing the Impact on the Safety, Security and Access to Justice Sector in Malawi and Developing Appropriate Mitigation Strategies*, Report prepared for MaSSAJ by the Institute for Security Studies (ISS) and the Malawi Institute of Management (MIM), May.

Malewezi, J. C. (2000), Keynote Address delivered at the first Conference to Expand Access to Anti-retroviral Therapy, Lilongwe, February.

Malewezi, J. C. (2001), Keynote Address delivered at the Government–Faith Community Consultation to Strengthen Collaboration in HIV Prevention and Care, February.

Ministry of Finance and Economic Planning (2002), Malawi Poverty Reduction and Strategy Paper.

Ministry of Health and Population (1999), National Health Plan.

Ministry of Health and Population (2002), *SWAps: Today, Tomorrow, Together*, SWAp Design Team Final Report, November.

Ministry of Health and Population (2003), *HIV Sentinel Surveillance Report*.

Ministry of Health and Population (2004), Joint Programme of Work.

Morris, James (2002), 'Mission Report on the Food Crisis in Southern Africa', World Food Programme.

Nullis, C. (2002), 'Global Fund against AIDS–TB needs more money', circulated by Breaking the Silence, October.

Périn, Inez and Amir Attaran (2003), 'Trading ideology for dialogue: an opportunity to fix international aid for health?', *The Lancet*, 361: 1216–19.

Stillwaggon, Eileen (2001), 'Determinants of HIV Transmission in Africa and Latin America', unpublished report.

de Waal, Alex (2002), 'New Variant Famine in Southern Africa', unpublished paper presented to SADC Vulnerability Assessment Committee Conference, Victoria Falls, October.

World Health Organization (2001), *Macroeconomics and Health: Investing in Health for Economic Development* (Geneva: WHO).

World Health Organization and Ministry of Health and Population (2002), *Evaluation of the Capacity of the Health Sector to Respond to the Food Crisis*, Lilongwe, Malawi.

4 ECONOMIC REGULATORY FRAMEWORKS FOR THE PHARMACEUTICAL SECTOR IN MIDDLE-INCOME COUNTRIES

Jim Attridge and Rifat Atun

INTRODUCTION

This chapter analyses approaches to regulating the pharmaceutical sector in different national contexts and identifies the features of those approaches that could be integrated into a coherent model for the regulation and successful development of this industry in emerging countries, thus ensuring affordable and equitable access to modern medicines. The model, or set of principles, proposed here is not meant to be prescriptive but it does offer a framework within which stakeholders in specific national settings can discuss future policy options.

There are a number of ways of classifying countries by income and stage of development. Commonly used classifications are that developed by the United Nations, which is based on a composite index (the human development index), and that devised by the World Bank (United Nations, 2000; World Bank, 1999 and 2000). The World Bank classifies countries by income. Economies are divided according to their gross national income (GNI) per capita for 2002, calculated using the World Bank Atlas method. The groups are: low income, $735 or less; lower-middle income, $736–2,935; upper-middle income, $2,936–9,075; and high income, $9,076 or more (see Annex 1) (World Bank, 2002). A formal grouping is the Organization for Economic Cooperation and Development (OECD), like-minded countries committed to a market economy and a pluralistic democracy. It has 30 members (see Annex 2), which produce two-thirds of the world's goods and services.[1]

The term 'emerging market', originally coined by the International Finance Corporation to describe a fairly narrow category of middle-to-higher-income economies among the developing countries, is also frequently used. Its meaning has since been expanded to include more or less all developing countries with a per capita GNI of $9,265 or less.

---

[1] *http://www.oecd.org*, accessed 1 August 2003.

This chapter develops a 'market-based' model for middle-income countries. This category includes major nations such as Brazil, China, Mexico and several post-Soviet countries of central and eastern Europe (CEE). The model is based on both the experience of the current situation in those countries and the relevant experience of the more affluent OECD states. The more fundamental needs of the low-income countries, for which 'market-based' approaches are widely acknowledged to be inadequate at the present time, are not included within this analysis.

A rational approach to a sector such as pharmaceuticals must be cognizant of the broader social, technological, economic and political environment. This is particularly relevant to middle-income countries undergoing a significant transition process in terms of political institutions and practice. For instance, one group of countries is moving from a communist state model with single-party systems to a multi-party democratic electoral system (Behrman and Rondinelli, 2000), and another group has moved to democracy from a long tradition of relatively unstable right-wing military or civil dictatorships (UNDP, 2001a).

Progress towards a Western-style democracy has been accompanied by a move, at varying speeds, towards Western-style capitalism. However, in many post-Soviet countries, the dismantling of monolithic state-owned industries and creation of a competitive dynamic capitalist market system with effective regulation has been slow. In countries emerging from dictatorships and oligarchies, strong regulation has prevented competition and greater economic efficiency.

Middle-income countries exhibit an enormous range of purchasing power across society, from the most affluent 5–10 per cent, whose disposable income is comparable with that of OECD countries, to a substantial group of the population, representing 30–40 per cent, who live in conditions of great poverty.

In recent years, many of these countries have shown strong growth in GDP: their annual rate of growth has been in the 4–8 per cent range, higher than the OECD average of 2–3 per cent. However, this growth rate masks widening income inequalities (e.g. in Russia and China), and variable progress in civil society development and the provision of basic education and health facilities (UNDP, 2001b). Even so, there are grounds for optimism that the wealth gap relative to OECD countries may be narrowed in the long term; and the anticipated growth rates of many middle-income countries will generate income levels that will enable them to develop comprehensive health systems for their citizens.

New technologies apparent in the OECD, if embraced and applied selectively, have an enormous potential to accelerate progress in middle-income countries. An example is the use of modern information and communication technologies (ICT) to improve the efficiency of many routine activities. For health care, a pragmatic and well-focused approach is needed in order to get the best value from relatively expensive new technologies, and the adoption of appropriate new technologies will depend on the availability of human resources and mechanisms that enable cost-effective and timely technology transfer.

From an economic perspective, despite the growth of the knowledge base, there has been little change in the principles of how best to improve the health of society through an effective healthcare system (Culyer and Jonsson, eds, 1986; Van de Ven et al., 1994). Integrated public healthcare systems funded through tax or compulsory social insurance are perceived, when the state is the service provider, to be more equitable and less efficient. By contrast, health systems based on voluntary insurance or out-of-pocket contributions and private providers are regarded as more efficient, owing to competitive market pressures, but less equitable.[2] Most health systems are now mixed: they comprise public and private elements and offer a degree of choice while attempting to provide equitable access to a core set of services.

The current debate about the funding and delivery of healthcare centres upon how to strike the right balance between public and private elements so as to deliver a system that is equitable, efficient and responsive and with appropriate stewardship (WHO, 1999 and 2000). Emphasis in the past has been skewed towards equity. Increasingly, however, the responsiveness of systems and the extent of choice they offer to the users are being emphasized. The approach to achieving these objectives will be influenced by national traditions, the history of the health system, the current and likely future macroenvironment, which will largely dictate what can be afforded, and electoral expectations. However, a number of other issues and trends are relevant to middle-income countries:

1. The funding and provision of health care is a major and sensitive political issue.
2. Middle-income countries generally have strong legislative frameworks for the funding and provision of health care.
3. Those advocating a purely public or private approach are few.
4. In the OECD countries, there is evidence of a convergence of thinking on the need to balance public and private funding.
5. For the provision and management of health care, even in the British National Health Service (NHS), there is a trend towards increased private-sector involvement.

Among the highly influential international agencies a wide range of views exists on the balance between the public and the private sector. In its recent publications the WHO continues to place great emphasis on the need for a

---

[2] For a contemporary example of this debate see Feacham et al. (2002); Schoen et al. (2000); Wagstaff et al. (1989); and Saltman and Figueras, eds (1997).

strong public role in the funding and provision of health care (WHO, 1998; Dumoulin et al., 1998; Sachs et al., 2001). It advocates international support from OECD countries to achieve 'health for all', defined as a fundamental human right and best served by effective public national infrastructures and health delivery systems. In contrast, others take a more pragmatic view, pointing out that the current public expenditure level in some middle-income countries is so low that even major injections of external funding will have limited impact on access to better health care (Preker et al., 1997; Harding and Preker, 2002). They suggest keeping an open mind when considering a public–private mix and evaluating private-sector projects objectively, especially if they add value even though their impact on equity may be limited. This view coincides with the increasing popularity and implementation of public–private partnerships in health in many countries, from the United Kingdom to many Latin American and post-Soviet countries.

This chapter is structured in six parts. The introduction has set the context. The second part presents an overview of medicines and the pharmaceutical sector. The third and fourth parts explore in detail the demand-side and supply-side policies for achieving equitable access to the best range of currently available modern medicines at fair and reasonable prices. The fifth section, on industry policy, examines regulatory and competitive landscape as well as issues surrounding intellectual property rights. The final section of the chapter presents a model that can be used in middle-income countries as a workable framework to develop supply- and demand-side policies for achieving equitable access.

Given the observed convergence of international health policy and health system reform initiatives in middle-income countries, the chapter assumes that middle-income countries will in general follow the broad trend observed in OECD countries. They will work towards health systems with a public–private mix, funded through social insurance or taxation, catering for the majority of the population.

MEDICINES AND THE PHARMACEUTICAL SECTOR

From a government perspective, the financing and provision of access to modern medicines is a key element of national health policy and the health system. National health policy and regulations, together with health system organization and financing, influence the demand for these medicines, whereas the supply side, namely the discovery, development, manufacture and distribution of medicines, is subject to industry policy regulations concerning competition (see Figure 4.1).

In middle-income countries supply-side behaviour and the structure of the pharmaceutical industry will be generally influenced by:

Figure 4.1: Macrodeterminants of pharmaceuticals policy

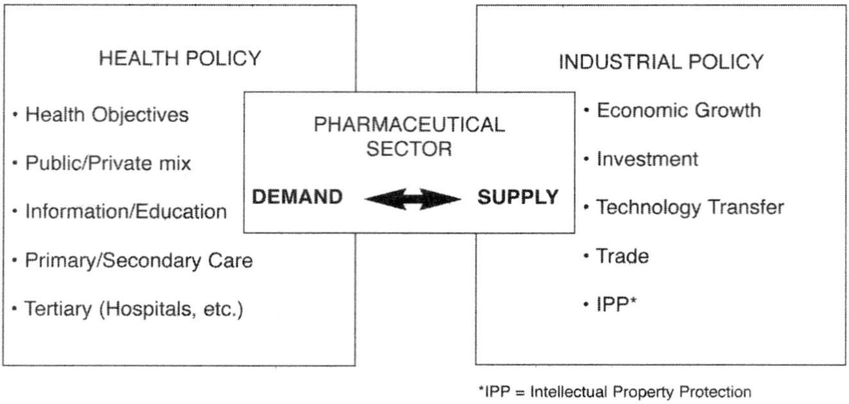

*IPP = Intellectual Property Protection

1. The science base: the higher education systems in the relevant sciences and associated centres of expertise that determine the availability of skilled graduate cadre and supporting staff;
2. The historical traditions of the national pharmaceutical industry that evolved over many years to serve the needs of the local population – for instance, Hungary, relative to other central European nations, has a very strong tradition in this field;
3. The scope for investment in manufacturing and R&D activities at national or regional levels;
4. Tariff or non-tariff trade barriers to imports and incentives for the export of medicines;
5. The intellectual property laws for product or process patents, trademarks and brand names;
6. The economic regulation of the sector, in particular competition law and the special provisions for mergers, acquisitions and alliances;
7. The availability of government funds and venture capital for entrepreneurial activity, new business ventures and the growth of small and medium-sized enterprises;
8. Discriminatory practices which provide protection or favourable treatment for national companies at the expense of international competitors.

This list is not exhaustive but it helps identify the diversity of factors that condition the shape, size and modus operandi of the industry over the long and short term. These factors will be explored further below.

Figure 4.2: A general pharmaceutical market model

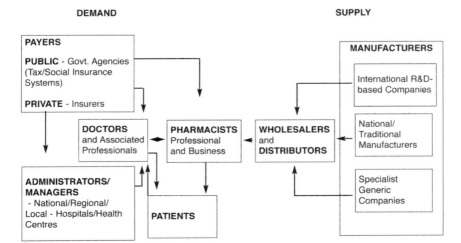

The pharmaceutical sector is characterized by the presence of a diverse set of stakeholders in both the demand and the supply sides, as shown in Figure 4.2. On the demand side there are five major primary stakeholders:

1. *Payers*: In both public and private contexts, payers participate in setting budget limits and mechanisms to contain costs, for instance through price controls and limited formulary lists.
2. *Policy-makers and managers*: Managers play an increasingly important role in setting priorities and ensuring rational use of limited resources at national and local levels.
3. *Doctors and other professionals*: In many developed-country health systems the doctors' voice, while still the most important factor in determining choices at individual patient level, is increasingly less dominant in shaping decisions about which medicines are included in drug formularies.
4. *Pharmacists*: Pharmacists could be placed in either the demand or the supply side of the equation. Their influence as key intermediaries in the delivery chain is increasing. For instance, in the NHS in Britain, their traditional role is being transformed from passive drug dispenser to first-line primary care professional, giving advice, treating minor ailments and with rights to prescribe (Department of Health, 2000).
5. *Patients*: Individually and collectively, patients are participating more in decision-making about choices of treatment (McCrae et al., 1995; WHO, 1995). This process has been accelerated by the increasing availability of information and the emergence of powerful patient and consumer groups.

Table 4.1: Increasing concentration in the R&D-based pharmaceutical sector, 1987–2000: % share by value of the world pharmaceutical market

	1987	1990	1994	1997	2000
No. 1 company	3.42	3.99	4.90	4.60	7.30
Top 10 companies	27.50	28.70	31.80	36.20	45.70
Top 20 companies	45.00	46.40	48.90	55.70	64.60
Top 50 companies	69.70	70.20	73.00	74.30	78.20

Source: Annual Statistics, IMS Health Ltd, Global Services, London.

On the supply side, the traditional boundaries between the roles have become blurred in many countries but four major categories of stakeholders are apparent:

1. *Wholesalers and distributors:* These intermediaries had an enabling role to improve supply-chain management by use of information and communication technologies. However, in recent years, they have significantly enhanced their position through a relatively rapid consolidation of small and medium-sized companies into a relatively few powerful international and national groups (OFT, 2003; Monopolies and Mergers Commission, 1996; and Keynote, 2001). Examples include Alliance Unichem and GEHE. Furthermore, price differentials for branded drugs in different countries have led to a considerable growth in international arbitrage, or parallel trade. These companies, now represented by increasingly effective international associations, look set to have a significant impact on national markets by promoting international trade in medicines (Martin, 2000).[3]

2. *International R&D-based companies:* Within the OECD, mergers and acquisitions have led to an increasing concentration in the pharmaceutical markets (see Table 4.1). Increasingly, the large R&D-based companies no longer operate from one national base but are genuinely transnational. Their primary activities (research, development, manufacturing and marketing) are located in varied geographies influenced by favourability of the business environment in different countries.

3. *National and traditional manufacturers:* A majority of middle-income countries have a long-established pharmaceutical sector. There are established companies in manufacturing, distribution and marketing whose activities are of varying scope and scale. In Hungary, for instance, there are companies which engage in modest but sophisticated R&D activities and also in the

---

[3] See also Annual Reports of International Federation of Pharmaceutical Wholesalers (IFPW) and Groupement International de la Répartition Pharmaceutique Européenne (GIRP).

regional and international marketing of their products. However, the bulk of the companies in this category manufacture and market long-established products under national brand names and some more modern ones licensed from multinationals. Some may continue to successfully exploit 'niche' markets in which they have a particular expertise. But many lack either the capital or the human resources necessary for innovation and face an uncertain future, given the constant supply of innovative products from the multinational companies and the increasing globalization of the trade in cheap generic medicines.

This sector is heterogeneous in composition and varies considerably from country to country. Owing to its diversity, middle-income countries need to audit the status and future sustainability of their national industry and formulate appropriate industrial policies and health policies aimed at improving access to modern medicines.

4. *Generic companies.* This category encompasses a broad range of companies. Globally, there is a growing trade in the bulk-active form of long-established and important medicines such as commonly used anti-microbials, rather than the tablet or packaged forms. This subsector of generic medicines is developing rapidly and is likely to be an ever more prominent feature of the world market. In contrast to the R&D-based multinationals, the driving force for competition in this sector is 'cost leadership'. This requires large and highly efficient plants with low-cost utilities and labour. In many middle-income countries these bulk-active products are still supplied by national companies specializing in the manufacture of low-cost generics in areas where they have appropriate technologies and established market positions. These companies recognize that they lack the funds to compete with multinationals, which invest heavily in R&D. This supplier class will in future be an important element in the supply side. Governments need to take account of the national and international implications of these companies in their forward strategy for the sector.

THE DEMAND SIDE: STRUCTURE AND KEY PROCESSES

Policy objectives

Health policy objectives vary among countries but a core set of objectives is emerging. It includes:

1. Improvement in longevity and quality of life for all citizens;
2. Greater access to health care and fairness that is culturally acceptable;
3. A healthcare system that is responsive to demands and acute crises at the societal and the individual levels;

4. Efficient deployment of public and/or private resources;
5. Appropriate and progressive adoption of medical innovations.

There are essentially two approaches to tracking the improvement of performance against these types of objective: first, establishing good historical national records of health status and care so as to measure progress over time; and, secondly, participating in the programmes of international bodies, with the possibility of benchmarking performance against other nations.

Increasingly, comparative information on health system performance is made available by international bodies such as the WHO, the UN, the OECD and the World Bank. It is now possible to track the performance of individual countries and benchmark one against another. However, the performance indicators used tend to be aggregate; they reflect national averages, which mask the extent of variation in health outcomes between different socio-economic groups. Achieving long-term health gains will depend on identifying the vulnerable sections of the population and the categories of disease that affect them most. These can then be appropriately targeted. For instance, in post-Soviet countries multiple-drug-resistant tuberculosis and HIV/AIDS are emerging as real priorities whereas many African and Asian countries are still trying to eradicate malaria while dealing with the formidable challenge of HIV/AIDS.

Public support and attitudes to equity vary in different countries, reflecting prevailing value systems. In many European countries, governments aim to achieve high levels of equity, in contrast to more *laissez-faire* models such as in the United States, where the individual is expected to take primary responsibility for funding his or her own health care. In many middle-income countries large disparities in socio-economic status are mirrored in inequality of access to modern health care. This is not ideal, and health policies should aim to reduce inequalities. But as this is a slow process, policy decisions should be made with reference to what is possible rather than to what is ideal.

Health policy objectives should address the issue of the availability of essential and innovative medicines. There is a growing recognition of the exceptional contribution innovative medicines can make to achieving health system objectives. Innovations that can make a significant contribution to reducing the disease burden and achieving health system objectives include an effective HIV/AIDS vaccine, new drugs to combat resistant strains of tuberculosis and more effective treatments for a range of cancers.

Therefore, high-level health policy objectives should specify a range of desirable aims and initiatives in organizing the demand side of healthcare funding and provision but also specify targets for innovation. Health and industrial policies, in terms of supply-side regulation and incentives, should aim to foster an enabling environment for innovation, for example by encouraging private-sector investment in R&D activities and effective protection of intellectual property rights.

Funding and budget mechanisms

The proportion of national expenditure devoted to health care is a challenging and politically sensitive decision. Among the factors influencing this decision are the recent trends in year-on-year increases in actual expenditure and percentage GNP expenditure on health in relation to other countries. The first may be distorted by short-term political expediency and the fluctuating fortunes of the national economy; but the second provides a more fundamental, long-term benchmark, and it is commonly used in international comparisons. This health expenditure level is available, and is often published in comparison to other sectors (see Table 4.2).

The governments of middle-income countries are only too well aware of the public and international pressure to upgrade and develop health services to OECD standards, but they have limited scope in increasing health expenditure from public sources. Thus, in many countries there is a debate on the role and scope of private health insurance and provision, especially for elective interventions and non-life-threatening conditions.

In addition to macroeconomic efficiency, the key issues for governments are allocative and technical efficiency: how the health expenditure should be channelled

Table 4.2: Health and other public-sector expenditure as a percentage of GNP: an international comparison

Country	Health (1998)	Education (1995–7)	Military (1999)
USA	5.8	5.4	3.0
Japan	5.9	3.6	1.0
France	7.3	6.0	2.7
UK	5.9	5.3	2.5
Turkey	2.2[a]	2.2	5.0
Hungary	5.2	4.6	1.4
Poland	4.7	7.5	2.0
Russia	2.5[a]	3.5	3.8
India	0.9[a]	3.2	2.4
China	2.1[a]	2.3	2.1
Brazil	2.9	5.1	1.3
Argentina	4.9	3.5	1.5
Philippines	1.7	3.4	1.2
Pakistan	0.9	2.7	4.4

[a] 1990.

Source: United Nations, *Human Development Report 2002*.

and where. This chapter is particularly concerned with two questions: how much of the available budgeted expenditure should be spent on pharmaceuticals; and should there be a separate budget specifically for pharmaceuticals at various levels within the public system?

In the OECD and the middle-income countries there are as yet no apparent answers nor consensus about answers to these questions. In many countries, health budgets tend to be integrated at the national level. However, the allocation of budgets to lower levels in the system, such as regional, local or provider-level budgets, is often accompanied by limits or targets for medicines. These targets often limit the use of new and more expensive medicines. For example, in the United Kingdom until 1997 the expenditure on medicines was non-cash-limited, with no specified ceiling on annual expenditure. In 2000, Italy introduced laws limiting expenditure on medicines to 13 per cent of total health expenditure.

Spending on medicines as a proportion of total health expenditure varies considerably from country to country and there is no obvious correlation with basic economic status. For instance, Japan devotes around 20 per cent of all health expenditure to medicines, compared to eight per cent in the United States (Preker et al., 1997).

Organizing and managing the demand side

For a modern health system to function effectively as purchaser of medicines, a number of key inputs are needed (see Figure 4.3). A distinctive feature of demand-side decision-making in pharmaceutical markets is that there is not one but three customers, namely the doctor, who makes the purchasing decision by prescribing; the payer, who pays the pharmacist; and the patient, who consumes or uses the product and obtains the therapeutic benefit.

In most markets, a single customer is responsible for evaluating both the price of the product and the quantity purchased. However, in most health systems the price paid for medicines is likely to be determined by regulation or some form of negotiation with central government or a payer-dominated customer sub-group, while the total volume purchased will be determined by the collective behaviour of a large number of doctors.

Therefore, in improving the efficiency of purchasing decisions, national public systems face two challenges: to invest in systems and structures that bring together these two elements of purchasing and at the same time to be responsive to ever more knowledgeable and vociferous patients, who want to understand and exercise choice about available treatments.

Historically, doctors have insisted upon their professional freedom to choose the best treatment for their patients from the products available in the market.

Figure 4.3: Organizing and managing the demand side

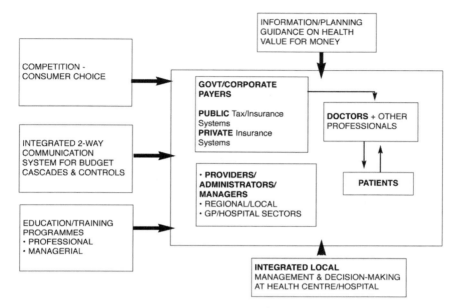

The payers and managers have found it very difficult, in most contexts, to influence this professional freedom. But, in recent years this professional freedom has been eroded, and managers and payers have a growing say in medical decisions. For instance, in the early 1980s, 70–80 per cent of US doctors were self-employed. By the early 1990s, 70–80 per cent were salaried employees of a range of healthcare providers who limited the freedom of clinicians by the imposition of limited drug formularies. Consequently, doctors were no longer able to choose any treatment for individual patients and pass the bill on to the private insurer or the Medicare system. If they wanted to do so, they had to justify their decisions on cost-effectiveness grounds. Similar trends have been observed in many European and middle-income countries. In Britain and Germany, for instance, a wide range of incentives, and on occasion penalties, have been deployed to encourage doctors to conform to guidelines and formularies, to set priorities and to manage within constrained budgets. The main tools used to influence clinicians' decisions have been evidence-based medicine (EBM) (Sackett, 1996), in which decisions are guided by the best available research evidence (usually based on randomized controlled trials) rather than opinions (Drummond, 1980).[4] In the UK, the application of EBM and economic evaluation methods culminated in the establishment of the

---

[4] See also Murray et al. (1999).

National Institute of Clinical Excellence (NICE). This makes recommendations to all NHS decision-makers on the relative clinical and economic merits of medicines using composite indices such as cost per quality-adjusted life-year (QALY) gained (Smith, 1999).[5]

QALY is an attractive and rational approach to resource allocation. However, it would be difficult to apply this index readily in middle-income countries, as the analysis requires a great deal of background cost data and specific cost data related to the treatment in question. Also, as the cost data are country-specific, extrapolation of findings from one country to another is problematic. Moreover, the medical norms and behaviour vary a great deal both within and between countries. Finally, population data are not available on outcomes and costs are not available. When assessing new medicines prior to their introduction for general use it is possible only to construct theoretical models using information from within limited clinical trials. This information can vary widely depending on the robustness of the data and the assumptions.

In an effort to demonstrate new medicines' value for money, the pharmaceutical industry has played a leading role in developing these economic evaluation methodologies. But they have not been used in subjecting older classes of drugs to rigorous scrutiny.

There is much interest in integrating economic evaluation methods into national decision-making processes about the prices of new medicines and the levels of reimbursement. However, despite the availability of high-quality studies, other considerations, such as equity, have to be taken into account when setting expenditure priorities. There is broad agreement that scarce resources should be used effectively, and the best available clinical and economic evidence is useful to guide evidence-based policies. Even so, is not clear whether it is feasible to establish structures similar to NICE in middle-income countries and to what extent the evidence from developed countries can be extrapolated to inform decisions in middle-income countries.

The effective functioning of the health system as a purchaser is also influenced by competition, consumer choice, information systems, and level of professional training (see Figure 4.3). In outline, there are two distinct features of this aspect of a health system, which require careful planning: first, appropriate management structures to enable integration of professional, technical support and managerial staff into committed and effective teams to implement strategies that achieve policy objectives; and, second, management structures that enable effective vertical and horizontal communication between different levels in the health system (see Figure 4.4).

---

[5] See also National Prescribing Centre (2001).

Figure 4.4: A typical health service hierarchy

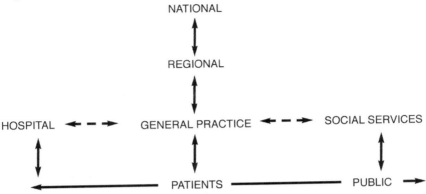

Most countries are engaged in a reform process to establish appropriate and efficient management structures, often with devolution of budgets and operational responsibility to the local level. There is also a tendency to change working practices, with the establishment of multidisciplinary health teams, to achieve a better balance between clinical and managerial leadership of large and complex organizations and to reduce the asymmetry of power between clinician and manager. A leading UK economist, Alan Maynard, has observed: 'professional and stable relationships between managers and doctors seem essential if efficiency is to be achieved cost effectively. If the medical profession could introduce a new Hippocratic Oath, which required practitioners to produce evidence based healthcare, this might improve resource allocation with lower transaction costs than those associated with the creation of competitive markets' (Maynard, 1994).

The process of achieving this balance is a slow and painful one, requiring long-term commitment to organizational development, establishing balanced decision-making structures and achieving cultural change. The experience of public health systems in Europe contrasts sharply with the US private sector, where clinicians, as employees of 'for profit' organizations, are subject to the same managerial and performance criteria and discipline as other employees.

An ageing population, increased consumerism and the availability of new technologies mean an inexorable rise in demand for health care as against a limited supply of resources. This mismatch means under-resourcing with inadequate incentives for staff and limited funds for the training and development of human resources. This perpetuates managerial inefficiencies and underperformance.

In many countries, the key to upgrading the performance of the health service over the long term lies in a radical improvement in the status and rewards for professional managers, and in establishing mechanisms to recruit, train, develop and retain high-calibre managers.

Since the 1990s there has been increasing patient pressure for choice. Patients want a choice of provider as well as information on the treatment options available. The demand for greater choice has been led by well-organized pressure groups of patients with a specific illness. It has yet to spread evenly to general users but the ready availability of information ensures that this demand will continue to grow. The balance between choice and responsibility, especially the extent of cost-sharing for services and medicines, is being debated. Cost-sharing is widely practised in OECD and middle-income countries. The level and scope of cost-sharing varies, often with none for drugs and services for life-threatening conditions but with different levels of cost-sharing for other services and medicines. Proponents of cost-sharing advocate high levels of cost-sharing for medicines that produce limited or no health gain. A case in point is medicines seen as 'lifestyle drugs', such as those for erectile dysfunction or obesity. Some countries have created criteria that restrict the reimbursement only to those at high risk of serious or catastrophic consequences if left untreated. Some of these drugs are being made available over the counter so that their full cost is met by the patient. In other countries, the management of these drugs, especially for chronic cases, is being passed to pharmacists after an initial consultation with the doctor, to reduce service delivery costs. However, cost-sharing is a blunt instrument for managing demand or raising additional revenues.

These trends have implications for regulators in middle-income countries, as some of the above cost-sharing practices are likely to be implemented given the pressures to manage short-term costs. Above all, there is a need to design selective patient co-payment systems that fairly balance cost and equity considerations while allowing access to important innovations.

A well-managed health policy for the demand side of medicines should be guided by a number of principles:

1. A public and private mix of funding and provision that offers the public a reasonable degree of choice;
2. A public-sector insurance funding system that ensures equitable access to modern treatment;
3. Transparent funding mechanisms, with responsibility for managing budgets delegated to those directly responsible for service but with efficient modern monitoring and control systems;
4. Both high-calibre, well-trained clinicians and managers working in integrated teams with a shared understanding of the clinical ideals and economic realities of the sector;
5. Funding and delivery processes that allow an increasing and flexible scope for patients to play a larger role in exercising choice over treatment and payment options.

THE SUPPLY SIDE: REGULATION AND PROCESSES

Technical regulation

Although this chapter is concerned primarily with market regulation, it is also necessary to address technical regulations that ensure efficacy, safety and quality for prescription medicines. The WHO's guidelines, *How to Develop and Implement a National Drug Policy*, with the emphasis on middle- and lower-income countries, provide an excellent set of principles for technical regulation (WHO, 2001).

The International Conference on Harmonization for technical regulation has made steady progress over the years and provides a 'gold standard' that middle-income countries can aspire to (IFPMA, 1997). But to develop and implement more sophisticated means of good manufacturing practice and good clinical practice for clinical research programmes, given the shortage of resources and high-calibre technical manpower, it may be preferable to rely on the work of leading regulatory agencies, such as the US Food and Drug Administration and the EU European Medicines Evaluation Agency, rather than to build a modern national regulatory system without assistance.

It is essential that a professional national regulatory agency be supported by an expert advisory committee network whose purpose is to develop and effectively manage an appropriate national formulary of modern medicines. This involves speedily appraising new medicines and, equally importantly, periodically reviewing older medicines that may no longer meet modern standards of efficacy, safety and quality.

In many middle-income countries, conducting reviews of older medicines and deleting them from the national formulary can be slow and tortuous. Many medicines will be favourites of older clinicians and may also be the mainstay of national manufacturers. Both these interest groups may offer strong resistance to an evidence-based medicine review process. Many CEE countries are now undertaking this type of review as a precursor to entry into the EU, and the German Medicines Agency has offered its technical expertise and experience by way of help. However, the process is fraught with difficulties owing to powerful interest groups. For instance, in both Germany and France there have been protracted, hard-fought campaigns against attempts to modernize national formularies.

In many countries there is a growing trend to adopt a more liberal policy on transferring some palliative or 'comfort' medicines into the over-the-counter (OTC) or 'pharmacy-only' (where the drug is dispensed by the pharmacist without a prescription) categories. This encourages a greater degree of self-medication and relieves pressure on primary-care physicians, as advice can be sought from pharmacists. In addition, these relatively inexpensive but widely used products can be paid for out-of-pocket, thereby allowing more state or insurance resources to be allocated to medicines for more serious conditions.

To achieve the highest standards of regulating medicines, it is essential that national agencies should operate to impartial and objective scientific standards, resisting attempts by third parties to influence decisions in order to achieve commercial or professional gain. In prioritizing medicines, the approach adopted by many national authorities includes assessment of clinical efficacy of the cost-effectiveness of alternative therapies and of affordability. These approaches will be further discussed later.

Economic regulation

Market dynamics

The main focus of supply-side regulation is the varying degrees of intervention on the prices charged for medicines. In some of the most affluent countries, such as France, there has been a trend towards negotiating forward supply contracts, with individual companies fixing prices on a product-by-product basis but also specifying maximum volumes, thereby effectively defining the maximum allowable increase in annual sales turnover.

The advantages and disadvantages of various forms of government economic control are the prime subject of a dialogue between government regulators and the health sector (Lasagna and Schulman, 1992).[6] In learning from the experience of different countries it is important to appreciate that mechanisms for price control are designed to work in a particular market structure with demand and supply characteristics peculiar to that country. Therefore, arbitrarily applying a price regulation scheme from one country to another could have unforeseen and undesired consequences on market behaviour (see the discussion below on 'reference price' control schemes and doctor–patient relationships).

Markets vary widely in character (Nagle, 1987). Suppliers in low-value-added, high-volume sectors, such as multi-product supermarket retailers, do not negotiate prices with individual customers. For a new product, suppliers effectively declare a price and await the outcome in terms of the mass customer response. As vast numbers of products are sold every day and there are regular repeat purchases, it is possible to adjust prices up or down in response to changing demand. At the other end of the spectrum are heavy industrial goods, such as power stations or aircraft carriers, for which the customer base is small, unit sales are low and unit costs are very high. In this situation, individual customers engage in protracted direct negotiation of prices and terms before agreeing a deal. There are, of course, many variations between these extremes.

[6] See also Mossialos et al. (1994).

In the health sector the customer is characterized as a continuum, extending from a single government payer to millions of individual patients (see Figure 4.5). But in the pharmaceutical sector, the payer–doctor duality immediately raises a problem about conventional models of market behaviour. If individual doctors are regarded as the decision-making customers, then suppliers will not negotiate prices with them individually. They will treat the doctors as a mass consumer market in which they freely post list prices and wait and see what volume of sales ensue. However, if an institutional payer, for instance the ministry of health or a health authority, is the customer then an industrial market and a monopsony structure prevails in which the paying customer negotiates prices with suppliers in advance of sales and there is no independent declaration of prices.

This dual-purchaser conundrum poses challenges, and attempts to resolve them have led to a range of creative approaches to arrive at what the interested parties regard as a 'fair price' for the new medicines. In effect, the prices and volumes of new medicines are determined by the decisions of the payer and the doctor. The extent of their influence depends on the power base of each group. The payer usually determines the price, and the doctor, through prescribing, the volume. When the patient is also a payer, through cost-sharing, he or she has a role to play in determining the price. In practice, however, fixed co-pay schemes leave no scope for patient choice, and variable reference price co-payment systems rarely function, because the doctor, as the key intermediary, has little incentive to spend precious time explaining to the patient the pros and cons of alternative products.

In France, a monopsony structure prevails in which the government and the drug companies agree annual contracts covering prices, volumes and sales value. By contrast, in Germany, which is more like a consumer market, there is no central control of prices but a sophisticated system of delegation of budgetary control to local doctors. The central health insurance system and the government act only indirectly on the market, through budgetary constraints. Although, in this case, there are also secondary constraints owing to a reference pricing scheme, this does not seriously infringe on the power of doctors at the local level to exercise choice within their allotted budgets.

Figure 4.5: Customers – the payer–doctor–patient continuum

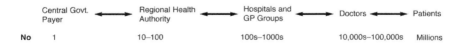

Central Govt. Payer		Regional Health Authority		Hospitals and GP Groups		Doctors		Patients
No 1		10–100		100s–1000s		10,000s–100,000s		Millions

Collective bargaining

It is worth noting at this point that in most countries the evolution of the supply-side regulatory framework involves a dialogue between the government and the pharmaceutical industry, often through some form of national industry association. In a sector where public purchasing is subject to high levels of economic control, this dialogue is clearly of great importance to both parties. However, the ability of governments to enact strong legislation tips the balance of power in their favour. *Force majeure* intervention by the state in the form of general price reductions is quite commonplace. Experience suggests that governments which regulate arbitrarily, with little or no consultation or negotiation, are in much greater danger of destabilizing markets, leading to risks to both the continuity of supply and an orderly industrial policy. By contrast, those governments which seek a close, ongoing dialogue with industry on supply-side regulation and sectoral policy are most likely to improve access to modern medicines on the demand side and a strong industrial base on the supply side.

The relationship between relevant government departments and the industry operates at two levels: collective dialogue or negotiation with industry associations[7] and negotiations with individual companies. In recent years, the dialogue with the industry association has become more complex as differences in interests between the international R&D-based companies, national companies and specialist generic companies (see Figure 4.2) have become more sharply defined and positions on issues have become more diverse. Typical issues of contention are the reform of the patent law and the de-listing of older products from reimbursement. It is not uncommon for each of these sub-groups to have its own association.

Pharmacists and wholesalers

Pharmacists, as independent, profit-maximizing businesses, and a group with a strong professional ethos and organization, are a powerful intermediary with whom other demand- and supply-side players must bargain.

Traditionally, pharmacists operated as small independent businesses (owner-managed single shops) and dealt in prescription medicines and a range of other health and consumer products. Their business model was based on that of a typical retailer: buying products at as low a price as possible and selling at a price the market would bear.

For prescription medicines, however, this business model soon changed. Public-sector prices are agreed on a formula or a fixed list-price basis, and in many countries pharmacists grouped together for collective bargaining, to negotiate a nationally fixed percentage margin mark-up on the price of each item dis-

---

[7] For a useful insight into the structure and role of pharmaceutical industry associations, see European Federation of Pharmaceutical Industries and Associations (2002).

pensed. Over the years, as the unit value of prescriptions increased greatly, this percentage mark-up approach was advantageous to pharmacists. In response, governments have tried to move slowly to a 'tapered' percentage margin system or to a formula with an emphasis on a fee-for-service plus cost allowance per item dispensed regardless of its price. Currently, the percentage margin approach is in place in most countries but with a scale of declining percentages for higher-value products. The jealously guarded tradition of one-pharmacist, one-shop, enshrined in law in many countries, clearly precludes the development of large pharmacy chains with scope for economies of scale and gains in efficiency. What to do about this is a key issue for most countries. A recent review in Britain relaxed the rules for opening new pharmacies, thereby increasing competition and the scope for large retailers to form chains of pharmacies (OFT, 2003).

Similar considerations apply to wholesalers, whose 'custom and practice' has in some countries led to generous fixed margins for small, inefficient warehousing and distribution businesses. Careful thought needs to be given to providing market incentives that improve efficiency in the value chain by the use of modern information and communication technologies and by achieving economies of scale.

In some middle-income countries two other significant ways of distribution exist: doctors, who also dispense medicines, and retail outlets unsupervised by qualified pharmacists but which sell a limited range of 'prescription' products. Both these distribution channels need regulation.

Market structure

Governments regulate pharmaceutical prices. The extent of regulation should depend on the level of competition. The pharmaceutical industry argues strongly that adequate competition exists for a majority of products. However, governments disagree.

Assessing a particular market requires careful examination of three factors:

1. How well organized are the customers?
2. What is the nature of the product segments that make up the market?
3. What is the structure of the supply side in terms of the type and number of competing companies?

The first of these questions has been addressed in the discussions of the payer–doctor–patient relationship. This section addresses the market structure in relation to product classes. Competitive structure will be dealt with in the section on industrial policy.

The pharmaceutical sector consists of a set of discrete sub-markets whose products are not substitutable and thus do not compete with one another. For example, one cannot substitute a heart drug with an anti-cancer drug. But, within sub-markets competition and substitution exist and three product classes prevail: innovative, patented, 'new-in-class' or pioneer products; close substitutes, the same in class but with different patented molecules; and a variety of non-patented brands and generic products.

The situation in which a radically new and patented product, clearly better than any existing ones, enjoys a monopoly position is becoming increasingly rare. This is because R&D activities are increasingly competitive, resulting in a cluster of new and similar patented molecules appearing soon after the first 'new-in-class' market entrant. A typical example is the Cox 2 inhibitor drugs for rheumatoid arthritis: competitor products followed the launch of 'first-in-class' within a few months. The perception that the possession of a patent provides a market monopoly position is no longer true for the pharmaceutical sector. In practice, it is increasingly common for there to be a number of patented entities with similar medical effects and side-effect profiles (Towse and Leighton, 1999). Consequently, if the demand-side customers are well organized and have good information on prices, it should be relatively easy to exploit the competition between suppliers by switching to the cheaper similar product without the need for formal supply-side controls.

In most countries, patented family classes account for only about 20 to 30 per cent of the total market by value. The rest consist of classes in which popular brands whose patents have expired must compete with identical generic copies (Senior et al., 1998). There is, therefore, the possibility for intense price-based competition for most drugs on the market. But in practice this degree of competition has not materialized. This limit to competition can be attributed to two principal factors. The first is a rigid bureaucratic system for determining prices. The relevant body, applying the simple logic that the same chemical entity should be given the same price, fixes the price of all brands of a given molecule at the same level, leaving suppliers virtually no scope or incentive to compete by lowering prices. The second factor is the unavailability of an industry sector that specializes in selling cheaper generic products. Even if price controls are relaxed, there are no companies which can take advantage of it.

Reference pricing

In recent years, reference pricing, one approach to pricing, has come into use in price regulation in various European countries, Australia and the Canadian province of British Columbia. It is an approach whereby the insurer covers only the prices of low-cost, benchmark drugs in a therapeutic class with a similar efficacy and side-effect profile. Patients who wish to use a higher-price substitute in a class must then pay the full difference between the retail price of that drug and the reference price covered by the insurer (Kanavos and Reinhardt, 2003).

Reference pricing was introduced in Germany in the late 1980s in order to overcome doctors' resistance to using cheaper brands of the same molecule (Zammit-Lucia and Dasgupta, 1995). Despite the availability of lower-price substitutes, the doctors preferred to use their favourite brands from well-known companies. The German Krankenkassen decided to force the issue by introducing a regime in which they chose a reference price for a given band of medicines, whereby two-thirds of the products would have prices above the reference price and one-third could have prices below it. They stipulated that they would reimburse pharmacists only at the reference price. If the doctor prescribed and the pharmacist dispensed one of the higher-price brands the patient would have to pay the difference. In effect, this would force doctor and patient to become joint decision-makers in selecting a brand at an acceptable price.

Doctors quickly adopted a policy of only using brands whose prices were at or below the reference price, as they did not have the time to explain to patients the pros and cons of different drugs in the same class. The ensuing loss of sales volume forced all the companies with higher prices to reduce these to the reference level. Then the reference prices were reduced further in order to achieve further cost savings. Although the health system did achieve considerable cost savings, prices were clustered very closely around the reference price without genuine competition among generics. It was only when doctors became budget holders that a true generics market with price competition evolved. Germany now has the highest use of generics of any developed country (Statistics 2000, 2001).

National reimbursement lists

A popular approach to sustaining effective budgetary control in public or private health systems with large numbers of quasi-independent doctors consists of defining an agreed list of products that will be reimbursed by the system. The extent to which doctors are expected to adhere to the prescribing list varies. In some countries this is mandatory. In others the list is in the form of a guideline, and there is some flexibility and a mechanism for doctors to make a special case to use drugs not included in it. The widespread use of such lists requires the regulatory authorities to address two key issues: how one decides which new products should be added to the list and what should be the scope and processes to remove products from the list. In some countries, different lists exist at national, regional and local levels.

A comprehensive account of the evolution of the use of lists is beyond the scope of this chapter. It is important to have a system that allows a dynamic inflow of innovative products into the system over time as well as the removal of older or obsolete drugs from the list (see Figure 4.6).

Figure 4.6: A dynamic reimbursement pipeline model

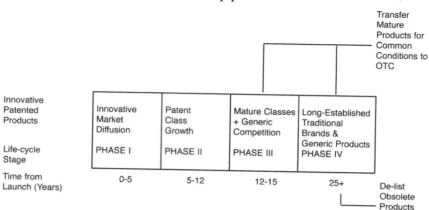

From time to time, demand-side decision-makers need to review and rebalance the reimbursement portfolio in its entirety in order to optimize its value in offering patients the best modern treatments. Unfortunately, in many national settings, where decision-making is dominated by short-term concern of payers to contain costs, the emphasis is on slowing down new entrants into the reimbursement lists by challenging their clinical efficacy and cost-effectiveness. This is not to suggest that customer groups should uncritically accept new products into general use without any evaluation. With a well-managed reimbursement 'pipeline' it should be possible to allow new products to enter the market at a suitable price relative to other members of a competitive patented class and then to evaluate retrospectively its cost-effectiveness over a period of years. Evidence supports the view that in Phase II of the life-cycle of a particular drug class (see Figure 4.6) there is sufficient competition to keep prices in check (Towse and Leighton, 1999; Schulman and Lasagna, 1998).

On the industry side, there can be no objection to impartial assessment of the comparative clinical efficacy and cost-effectiveness of products at regular intervals and to the dissemination of this information to budget holders and individual clinicians as guidance but not mandatory instruction. Where a well-ordered demand side exists with a transparent flow of funds and information, it should be possible for central payers to trust local decision-makers to act on such information and select the best products.

Cost containment: alternative policies and regulatory measures

There are many alternative options for containing pharmaceutical costs, and the academic health literature and specialist pharmaceutical literature discuss their advantages and disadvantages in detail (Rapple, ed., 2000). Table 4.3 summarizes alternative policy options on the demand and supply sides.

For middle-income countries the challenge is to develop coherent pharmaceutical and health policies with mechanisms that allow cost containment and also the introduction of innovative medicines. The 'pick 'n' mix' approach whereby different mechanisms are incrementally added to the existing menu of controls without systematic thinking is inappropriate.

Typically, in many countries, cost-effectiveness assessment or reference pricing is introduced without any change to the existing controls. The net effect is an accumulation of a complex array of regulatory measures whose interactions and overall impact on health system objectives are poorly understood by all the stakeholders.

A balanced approach, which would meet the twin objectives of giving patients good access to the best modern medicines while managing expenditure growth within reasonable limits, is proposed (see Figure 4.7).

Table 4.3: The impact of economic regulation on the demand and supply sides

Supply side	Demand and supply side	Demand side
Control of increases in annual company sales	Pharmacist reimbursement charges – tapered percentage margins – fee for service systems	Annual budget limits – national, which cascade down to operational level
Retrospective customer 'pay back' contracts	Government price information systems	
Annual company profitability controls	Generic competition incentives	National reimbursement lists
New product price controls	Cost-effectiveness appraisals and guidelines	Local hospital/GP group reimbursement lists
Periodic price reductions	Periodic de-listing of obsolete products	Patient co-payment – fixed or variable percentage models
Tax restraints on promotional expenditure	Periodic transfer of mature products to OTC	
International price comparisons	Referencing pricing systems	Additional variable co-pay based on reference price

Figure 4.7: Supply-side policies and regulation

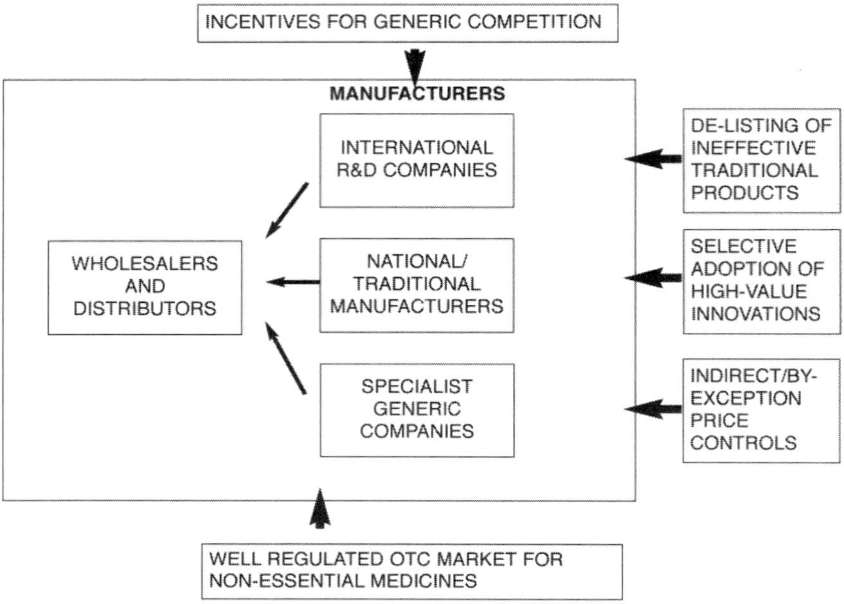

Information systems and promotion

Most countries adopt a pluralistic approach to providing information on medicines. For instance, the government provides information to health professionals through a national network and to the pharmaceutical industry through direct contacts, conferences and media advertising.

Pharmaceutical industry behaviour is tightly managed with self-regulatory codes of conduct for industry promotional activities. The balance of what information should be provided by the government and what by the industry is an unresolved issue. Government-initiated information is seen to be biased, as is that provided by individual companies. However, as many pharmaceutical companies provide information, health professionals are able to compare and contrast it. In recent times, a number of government authorities in Europe have sought to constrain industry expenditure on promotion through supply-side interventions such as changing the limits of what is allowable as a taxable expense. Such blunt instruments are no substitute to improving the demand side's ability to discriminate effectively between alternative offerings.

At first sight, the idea of a publicly funded national appraisal system using modern information communication technologies to review clinical trials and experiences and cost-effective studies appears attractive. However, given the preoccupation with cost containment, this approach may not be immune from bias and may also prove to be very costly. A balance should be struck between information provided by the government, the industry and consumer groups. The application of electronic communication technologies should provide new and more efficient communication channels to promote balance, although its impact on traditional approaches appears to be limited.[8]

There is general agreement that users should be provided with better medical information in order to empower them to take greater responsibility for their health and to participate in decisions related to treatment options.

A better-educated population with access to sophisticated ICT, transparency of information on the best available treatments and direct-to-consumer advertising have increased the demand for innovative and more costly drugs. Patients want to have what is best for them. This is alarming for health system managers trying to contain the costs of medicines. Therefore, greater explicit rationing is increasingly an option entertained by policy-makers.

INDUSTRY POLICY

At the beginning of this chapter it was argued that the behaviour of the pharmaceutical sector and effective regulation depended on both the health and industry policy objectives. Health policies have been discussed. Industry policies fall into two general categories: first, laws and regulations to control industry to protect consumer or public interest; and, second, policies to promote and encourage industrial investment and activities for wealth creation and employment. In the first area competition policy and laws, and intellectual property laws plus their enforcement, are particularly important for the pharmaceutical sector.

Competition law

Many middle-income countries, in particular the post-Soviet countries, are developing national competition regulations and, importantly, establishing suitable competition authorities to enforce them. In the case of the pharmaceutical sector there are numerous regulatory systems for dealing with price negotiation or control. The proponents of strong sector-specific controls often overlook the fact that a well-constituted national competition law should provide a framework for protecting the interest of the state and the public at large. Specifically, competition law should protect against the abuse of a dominant position (control of a large share of a defined market sector), excessive or predatory pricing practices, operation of price cartels between companies, the partitioning of markets between companies and the creation of monopolies in specific markets through mergers and acquisitions.

[8] For a review of issues affecting the sector, see Levy (1995).

As paying customers, government health agencies should ensure that they are well equipped with expert legal advice so as to seek remedies, through the courts if necessary, before using the state's power to promulgate specific regulations for the pharmaceutical sector. Attempts to use sector-specific formulas to serve the interest of the government as customer may have unforeseen consequences for the development of competitive markets.

Intellectual property law

There is currently a high-profile international debate at the WTO about how the template for national intellectual property (IP) law agreed in the 1995 GATT round, namely the Trade-Related Intellectual Property Rights agreement (TRIPS), might be interpreted or translated into national law in middle- and low-income countries (WTO, 2001; Bale, 2000). Pharmaceuticals have become a major focal point of this debate. First, they are widely recognized to be the industry most heavily dependent on patents to protect inventions (Mansfield, 1986 and 1996). Secondly, there is strong pressure from some emerging countries, most notably India. They argue against international patent laws on a number of points: to improve access to patented medicines cheaply for the local population; to offer cheap local copies and thereby promote local manufacturing industry; to transfer technology cheaply; and to save on import costs.

TRIPS has provisions which stipulate that in the event of a national emergency, the rights of IP owners can be overridden by a process of compulsory licensing to other (local) manufacturers. The HIV/AIDS epidemic in emerging countries has been identified as just such a crisis. The Brazilian government has overridden IP rights and invested directly in copy manufacture, producing the drugs locally. In response, many R&D-based company patent owners with anti-retroviral treatment for AIDS have offered to supply products to emerging countries at deeply discounted prices, at a level approaching direct manufacturing costs. A prominent example is GlaxoSmithKline in Africa.

For many middle-income countries which aspire to join the EU and which are required to upgrade their patent protection laws to European levels, this approach is unlikely to be an issue. Nor is it an issue for the poorest low-income countries, as they lack the necessary infrastructure for local manufacture. Much more in question is what may happen in large emerging countries such as India, China and Brazil which have recently patented innovations in key disease areas such as malaria and TB. It is currently debatable whether under new national IP laws, which are nominally TRIPS-compliant, those products will be declared as essential to deal with health emergencies and be subject to compulsory licensing for local manufacture. This is of particular concern to India, which has a vast poor population and an influential local manufacturing industry (Watal, 2000).[9]

[9] See also Lanjouw (1999).

Many alternative scenarios exist as to how this issue of overriding the rights of IP owners will play out in future. We argue that a basic TRIPS-compliant law, which would provide sound product patent protection for medicines, is also an essential minimum requirement for the long-term development of the supply side of the national pharmaceutical sector. For countries hoping to attract inward investment for their pharmaceutical sector, the adoption of regulations and policies that attempt to deal with existing health challenges by overriding patent laws appears to be counter-productive. A policy of professional but tough commercial negotiation, which has been notably successful for AIDS drugs in many countries, would appear to be a far more attractive option.

Industry investment: promotion and incentives

Developing a successful pharmaceutical sector also depends on promoting investment and industry activity, which raises three issues for that sector: investment promotion – both national industry investment and inward investment from overseas; transfer of medical technologies, manufacturing technologies and R&D technologies; and trade policies – import tariffs and anti-dumping regulations, manufacturing restrictions and interpretations of international IP issues.

Earlier in this chapter we divided pharmaceutical industry manufacturers into three distinct groups, namely the international R&D-based industry, traditional established national manufacturers, and the manufacturers and suppliers of special generic products. Special generic product manufacturers will continue to grow, but the immediate policy challenge facing middle-income countries is how to balance the different interests of the first two groups. Not all companies or countries fit neatly into these categories. Hungary, for example, has a relatively strong national industry, and in selected areas it has a world-class R&D capability (Gogl, 1998). However, most middle-income countries have national companies which have concentrated on investing in manufacturing in order to supply their national market and which have little or no significant R&D investment or export sales. Their product portfolios are concentrated at the mature end of the spectrum (see Figure 4.6) with a significant proportion of their products approaching obsolescence. Their main assets are their special knowledge of and relationships with customers and regulators in the national market and their 'know-how' in the registration of new products. In contrast, the major multinationals, which operate locally through an affiliate or a national distributor/manufacturer, have the benefits of enormous economies of scope and scale, and through intensive R&D investment over many years they dominate the new product end of the market range.

Despite differences, in many countries these two groups have established a relatively harmonious *modus vivendi*, within which licensing, co-marketing and manufacturing collaborations have flourished. However, this relationship has often resulted from government pressure or regulation of the multinationals.

In trading off health and industry policies, governments face some difficult decisions. Industry policies in the past have championed and defended national companies, often with discriminatory practices in their favour, albeit within the limits of international trade conventions. In the pharmaceutical sector a classic example of this is to write into the laws governing the technical approval of medicines or IP rights a stipulation that the product must be manufactured within the country. This invariably requires multinational companies, which may not have local manufacturing plants, either to invest locally or to enter into some kind of partnership agreement with a national company to manufacture on its behalf.

Investment promotion

Successful promotion of inward investment for the pharmaceutical sector will be influenced by the availability of a core pharmaceutical manufacturing base, medical 'centres of excellence', which can undertake clinical trials to international standards, and academic institutions and public–private partnerships that develop a national knowledge base in the new field of bioscience.

The pharmaceutical manufacturing base should be consolidated in a way that allows competition in international markets but eliminates non-competitive elements. In larger countries, consolidation and restructuring have been achieved through partnerships with multinational companies. These partnerships offer the advantages of inward investment and state-of-the-art technology transfer. Their obvious disadvantages are that corporate ownership lies beyond national boundaries and that old allegiances are eroded.

Some middle-income countries in eastern Europe (Hungary) and Asia (China) have been remarkably successful in attracting multinational companies to undertake clinical trials. Ironically, these companies' motivation for this is not only the host's centres of expertise, which are less expensive, but also the large untapped reservoir of patients in specific disease categories. There is great pressure on them to conduct larger clinical trials and produce better statistical evidence of efficacy and safety. This is an attractive area, in which a successful national policy will bring the dual benefits of medical technology transfer and international revenue streams directly into the health system.

Many middle-income countries are also trying to emulate the developed ones in using scientific research in academic centres to develop innovative technology-based sectors for small to medium-sized enterprises. For example,

Kazakhstan has established a $50 million fund to invest in companies operating in bioscience. The rapid advances in this field have made it particularly attractive for research, but in investing scarce national funds in bioscience, middle-income countries must recognize that the knowledge gap relative to the United States and Europe may be very wide. The balance between risk and industry or trade pay-off is likely to be only favourable in niche areas and even then, only over the very long term (10 to 20 years). Thus policies need to focus precious resources on a few of the more promising areas or centres. Limited resources spread thinly across many specialities and centres are unlikely to be effective in bridging the competitive gap with the developed world.

Technology transfer

Middle-income governments need to recognize the distinction between health policies aimed at medical technology transfer and industry policies that seek to achieve manufacturing technology transfer. In some countries there is a strong belief that sustaining or acquiring a manufacturing base to supply the national market with medicines will improve patient access to medicines and industrial self-sufficiency. Although this policy may have had some utility in the past, it is unlikely to be optimal in a world with multiple advances in medical technology and open, competitive trade in medicines. Given that 60–70 per cent of the demand for medicines will be for mature generics, success in this market will be influenced by a low-cost manufacturing capability and very large domestic markets, which allow large manufacturing facilities with scale economies. The obvious candidates, which are already well advanced in this regard for primary (active ingredient) manufacture, are Argentina, Brazil, China and India. Even though niche areas of production may allow exceptions, it would be unwise for the majority of other middle-income countries to stake their industrial future on manufacturing pharmaceuticals.

Much more important is to recognize the value of medical technology transfer through a well-designed industry policy that enables integration of the international R&D-based sector with the national sector. One strategy pursued by a number of middle-income countries encourages some sections of the existing national manufacturing base to specialize in low-cost generic medicine production. This policy, accompanied by demand-side health reforms, can encourage the use of good-quality but much cheaper generics for off-patent products. It can make an important contribution to controlling the cost of medicines and helping to ease the transition of traditional manufacturers to a more viable long-term future.

Trade policies

Emerging countries face difficult choices in managing their economies. Modern ICT enables their citizens to see what is available in developed countries and to create demand for new products. Excess demand, and imports to meet it, can create trade imbalances and deficits, with adverse consequences for the economy. Trade policies that aim to curb demand through barriers such as tariffs can in the long run be counter-productive, especially if they encourage the growth of low-quality producers who are unfairly protected. This certainly applies to pharmaceuticals, where protecting inefficient national medicines manufacturers against cheaper and better-quality substitutes will reduce access to high-quality drugs and prevent progress by the local pharmaceutical economy.

PHARMACEUTICALS: AN OUTLINE SUPPLY- AND DEMAND-SIDE MODEL TO AID POLICY-MAKING

Given the complexities associated with pharmaceutical markets, it is necessary to have a model that will enable policy-makers to discuss in a systematic way the policy options on the supply and demand sides when developing pharmaceutical policies. This model can be used as a vehicle to discuss reform options in real health systems. When developing a model, policy-makers should ensure that the boundaries are well defined and focus on the pharmaceutical sector, not the entire health policy domain.

We propose a model that provides a workable framework for achieving equitable access to the best range of currently available modern medicines at fair and reasonable prices. The model takes into account two economic realities. First, funds will be constrained through some form of budgetary system. Secondly, innovative medicines will be more expensive, reflecting both their greater value relative to existing ones and the need to provide incentives for further investment in R&D to enable future advances in medicine.

The demand–supply balance

From a government perspective, there is a need to carefully balance demand-side structures with appropriate incentives and supply-side regulation. The demand- and the supply-side policies must be compatible and evolve continually in response to macro-level economic changes.

An appropriate combination of policies can provide a basis for a sustainable supply of innovative medicines at prices that are affordable, even within highly constrained healthcare budgets. This requires integration of respective policies for the demand and the supply sides (see Figure 4.8). There must also be both mechanisms for achieving solidarity (such as in financing and risk pooling), so as to ensure equitable access through coherent controls on the demand side, and supply-side interventions in the market to allow competitive forces to operate and impose efficiency.

On the demand side, there is a need to develop and refine the delicate system of checks and balances governing the principles of affordability and to emphasize the ethical responsibilities of professionals to deliver high-quality care.

On the supply side, it is crucial to recognize early on the benefits of therapeutic and cost-saving innovations and to negotiate robustly with suppliers and seek to accommodate them within limited budgets. This can be done by rebalancing the reimbursement pipeline, rather than by blocking or delaying medical progress on the grounds of inadequate funding. Many real-world systems fail to address this issue objectively.

Two strategies release resources and stimulate the provision of modern medicines: the implementation of rigorous policies for de-listing older, less effective medicines from both nationally technically approved and state reimbursement lists, and the prompt transfer of long-established, safe and relatively cheap treatments for minor ailments and non-life-threatening chronic conditions to an OTC basis. These may be limited to regulated pharmacy outlets or, as in many developed countries, made more generally available in supermarkets.

A third strategy, currently under way in Britain, transfers prescribing responsibility for 'high-volume' preventive treatments for chronic conditions (such as 'cholesterol reducers') to pharmacy-only prescribing and monitoring. This will open up the possibility of shifting some costs to the public by way of cost-sharing.

A significant proportion of the population spends substantial amounts of its disposable income on 'self-medication', in the form of traditional formulated remedies, vitamins and tonics. There may be considerable scope to displace some of these products with those transferred from the prescription-only sector. Also, as disposable income rises, there is considerable scope for this expenditure to increase. Governments should provide health education to the population in order to help them discriminate between cost-effective drugs in the growing OTC 'self-medication' market.

For middle-income countries, selective adoption of high-value innovations constitutes a big challenge and raises a number of questions. Who should be responsible for assessing the value of new products in normal use? What principles and criteria should be employed? Should there be a national policy that fosters 'best clinical practice' for the treatment of illnesses?

In the past decade, there has been a dramatic evolution of thinking to encourage adoption of innovations and 'best developed practice'. These range from a *laissez-faire* approach with maximum professional autonomy, to a concept of 'evidence-based medicine', and then to current practice of a balanced assess-

Figure 4.8: Demand and supply: an integrated schematic model

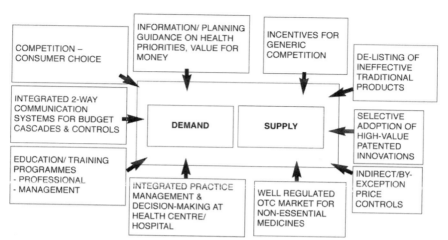

ment of both clinical effectiveness and cost-effectiveness. The availability of clinical and cost-effectiveness information varies markedly in different countries. In middle-income countries this information is often not available and the extent to which findings from other countries can be generalized is open to debate.

For new products in particular, the data will be limited. Mechanisms should be put in place that, instead of imposing blanket restrictions on these products, allow the diffusion process for innovations to take place and enable the system to gather locally generated information for the subsequent analysis of clinical effectiveness and cost-effectiveness. Another contentious area between the demand and the supply sides is the price of new products and how these prices should be determined. Our model rests on the premise that with a well-organized demand-side system, it is not necessary to have a formal product-by-product national price control mechanism based on highly complex and bureaucratic methods.

For this approach to work effectively there are prerequisites. On the demand side, in large tax or social insurance systems, core policies are established on health priorities, and budgets are earmarked accordingly in a transparent manner. These budgets are cascaded to local operating units, accompanied by guidance on national priorities. The local operating units, in the form of teams of doctors, managers and other professionals, can use the national guidelines and local knowledge and identify their own expenditure priorities so as best to meet the needs of local patient populations.

The active participation of individual doctors in these teams, along with modern managerial and information systems, will ensure cost-effective prescribing decisions and effective price control. Local teams will make two types of 'price-sensitive' decision: first for non-patented products – whether to prescribe the cheapest approved generic product; and secondly for patented classes of 'close substitute' products – whether to use the cheapest one if a special benefit can be gained for an individual patient by using a more expensive alternative.

If these principles are followed, exposure to the risk of 'excessive pricing' by suppliers is limited to two possibilities. The first is resort to 'first-in-class' products for which there is no effective alternative product and for which the treatment cost is very high. The evidence from the past 20 years clearly shows that this is now rare and if it happens it is transitory. Regardless of the prices charged, the impact on the total expenditure of these medicines is likely to be limited. Secondly, in patented classes for significant therapeutic advances with only a few competitors there is a potential for oligopolistic, 'cartel-like', behaviour: the small number of competing companies may, in certain circumstances, perceive a common interest in posting and sustaining uniformly high prices.

These possibilities do not require or justify pharmaceutical sector-specific controls or regulation. Uncompetitive behaviour is subject to the general law on competition and regulation by the national competition authorities. In most countries, these authorities have extensive powers to investigate, to enforce price reductions and levy fines on those who offend the general principles of fair competition.

Industry policy: the broader perspective

From the perspective of a government, regulation of the pharmaceutical industry involves trade-offs between health and industry policies. Earlier in this chapter we explored the relationships and the regulation of the pharmaceutical sector primarily from the viewpoint of the healthcare system. In this section, we focus on a much broader range of government policies and regulatory roles that impinge upon the industry, as shown in Figure 4.9. All four key government agencies – health, finance, industry and education – can play an important role in ensuring that a country has a thriving and, to a degree, innovative pharmaceutical industry. Thus a model system for the development of the industry must also pay careful attention to industrial, educational and financial policies.

Industrial policies

Four facets of industrial policy require consideration:

1. *Competition law.* Many middle-income countries lack a strong tradition of competition law and its enforcement. It is important for them to recognize that the development of robust competition laws is essential for the

Figure 4.9: The complete industry policy and regulatory framework

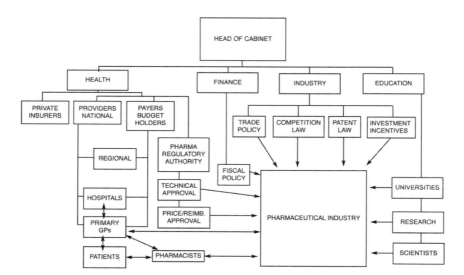

development of the economy. These laws can address many of the concerns expressed by healthcare administrators without a need for complex controls that are specific to the pharmaceutical sector.

2. *Patent law.* An essential feature of a sound national framework for a modern 'high-tech' industry, such as pharmaceuticals, is a strong and effective patent system, to provide incentives for innovation. Frequently, the introduction of an effective product patent system is a divisive issue, both for government policy-makers and within the industry. Policy-makers will be divided between those who favour avoiding patent protection so as to facilitate rapid access to cheaper, locally manufactured copies in the short term, and those who recognize the long-term value of providing incentives for future innovations. Similarly, within the industry, there may be corresponding tension between established national companies and inward-investing multinationals. For emerging countries which aspire over the long term to develop their own modern industrial base, progress to meet the requirements of the TRIPS agreement is essential.

3. *Trade policy.* National circumstances may vary considerably in terms of overall economic development and the trade balance. Appropriate economic controls and discipline are vitally important. However, in the specific case of medicines that bring a range of wider economic benefits, it is counter-

productive to use tariff and non-tariff barriers to protect ageing national industries and deprive society of the benefits of medical advances.

4. *Investment incentives.* There is increasing competition between nations for inward investment in their industries. Policies that encourage inward investment in the pharmaceutical sector must be aligned with policies that influence other factors, notably the education, science and medical infrastructures. Many governments still cling to outmoded policies which focus on investment in manufacturing as a key objective. They fail to recognize that forcing multinational companies to invest in a multiplicity of small, inefficient national plants in order to achieve very modest gains in local employment and capital investment is likely to be sub-optimal for both parties over the long term.

Of course, governments should still seek to make the most of existing local skills and capabilities. A proactive policy that facilitates the restructuring of the pharmaceutical industry through mergers and acquisitions between quality national companies and inward-investing multinationals is an alternative to old-fashioned protectionism for declining national companies. Grants and incentives to facilitate activities in this area should be provided within a clearly articulated national framework. The aim, however, should be to support only those ventures that have a real possibility of competing in an increasingly open world economy.

The same principles apply to R&D investment. Even in the developed world, countries are facing the harsh realities that only the best centres of excellence, be they in basic research development or the clinical field, will be able to survive in international competition. Thus a ruthlessly objective and selective approach is needed when deploying limited state funds and resources.

The education system

It is self-evident that even a basic national pharmaceutical sector requires a cadre of well-trained scientists and technicians. Investment in education and research is needed in order to encourage developments in the field of bioscience. In the near term, few countries can realistically hope to emulate the achievements of the US and, to a lesser degree, the European academia–industry–science community clusters. However, the pace of advance in bioscience and some medical fields is such that the possibility of capturing a position in 'niche' areas should not be overlooked. Again, fostering initiatives in this area requires robust intellectual property protection regulations.

Financial incentives and taxation

Many countries offer special tax incentives for both manufacturing and R&D investment. In practice, it is more and more difficult to offer exceptional packages that are clearly different from others as any incentives offered by countries are rapidly identified by others and replicated.

CONCLUDING REMARKS

Given the various elements and the complex nature of the policy setting of the pharmaceutical industry, our model provides a useful framework for discussing policy options. These must be addressed not in isolation but as a coherent whole, and they must consider the demand and the supply sides, both trade and sector-specific policies, and all those variables that impact on the demand and the supply sides. A holistic approach to policy-making is necessary to establish and sustain a pharmaceutical sector and an environment that will allow equitable access to innovative medicines.

The sector's success will also be determined by:

1. A clear and well-communicated vision of the long-term aims for the sector;
2. Well-thought-out and carefully designed programmes for change implemented both horizontally and vertically within government, the health system and the industry;
3. Strong and positive relationships between key government agencies, the health system, the pharmaceutical industry and the national pharmaceutical industry associations;
4. Pragmatism, flexibility and a continued dialogue between key stakeholders in dealing with unforeseen crises.

ANNEX I: CLASSIFICATION OF COUNTRIES BY INCOME

High-income OECD economies (24)

Australia	Greece	New Zealand
Austria	Iceland	Norway
Belgium	Ireland	Portugal
Canada	Italy	Spain
Denmark	Japan	Sweden
Finland	South Korea	Switzerland
France	Luxembourg	United Kingdom
Germany	Netherlands	United States

High-income economies (56)

Andorra	French Polynesia	Netherlands
Antigua and Barbuda	Germany	Netherlands Antilles
Aruba	Greece	New Caledonia
Australia	Greenland	New Zealand
Austria	Guam	Norway
Bahamas	Hong Kong (China)	Portugal
Bahrain	Iceland	Puerto Rico
Barbados	Ireland	Qatar
Belgium	Isle of Man (UK)	San Marino
Bermuda	Israel	Singapore
Brunei	Italy	Slovenia
Canada	Japan	Spain
Cayman Islands	Korea (Republic of)	Sweden
Channel Islands (UK)	Kuwait	Switzerland
Cyprus	Liechtenstein	United Arab Emirates
Denmark	Luxembourg	United Kingdom
Faeroe Islands	Macao (China)	United States
Finland	Malta	Virgin Islands (US)
France	Monaco	

Upper-middle-income economies (34)

American Samoa	Czech Republic	Lebanon
Argentina	Dominica	Libya
Belize	Estonia	Lithuania
Botswana	Gabon	Malaysia
Chile	Grenada	Mauritius
Costa Rica	Hungary	Mayotte
Croatia	Latvia	Mexico

Northern Mariana Islands Saudi Arabia St Lucia
Oman Seychelles Trinidad and Tobago
Palau Slovak Republic Uruguay
Panama St Kitts and Nevis Venezuela
Poland

Lower-middle-income economies (54)

Albania Guyana Russian Federation
Algeria Honduras Samoa
Armenia Iran Serbia and Montenegro
Belarus Iraq South Africa
Bolivia Jamaica Sri Lanka
Bosnia and Herzegovina Jordan St Vincent and the
Brazil Kazakhstan Grenadines
Bulgaria Kiribati Suriname
Cape Verde Macedonia Swaziland
China Maldives Syrian Arab Republic
Colombia Marshall Islands Thailand
Cuba Micronesia Tonga
Djibouti Morocco Tunisia
Dominican Republic Namibia Turkey
Ecuador Paraguay Turkmenistan
Egypt Peru Ukraine
El Salvador Philippines Vanuatu
Fiji Romania West Bank and Gaza
Guatemala

Low-income economies (64)

Afghanistan Congo (Kinshasa) Indonesia
Angola Congo (Brazzaville) Kenya
Azerbaijan Côte d'Ivoire North Korea
Bangladesh Equatorial Guinea Kyrgyz Republic
Benin Eritrea Laos
Bhutan Ethiopia Lesotho
Burkina Faso Gambia Liberia
Burundi Georgia Madagascar
Cambodia Ghana Malawi
Cameroon Guinea Mali
Central African Republic Guinea-Bissau Mauritania
Chad Haiti Moldova
Comoros India Mongolia

Mozambique
Myanmar
Nepal
Nicaragua
Niger
Nigeria
Pakistan
Papua New Guinea
Rwanda

São Tomé and Príncipe
Senegal
Sierra Leone
Solomon Islands
Somalia
Sudan
Tajikistan
Tanzania

Timor-Leste
Togo
Uganda
Uzbekistan
Vietnam
Yemen
Zambia
Zimbabwe

Source: World Bank – *http://www.worldbank.org/data/countryclass/classgroups.htm*, accessed 1 August 2003.

ANNEX 2: OECD COUNTRIES

Australia
Austria
Belgium
Canada
Denmark
Czech Republic
Finland
France
Germany
Greece

Hungary
Iceland
Ireland
Italy
Japan
Luxembourg
Mexico
Netherlands
New Zealand
Norway

Poland
Portugal
Slovak Republic
South Korea
Spain
Sweden
Switzerland
Turkey
United Kingdom
United States

REFERENCES

Bale, H. (2000), *TRIPS, Pharmaceuticals and Developing Countries* (Geneva: International Pharmaceutical Manufacturers Association).

Behrman, J. N. and D. A. Rondinelli (2000), 'The transition to market-oriented economies in Central and Eastern Europe', *European Business Journal*, 12: 87.

Culyer, A. J. and B. Jonsson (eds) (1986), *Public and Private Health Services* (Oxford: Blackwell).

Department of Health (2000), *Pharmacy in the Future – Implementing the NHS Plan* (London: DoH).

Drummond, M. F. (1980), *Principles of Economic Appraisal in Healthcare* (Oxford: Oxford University Press).

Dumoulin, J., M. Kaddar and G. Velasquez (1998), *Guide to Drug Financing Mechanisms* (Geneva: World Health Organization).

European Federation of Pharmaceutical Industries and Associations (2002), *The Pharmaceutical Industry in Figures* (Brussels: EFPIA).

Feacham, R. G. A., N. K. Sekhri and K. L White (2002), 'Getting more for their dollar: a comparison of the NHS with California's Kaiser Permanente', *British Medical Journal*, 324: 135–43.

Gogl, A. (1998), 'Health and enlargement of the EU: views of a candidate country (Hungary)', *EuroHealth*, 4: 18.

Harding, A. and A. S. Preker (2002), *Private Participation in Health Services Handbook*, Human Development Network (Washington, DC: World Bank).

IFPMA (1997), International Conference on Harmonization on Technical Requirements for Registration of Pharmaceuticals for Human Use, *Background and Status of Harmonisation Report* (Geneva: IFPMA Secretariat).

Kanavos, P. and U. Reinhardt (2003), 'Reference pricing for drugs: is it compatible with U.S. health care?', *Health Affairs*, 22: 16–30.

Keynote (2001), Keynote Market Reports, Retail Chemists and Drugstores.

Lanjouw, J. O. (1999), 'The Introduction of Pharmaceutical Product Patents in India: Heartless Exploitation of the Poor and Suffering?', Paper 6366, US National Bureau of Economic Research, Washington, DC.

Lasagna, L. and S. Schulman (1992), 'Cost containment and pharmaceuticals: issues for research', *PharmacoEconomics*, 1, Suppl. 1.

Levy, R. (1995), *The Pharmaceutical Industry – A Discussion of Competitive and Anti-Trust Issues in an Environment of Change*, Staff Report, Bureau of Economics, US Federal Trade Commission, Washington, DC.

McCrae, S. E., N. Mattison, J. L. Sturchio and P. B. Catterall (eds) (1995), *Healthcare – The Patients' Perspective, Proceedings of the Patients Charter Conference*, Georgia, USA.

Mansfield, E. (1986), 'Patents and innovation: an empirical study', *Management Science*, 32(2): 173–81.

Mansfield, E. (1996), *Intellectual Property Protection, Foreign Direct Investment and Technology Transfer*, Discussion Paper 19, International Finance Corporation (Washington, DC: World Bank).

Mansfield, E. and A. Romeo (1980), 'Technology transfer to overseas subsidiaries by US-based firms', *Quarterly Journal of Economics*, 95: 737.

Martin, V. (2000), *The Future of European Pharmaceutical Distribution*, Pharmaceutical Industry Report, Informa Publishing Group Ltd.

Maynard, A. (1994), 'Can competition enhance efficiency in healthcare?', *Social Science and Medicine*, 39: 1433.

Monopolies and Mergers Commission (1996), *UniChem PLC/Lloyds Chemists plc and GEHE AG/Lloyds Chemists plc: A Report on the Proposed Mergers*, Cm 3344 (London: HMSO).

Mossialos, E., C. Ranos and B. Abel-Smith (1994), *Cost Containment, Pricing and Financing of Pharmaceuticals*, LSE Health and Pharmetrica S.A.

Murray, C. J. L., D. B. Evans, A. Acharya and R. M. P. M. Baltussen (1999), *Development of*

WHO Guidelines on Generalised Cost-effectiveness Analysis, GDE Discussion Paper No. 4 (Geneva: World Health Organization); also in *Health Economics* 9(3): 235–51 (2000).

Nagle, T. T. (1987), *The Strategy and Tactics of Pricing* ((Englewood Cliffs, NJ: Prentice Hall).

National Prescribing Centre (2001), *Implementing NICE Guidance*, NHS (Abingdon, UK: Radcliffe Medical Press).

OECD (2000), *Health Data: A Comparative Analysis of 29 Countries* (Paris: OECD).

OFT (2003), *The Office of Fair Trading Report: The Control of Entry Regulations and Retail Pharmacy Services in the UK* (London: Office of Fair Trading), January.

Preker, A. S., R. G. Feacham and D. de Ferranti (1997), *Sector Strategy: Health, Nutrition and Population*, The Human Development Network (Washington, DC: World Bank).

Rapple, T. (ed.) (2000), *Internet Advertising of Pharmaceuticals in Europe* (Heidelberg: C. F. Muller Verlag, Huthig GmbH).

Sachs, J. D. et al. (2001), *Macroeconomics and Health: Investing in Health for Economic Development* (Geneva: World Health Organization).

Sackett, D. (1996), *The Doctor's Ethical and Economic Dilemma* (London: Office of Health Economics).

Saltman, R. and J. Figueres (eds) (1997), *European Health Care Reform: Analysis of Current Strategies* (Copenhagen: WHO Regional Publications).

Schoen, C., K. Davis, C. Des Roches, K. Donelan and R. Blendon (2000), 'Health insurance markets and income inequality: findings from an international health policy survey', *Health Policy*, 51(2): 67–85.

Schulman, R. and L. Lasagna (1998), 'Dynamics of the international pharmaceutical market-place: major forces in the late 1990's', *PharmacoEconomics*, Supplement 14: 1–146.

Senior, I., S. Kon et al. (1998), *Policy Relating to Generic Medicines in the OECD – Report for the European Commission*, III/E/3.

Smith, R. (1999), 'NICE – A Panacea for the NHS?', *British Medical Journal*, 313: 824.

Statistics 2000 (2001), *The Pharmaceutical Industry in Germany* (Berlin: Verband Forschender Arzneimittelhersteller).

Towse, A. and T. Leighton (1999), 'The Changing Nature of NCE Pricing of Second and Subsequent Entrants', in J. Sussex and N. Marchant (eds), *Risk and Return in the Pharmaceutical Industry* (London: Office of Health Economics Monograph, OHE).

TRIPS (1998), Special Issue, *Journal of International Economic Law*, 1(4): 497–690.

United Nations (2000), 'Trends and Policies in the World Economy', *World Economic and Social Survey* (New York: United Nations).

United Nations Development Programme (2001a), *Human Development Report* (New York: Oxford University Press for UNDP).

United Nations Development Programme (2001b), *Human Development Regional Reports – Latin America* (New York: Oxford University Press for UNDP).

Van de Ven, W. P. M., F. T. Schut and F. F. H. Rutten (1994), 'Forming and reforming the market for third party purchasing of healthcare', *Social Science and Medicine*, 39: 1405.

Wagstaff, Adam, Eddy van Doorslaar and Pierella Paci (1989), 'Equity in finance and delivery of health care: some tentative cross-country comparisons', *Oxford Review of Economic Policy*, 5(1): 89–112.

Watal, J. (2000), 'Pharmaceutical patents, prices and welfare losses: a simulation study of policy options for India under the WTO TRIPS agreement', *The World Economy*, 23 (5): 733–52.

World Bank (1999 and 2000), *World Development Report* (New York: World Bank/Oxford University Press).

World Bank (2002), *Global Economic Prospects and the Developing Countries* (Washington, DC: World Bank).

World Health Organization (1995), *Promotion of the Rights of Patients in Europe: Proceedings of a WHO Consultation* (The Hague: Kluwer Law International).

World Health Organization (1998), *Health Economics and Drugs*, DAP Series No. 6 (Geneva: WHO).

World Health Organization (1999), *The World Health Report: Making a Difference* (Geneva: WHO).

World Health Organization (2000), *The World Health Report: Health Systems: Improving Performance* (Geneva: WHO).

World Health Organization (2001), *How to Develop and Implement a National Drug Policy* (2nd edn) (Geneva: WHO).

World Trade Organization (2001), *TRIPS and Pharmaceutical Patents*, World Trade Organization Fact Sheet (Geneva: WTO).

Zammit-Lucia, J. and R. Dasgupta (1995), *Referencing Pricing – The European Experience*, Health Policy Review Paper No. 10, Health Policy Unit, Imperial College, London.

PART III
WORKING BETTER,
WORKING TOGETHER

5 JOINT PUBLIC–PRIVATE INITIATIVES AND DEVELOPING-COUNTRY HEALTH SYSTEMS

Annie Heaton

Despite the unparalleled health achievements of the twentieth century, over 800 million people around the world have no access to basic health services (UNDP, 1997). Every year some 10 million children still die from preventable diseases, and in a number of countries, such as Kenya, Colombia and Cameroon, the number of child deaths actually began to rise during the 1990s.[1] One of the Millennium Development Goals was to reduce child mortality by two-thirds by 2015. At present rates, sub-Saharan Africa will not achieve this for over 150 years.

This stark reality has prompted vociferous calls for better access to health care for the poor. One popular response from the private sector, in collaboration with UN agencies, bilateral and multilateral donors, has been Joint Public–Private Initiatives (JPPIs). These JPPIs have certainly increased global public awareness of the health crisis in the poorest countries. The direct benefits to the lives of their beneficiaries, however, are likely to be short term, since few have been effectively integrated into national health systems, with the exception of the Mectizan drug donation programme for onchocerciasis. The rise of this new form of health intervention has generated questions relating to the broader impacts of JPPIs, and their mechanisms for regulation and accountability. It is vital, therefore, that the impact of JPPIs is subjected to open scrutiny. They need to be assessed by means of a multi-stakeholder process that does not simply look at the number of people receiving medicines but considers the qualitative impact of these initiatives on the workings of broader health systems: on staff workload and morale, the quality of data systems, the effectiveness of equipment, health budgets and so on.

This chapter examines briefly the role of JPPIs in the context of the global health crisis. It outlines their initial design characteristics and the nature of

---

[1] These countries actually saw the death rates increase in children both under one year and under five years of age. Analysis of Demographic and Health Survey data by Medact and Save the Children, published in *The Bitterest Pill of All: The Collapse of Africa's Health Systems* (London: Save the Children & Medact, 2001).

private-sector commitments to them, while exploring their often-overlooked impact on developing-country health systems. It focuses on those disease-specific programmes that aim to supply selected commodities, whether by donation (such as Pfizer's Diflucan Donation Programme for opportunistic infections associated with HIV/AIDS and GSK's former Malarone Donation Programme for malaria), by discounted price offers (such as the Accelerating Access Initiative for HIV/AIDS), or by financing the cost of products procured by commercial tender (such as the Global Alliance for Vaccines and Immunization, GAVI). Although they are product- or disease-oriented, these kinds of JPPIs have important – if sometimes overlooked – impacts on health systems. JPPIs concerned with R&D are not considered here.

COLLAPSING HEALTH SYSTEMS – SAVE THE CHILDREN'S EXPERIENCE

Save the Children UK's experience of working directly with developing-country health systems at all levels has taught us that a long chain with many links is needed for the effective delivery of basic health care. Access to effective medicines is one essential link in this chain, but equally crucial are the availability of qualified, supervised and supported health staff, well-fuelled and well-maintained vehicles enabling them to access communities, refrigeration for the transport and storage of vaccines, safe and effective disposal systems for clinical waste, diagnostic equipment and so on. The entire health system relies on skilled efficient and participative management to ensure effective strategies, logistics and financial flows.

This healthcare chain is only as strong as its weakest link. If any of the links is broken, no services will be delivered – whether for malaria, tuberculosis, HIV/AIDS or any other disease. In the poorest countries, the chain has already broken: health systems have collapsed. Throughout the 1990s, numerous reports by the World Bank described this situation. In Niger, for example, it found that 'the poor have virtually no access to health care', and in Cameroon that 'the collapse has been one of the most painful any country has suffered' (Save the Children and Medact, 2001: p. 4).

The Debresina district in the highlands of Ethiopia, where Save the Children UK works, provides a stark illustration of a health system in a state of collapse. The government has less than $1.35 per person to spend on health per year.[2] As a result, there is only one health centre and one fully qualified doctor for 150,000 people. Health workers have little support and there is no money

---

[2] This is despite its spending some 20% of its budget on basic services. The WHO's 2001 recommendation states that a minimum of $30–40 per person is needed for an Essential Healthcare Package.

for training. There are regular drug shortages, no surgical facilities exist, nor is there any vehicle to transport urgent cases to hospital 180km away (Save the Children UK, 2003).

There are three main reasons for the collapse of these health systems. First, there has been a gross failure not only by national governments but by their donors to allow adequate investment in health systems.[3] Secondly, for far too long there has been a failure to finance the *recurrent* costs of health systems. Product-specific JPPIs are a response to one important kind of recurrent cost, that of drugs and vaccines, but this still makes up only a small proportion of the entire bill each health system faces, including such costs as staff salaries and training, fuel and maintenance for refrigerators and vehicles, data systems and management. Thirdly, what investment there is has typically been fragmented, short term and uncoordinated. Initiatives have tended to be conceived, led and managed at the global level – thus creating vertical programmes, each concentrating on achieving its own specific targets, each expecting new accountable systems to be set up to ensure its short-term targets are achieved.

The new wave of product-specific JPPIs tends to be characterized by all three of the failures above. Yet they are increasingly seen as the way forward in healthcare investment. Why?

COMMON CHARACTERISTICS OF JPPIS

These JPPIs have four features in common. They have tended to be *product-focused, high-profile, globally led* and, frequently, *time-limited.*

The end of the 1990s saw the emergence of a series of new JPPIs that concentrated the efforts of partners on the distribution of particular drugs for particular diseases, such as the donation of Malarone for malaria, Diflucan for cryptococcal meningitis and oesophageal infections related to HIV/AIDS, and Viramune for the prevention of mother-to-child transmission of HIV. These programmes became product-focused.

The pharmaceutical companies involved, charged with putting profit before people, have staked their philanthropic reputation on these programmes, which have consequently been the subject of much publicity. Such a high profile has meant that expectations, and thus the pressure to report success, are also high.

Most JPPIs, motivated by a global analysis of the disease burden in developing countries, were conceived at the global level. They were therefore designed by the headquarters of their partners, often failing to genuinely involve national governments and other local stakeholders. Consequently, the management of many JPPIs has remained at global level, resulting in top-down

---

[3] See, for example, Save the Children UK (1997 and 2002); Save the Children UK and Medact (2001).

programmes that lack the expertise and sensitivity to local needs and conditions that the national level would provide. The best-researched example of this problem is the Malarone Donation Programme (Shretta et al., 2001).

Many early JPPIs appeared to be established without any focus on the long term: GSK's Malarone Donation Programme was set up for just two years, and Pfizer's Diflucan donation offer to South Africa was originally of similar duration. A greater number specified a five-year timeframe, for example Boehringer Ingelheim's Viramune donation, GAVI and subsequently Merck's vaccine donation to GAVI. Only a small number, such as Merck's donation of Mectizan for river blindness and GSK's donation of albendazole for lymphatic filariasis, have stood out for their long-term commitment: both have been made until the disease is controlled or eliminated as a public-health problem.

CONCERNS OVER IMPACT OF JPPIS

As a result of the four features identified, JPPIs are apt to demand quick results based on easily identifiable targets. If that means concentrating simply on the number of tablets distributed rather than on the underlying capacity of health staff to reach villages, then the improvements will be superficial.[4] If it means focusing on regions with the strongest health systems, where results will come more easily, then the poorest may miss out.[5] And if it means seconding the capacity needed for a JPPI away from the routine health system, then the JPPIs, like the many vertical programmes that have gone before, will not only fail to build the blocks of the health system needed in the long term but may also undermine in the short term what already exists.

Further concerns exist about the secondary influence of drug donors on recipient governments. What, for example, will a government give up in order to accept and deliver donated drugs? Will it change its strategic priorities and modify its therapeutic guidelines? Will it cede influence on other drug procurement matters to the donor? What happens when the donation ends? What about accountability and regulation? These uncomfortable questions need to be addressed in the public debate about JPPIs (Heaton, 2001).

---

[4] Pfizer, for example, has said that it 'is focusing its efforts on product donations which, in our view, provide the most direct, least costly, and fastest means to address access problems in developing countries without extensive public infrastructure'. GAVI provides financial rewards to countries reporting improved immunization coverage, thus depending on data of often highly questionable quality. On the other hand, Merck reports on its Mectizan donation programme not only in quantitative terms, but also by attempting to reflect sustainable improvements to health care. See Oxfam, VSO and Save the Children UK (2002, pp. 18–19).
[5] Research on GAVI carried out in 2001, cited later in this chapter, recognizes that GAVI's system of rewarding countries that achieve immunization coverage targets 'may also encourage countries to use funds to raise overall coverage, rather than to address some of the inequities within countries'. See Starling et al. (2002, p. 49).

LESSONS FROM RESEARCH

In an effort to discover the reality behind some of these concerns, Save the Children UK worked with the London School of Hygiene and Tropical Medicine (LSHTM) in 2001 on a research project looking at the initial impact of GAVI as an example of a high-profile, product-focused, globally led and time-limited JPPI (Starling et al., 2002). GAVI was originally set up to promote three 'underused' vaccines in developing countries over five years. By establishing a demand for these vaccines in a number of poor countries, GAVI has been able to persuade the pharmaceutical industry to produce the quantity of vaccines needed, by a process of commercial tender.[6] GAVI then underwrites the cost of the vaccines for the recipient countries.

The LSHTM/Save the Children UK research examined the picture at ministry and district level in four African countries.[7] It found that although GAVI had provided a welcome boost to the profile of immunization among health ministries, some aspects of GAVI's implementation were a cause for concern. For example, some countries had been put under pressure to change their choice of vaccine because GAVI was experiencing problems in supplying their preferred choice. In the case of Ghana, a decision about whether to accept an alternative was requested within 10 days; yet this decision increased the implicit cost of the country's entire immunization budget between two and three times (Starling et al., 2002, pp. 40–41). At the time, GAVI – and the budgetary support for vaccines that it provided – only had plans to exist for five years.

The research also found that the cold chain system needed to support the safe delivery of vaccines was often broken and not maintained, and that the disposal of the auto-destruct syringes provided by GAVI was not always reliable. Some Health Ministry staff spent a lot of their time meeting the application requirements for GAVI – a common problem among vertical programmes, each of which places new demands on systems that are already overstretched.

These findings support Save the Children UK's concerns that JPPIs need to look much more carefully at their potential to distort national priorities and at the costs they incur for an entire health system. It is crucial that they are led by and integrated into the existing health plans of recipient countries and that, most importantly, they genuinely contribute to the longer-term, shared goal of strengthening national health systems.

Are such changes possible? Are pharmaceutical companies prepared to cede influence over the design of JPPIs? Can they be motivated to make longer-term contributions to programmes that focus on the whole chain of healthcare delivery rather than on their particular product and that are not stand-alone

---

[6] Limited amounts of vaccines have also been donated, for example by Merck.
[7] Ghana, Tanzania, Lesotho and Mozambique.

programmes but are integrated into the efforts of all donors and ministries? Or will they prefer JPPIs to remain supply-led, vertical programmes demanding quick results?

The answer largely depends on what drives a pharmaceutical company's philanthropy. As with all partnerships, it is important to recognize the various objectives of the different parties, because these will affect what the partners will commit to, how a JPPI is designed and, ultimately, how it impacts on health systems. If a company is involved in order to raise staff morale, or shareholder value, then its commitment may depend on getting the results the employees and shareholders want to see. If, on the other hand, it wants to develop better relationships with donors and recipient governments by means of regular contact through the JPPI, then a long-term commitment will achieve this more effectively. If commercial considerations are involved, such as the protection of a company's product market through donations or price discounts, then its objectives in the JPPI may be very limited and product-oriented. But if its philanthropy is driven by the personal conviction of its leadership that it should genuinely contribute to tackling the global health crisis tomorrow as well as today, then it cannot fail to see that JPPIs have to be more integrated and longer term.

At the start of the twenty-first century, there have been encouraging developments. GAVI is looking to fund itself beyond its initial five-year plan, and has recognized how essential functioning health systems and robust health information systems are to achieving its objectives. The Malarone Donation Programme, much criticized for being vertical, top-down and limited to two years, has ceased, and GSK has adopted tiered pricing as a more sustainable and systematic way forward for supplying its drugs according to countries' ability to pay. Pfizer's donation of Diflucan to South Africa has become an indefinite commitment; and Novartis has committed itself to supplying its new malaria drug CoArtem at a discounted price to the World Health Organization's malaria programmes instead of establishing a new vertical programme for its delivery. The public debate about appropriate commitment from pharmaceutical companies is clearly constructive: as these cases show, the industry has responded to criticism in an encouraging way.

As joint initiatives between the public and private sectors become more common as a form of response to public health crises, attention must be paid to their broader impacts. This chapter has outlined some of the concerns that have arisen about the generation of JPPIs that emerged towards the end of the 1990s. These JPPIs tended to be product-focused, high-profile, globally led and time-limited. These features jeopardize the health improvements the initiatives might bring because they encourage quick and easily reported results rather than the rebuilding of the developing world's crumbling health systems. Research on the impact of GAVI illustrated the need to integrate JPPIs into broader health strategies, to consider their wider impacts and to rely less on narrow quantitative reporting data. Following this research, GAVI is now looking at ways of reducing systems barriers to the delivery of its vaccines and improving the functioning of health systems.

The emergence of encouraging changes in the way JPPIs are designed is noted as evidence that a more evidence-based, nationally owned approach is possible, particularly if JPPIs are made more accountable. It is also vital that the leaders of the pharmaceutical industry are committed to sustainable health care in the developing world. Indeed, if we are to avoid yet further collapse of developing-country healthcare systems, and the terrible impact that would have, particularly on Africa's women and children, it is crucial that all JPPIs adopt a more sensitive, integrated, long-term and broadly accountable approach to tackling the health crisis in the developing world.

REFERENCES

Heaton, A. (2001), *Joint Public-Private Initiatives: Meeting Children's Right to Health?* (London: Save the Children UK).

Oxfam, VSO and Save the Children (2002), *Beyond Philanthropy: The Pharmaceutical Industry, Corporate Social Responsibility and the Developing World* (London: Oxfam, VSO and Save the Children UK).

Save the Children UK (1997), *Poor in Health* (London: Save the Children UK).

Save the Children UK (2003), *Paying the Price: The Case for Investment and Education* (London: Save the Children UK).

Save the Children and Medact (2001), *The Bitterest Pill of All: The Collapse of Africa's Health Systems* (London: Save the Children UK and Medact).

Shretta, R., G. Walt, R. Brugha and R.W. Snow (2001), 'A political analysis of corporate drug donations: the example of Malarone in Kenya', *Health Policy and Planning*, 16(2): 161–70, June.

Starling, M., R. Brugha and G. Walt (2002) (with contributions from A. Heaton and R. Keith), *New Products into Old Systems: The Initial Impact of the Global Alliance for Vaccines and Immunisation at Country Level* (London: London School of Hygiene and Tropical Medicine and Save the Children UK).

UNDP (1997), *Human Development Report* (New York: United Nations).

6 PARTNERSHIP FOR ACTION: THE EXPERIENCE OF THE ACCELERATING ACCESS INITIATIVE, 2000–04, AND LESSONS LEARNED

*Jeffrey L. Sturchio**

In 1990, the World Health Organization (WHO) estimated that roughly 8–10 million people were living with HIV/AIDS worldwide (Chin, 1990). By 2000, the HIV/AIDS epidemic had affected some 36.1 million people worldwide, exceeding by 50 per cent the best available 1991 projection made by the WHO's Global Programme on AIDS (UNAIDS/WHO, 2000, p. 4). Of these, 95 per cent lived in developing countries, and there is reason to believe that an equally large percentage of them were unaware of their HIV status. An estimated 5.3 million people were newly infected in 2000; 3 million died, bringing total deaths since the beginning of the epidemic to more than 20 million people. By the end of 2003, UNAIDS estimated that 38 million people were living with HIV/AIDS (UNAIDS/WHO, 2000, p. 3; UNAIDS, 2004, pp. 10, 24–5, Table 1, p. 190). Without an effective global prevention effort, an additional 45 million people in 126 low- and middle-income countries are likely to become infected by 2010 (UNAIDS, 2002a, p. 5).

The grim statistics of the global AIDS epidemic are well known. Yet they fail to convey in human terms the critical challenges that HIV and AIDS present to those countries hardest hit by the epidemic, challenges that go to the heart of social, economic and human development. In the face of these challenges, as Médecins Sans Frontières, among others, has observed: 'We must strive collectively to make effective HIV/AIDS treatment a reality for the millions of people who need it.' (MSF, 2002, p. 2) This goal is shared by the partners in the Accelerating Access Initiative, a country-led process bringing together resources and expertise from both the private and public sectors to improve HIV/AIDS care and treatment in the developing world.

There has been considerable progress since the Durban International AIDS Conference in 2000. HIV/AIDS has been placed squarely on the political

*Merck & Co., Inc., on behalf of the seven companies participating in the Accelerating Access Initiative.

agenda. New resources are being mobilized – through the advocacy of the WHO and UNAIDS for the 3 x 5 initiative (three million people on anti-retroviral treatment by 2005), through bilateral efforts such as the US President's Emergency Plan for AIDS Relief, through the World Bank's Multi-Country AIDS Program, and through the Global Fund to Fight AIDS, TB and Malaria, among others. The prices of anti-retroviral medicines have declined significantly. Companies acting individually have implemented differential pricing, which has helped to extend care and treatment.

Yet everyone involved in the AAI agrees that the gap between those who need care and those who receive it it is still unacceptable. More must be done by all stakeholders to achieve the goal set by the WHO of three million people on anti-retroviral treatment by 2005. We are all working hard to help achieve this ambitious goal. This paper sets out some of the results achieved to date and the lessons we have all learned from this experience.

THE ACCELERATING ACCESS INITIATIVE: CREATION, PURPOSE AND PRINCIPLES

The Accelerating Access Initiative (AAI) was formed in May 2000, following several months of intense dialogue. At the time, there was still scepticism in some circles about the feasibility of anti-retroviral treatment in resource-constrained settings, although the results of the UNAIDS-sponsored Drug Access Initiative (begun in 1998) and other early pilot projects were encouraging.[1] Over the next year, sparked in part by the advocacy surrounding the International AIDS Conference in Durban in the summer of 2000 and the UN General Assembly Special Session on HIV/AIDS in June 2001, a new consensus emerged in the international community on the complementarity of prevention and treatment and the urgency of addressing the needs of the developing world. But in early 2000 – at the time that discussions began on how the research-based pharmaceutical industry and the UN organizations might collaborate to improve access to HIV/AIDS care and treatment – there was still relatively little experience with treatment programmes in those developing countries hardest hit by the AIDS epidemic. Very few patients were on therapy – for a range of reasons having to do with the lack of resources, inadequate healthcare infrastructure, scepticism within the global health community, and the costs of chronic therapy.

In that context, it was an important step forward when five major research-based pharmaceutical companiese – Boehringer-Ingelheim, Bristol-Myers Squibb, GlaxoSmithKline, Merck & Co., Inc., and F. Hoffmann-La Roche – joined later

[1] For a thorough evaluation of the Drug Access Initiative in Côte d'Ivoire, Senegal and Uganda, see Katzenstein et al. (2003).

by Abbott Laboratories and Gilead Sciences, responded to calls by the leaders of several UN organizations for a new public–private partnership to expand the global response to AIDS (UNAIDS, 2000a). The UN organizations included the UNAIDS Secretariat, the World Health Organization, the United Nations Children's Fund (UNICEF), the World Bank and the United Nations Fund for Population Activities (UNFPA). These bodies and the five companies were the initial partners, but others from the public and private sector were encouraged to join; Abbott and Gilead did so in 2001 and 2004, respectively.

According to the 'Joint Statement of Intent' agreed by the AAI's private and public partners (see Annex 6.2), the 'new effort [was] undertaken to enhance progressively the capacity of countries to increase access to, and use of, sustainable, comprehensive and quality HIV/AIDS interventions across the entire spectrum of prevention, treatment, patient care and support (including prevention of perinatal transmission)'. Focusing on developing countries, particularly those of sub-Saharan Africa in the first instance, the AAI set out to:

- accelerate sustained access to and increased use of 'appropriate, good quality interventions';
- strive to reach significantly greater numbers of people in need through 'new alliances involving committed governments, private industry, the UN system, development assistance agencies, non-governmental organizations and people living with HIV/AIDS'; and to
- implement this programme 'in ways that respond to the specific needs and requests of individual countries, with respect for human rights, equity, transparency and accountability'.

The six principles adopted to guide the AAI reflect the broad range of conditions that ultimately determine the success of all efforts to address the AIDS epidemic in an effective and sustainable way:

1. to have the 'unequivocal' and sustained political commitment of the national governments involved in the initiative;
2. to build a 'strengthened national capacity' in the developing countries, including well-designed strategies and a strong infrastructure, both essential to the delivery of care and treatment;
3. to achieve the 'engagement of all sectors of national society and the global community' in facilitating access to treatment;
4. to develop 'efficient, reliable and secure distribution systems' to ensure that medicines reach the people for whom they are intended;
5. to acquire 'significant additional funding from national and international sources', at a level commensurate with the epidemic's challenges; and
6. to have 'continued investment in research and development by the pharmaceutical industry' to meet the challenges of the epidemic today and tomorrow.

THE AAI PROCESS

The AAI proceeded along two intersecting tracks. The first was the development of a national plan for each developing country involved, with technical collaboration provided through the UN system. The second involved dialogue with the individual pharmaceutical companies in the partnership so as to conclude supply agreements for specific anti-retroviral drugs (ARVs) (WHO/UNAIDS, 2002, pp. 5–7).

At the outset, governments were informed about the initiative and were offered support for planning by the UN. Those indicating an interest in participation were contacted by UN staff (primarily from UNAIDS and the WHO) who formed a country support working group, which assisted in developing a plan tailored to the particular country. These plans were not limited to anti-retroviral therapy (ART), but also included comprehensive approaches to care and information about procurement options covering both branded products and generics. Completed plans were transmitted by UNAIDS to those pharmaceutical companies with which the government wished to open discussions. Price was discussed in some, but not all, bilateral talks; supply arrangements were a primary focus. Discussions involved representatives of the government and individual pharmaceutical companies and were facilitated by the UN staff in the country support working group. From the outset the AAI was a country-led process, responding to the priorities and needs identified at the national level and at a pace established by the country. As regional and subregional collaborations developed, the same procedure was used to ensure technical support.

To encourage the involvement of all stakeholders, the UNAIDS Contact Group on Accelerating Access to HIV/AIDS Care and Support was formed in June 2000. It comprised representatives of governments of donor and low- and middle-income countries, civil society, the private sector and various multilateral organizations. Its purpose was to provide a forum for exchanging 'information and views, for consultation and to articulate needs and expectations, especially those emanating from governments, and to provide advice and guidance to the UNAIDS Secretariat, WHO, UNICEF, UNFPA and [the] World Bank on principles, policy and practice that will apply to the accelerating access endeavour' (UNAIDS, 2000b).

THE AAI'S IMPACT

The experience of the AAI has clearly demonstrated that with determined leadership, good planning and sufficient support, a developing country can achieve improved access to care and treatment in resource-limited settings. At the time the AAI was created, sub-Saharan Africa accounted for 70 per cent of people living with HIV/AIDS. Thus its initial efforts focused on this region but were not limited to it (UNAIDS/WHO, 2000, p. 5).[2] Countries in the Caribbean and eastern and central Europe also approached the AAI during its first two years of operation and there were also discussions at regional level. In July 2002 during the International AIDS Conference in Barcelona, for example, the ECOWAS and CARICOM countries signed statements of intent with the AAI companies. By mid-2003, 84 countries had expressed an interest in Accelerating Access; of these, 50 had developed plans of action and concluded discussions about supply agreements.[3]

As Figure 6.1 illustrates, in line with the principles articulated by the AAI, from mid-2000 there was a dramatic decline in the prices of anti-retrovirals (through individual company actions). Following the activities undertaken in the framework of the AAI, generic companies also began to offer price reductions, so that the costs of combination anti-retroviral therapy, at least in sub-Saharan Africa, had fallen by 90 per cent or more by early 2001 (as indicated, for example, by the experience in Uganda shown in Figure 6.1).[4]

This sea change in the affordability of anti-retroviral therapy began to spark action at the country level. Working with Axios International, a public-health consultancy specializing in developing countries, the AAI companies have developed and reported estimates of the number of patients treated with anti-retrovirals supplied by the AAI in the countries of Africa, the geographic region most affected by the HIV/AIDS epidemic and the region in which efforts by the AAI have been concentrated.[5] In the eighteen months between the third quarter of 2000 and the end of the first quarter of 2002, access to ARVs in Africa increased fourfold, from an estimated 9,300 to about 36,000 people, as a result of the efforts of the AAI (see Figure 6.2 and Table 6.1). The data also show that the proportion of patients on triple combination therapy grew over that period from one-third to nearly two-thirds, indicating a concomitant increase in the

[2] Initially, countries in Africa were slow to sign up for the AAI – by January 2001, only Uganda, Senegal and Rwanda had agreed on national treatment plans and held discussions with the pharmaceutical companies. For an informative discussion of the issues around the AAI in Uganda, see Fine et al. (2001).
[3] For a complete listing of countries, see Annex 6.3. The CARICOM and ECOWAS statements of intent can be found on the WHO website at *http://www.who.int/hiv/pub/prev_care/en/Caribbean.jpg* and *http://www.who.int/hiv/pub/prev_care/en/west_africa.jpg*.
[4] For the most recent survey of the prices of anti-retroviral medicines in developing countries, see UNICEF/UNAIDS/WHO/MSF (2004), which includes the 6th edition of MSF's *Untangling the Web of Price Reductions: A Pricing Guide for the Purchase of ARVs for Developing Countries*. For an analysis demonstrating that the prices of branded ARVs are now often less than or comparable to generic versions in developing countries, see Adelman, Norris and Weicher (2004).
[5] See Annex 6.1 at the end of this chapter and Annex 3 (pp. 25–29) of WHO/UNAIDS (2002) for an explanation of the methodology employed by Axios in developing these estimates. We thank Dr Joseph Saba and his colleagues for their help with the analyses.

Figure 6.1: Prices (US$/year) of a first-line anti-retroviral regimen in Uganda, 1998–2001

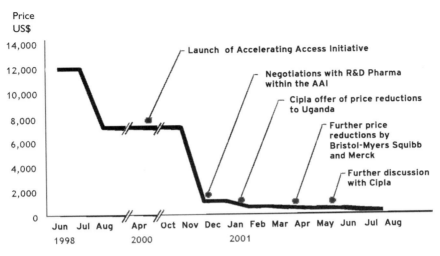

Source: UNAIDS (2002b), p. 146, Figure 34. Reproduced with permission.

quality of ART (See Figure 6.3 and Table 6.2). This compares with the WHO's estimate of some 50,000 people in Africa who had gained access to HIV therapy by the end of 2002 (International HIV Treatment Access Coalition, 2002, p. 1).

A little more than a year later (by the end of June 2003), Axios estimated that the six companies then involved in Accelerating Access supplied treatment to at least 76,300 people in Africa, an eight-fold increase since the programme began in May 2000 and roughly a doubling since the first quarter of 2002. The data also showed that the proportion of patients on triple combination therapy over that period continued to increase, to about four of every five patients, indicating a continuing improvement in the quality of anti-retroviral treatment. As indicated in Figure 6.2, this analysis also shows that the West Africa and Southern Africa regions had the greatest increase in the numbers of patients gaining access to ARVs.

By December 2003, on the basis of sales data, the number of HIV patients in Africa receiving anti-retroviral treatments provided by the AAI companies had doubled again in just six months, to an estimate of more than 150,000 people. As Figure 6.3 shows, at least three of every five patients were on triple combination therapy (the decline in this proportion from June 2002 probably indicates that more patients were using generic medicines for the third drug in the combination). While the actual number of patients on treatment could be

Figure 6.2: Estimated number of patients in Africa treated with ARV medicines supplied by AAI companies, by region, July 2000–December 2003

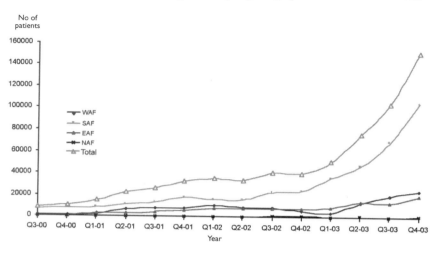

Figure 6.3: Estimated number of patients treated in Africa with ARVs supplied by AAI companies, triple combination therapy vs at least 2 NRTIs, July 2000–December 2003

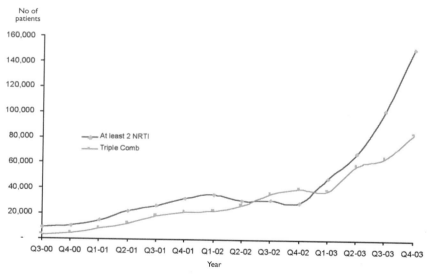

Source: Axios analysis of data provided by the seven companies in the Accelerating Access Initiative.

Table 6.1: Estimated number of patients in Africa treated with ARVs provided by AAI companies, by region, July 2000–December 2003

Quarter	Regions				Total
	WAF	SAF	EAF	NAF	
Q3-00	1,554	6,670	866	174	9,264
Q4-00	1,094	8,367	895	684	11,040
Q1-01	2,778	8,530	3,438	488	15,234
Q2-01	7,032	11,512	3,093	767	22,404
Q3-01	7,632	13,549	4,714	648	26,543
Q4-01	8,189	17,789	6,195	481	32,654
Q1-02	11,064	16,396	7,614	477	35,551
Q2-02	8,998	16,340	8,024	713	34,075
Q3-02	8,568	23,282	8,349	1,158	41,357
Q4-02	6,214	24,811	7,875	1,499	40,399
Q1-03	4,754	36,595	9,200	623	51,172
Q2-03	13,667	47,476	14,248	924	76,315
Q3-03	20,361	69,638	13,580	682	104,261
Q4-03	25,154	105,067	20,169	1,384	151,774

Definition of regions in Africa

WAF = West Africa: Benin, Burkina Faso, Cameroon, Central African Republic, Congo, Côte d'Ivoire, Democratic Republic of Congo, Gabon, The Gambia, Ghana, Guinea, Mali, Niger, Nigeria, Senegal, Sierra Leone, Togo.
SAF = Southern Africa: Angola, Botswana, Lesotho, Mozambique, Namibia, South Africa, Swaziland, Zambia, Zimbabwe.
EAF = East Africa: Burundi, Djibouti, Ethiopia, Kenya, Madagascar, Malawi, Mauritius, Rwanda, Seychelles, United Republic of Tanzania, Uganda.
NAF = Northern Africa: Algeria, Chad, Egypt, Libyan Arab Jamahiriya, Morocco, Tunisia.
Source: Axios analysis of data provided by the seven companies in the AAI.

either higher or lower than these data indicate – they are based on unit sales during the period, and do not include patients being treated with products from non-R&D companies – the trend is clear and unequivocal. There has been more than a 15-fold increase in patients treated since the AAI began in May 2000.

The encouraging early progress of the AAI is only the beginning of a much longer, demanding battle against the AIDS epidemic, and it pales in comparison with the estimated total need. As indicated above, the WHO has set an ambitious goal of three million people receiving ART by 2005. For Africa alone, 3.84 million adults were estimated to need ART in 2004–05. In all developing countries, an estimated 5.5 million adults will need ART by the close of 2005. Some 440,000 were receiving it by mid-2004, nearly one-third of them in Brazil (WHO, 2004a; WHO, 2004c, pp. 11, 62).

Table 6.2: Estimated number of patients treated in Africa with ARVs supplied by AAI companies, triple combination therapy vs at least 2 NRTIs, July 2000– December 2003

Quarter	At least 2 NRTIs	Triple Combinations
Q3-00	9,264	3,377
Q4-00	11,040	5,174
Q1-01	15,234	8,371
Q2-01	22,404	12,788
Q3-01	26,543	18,751
Q4-01	32,654	21,790
Q1-02	35,551	22,882
Q2-02	31,123	27,175
Q3-02	31,550	36,555
Q4-02	29,521	40,399
Q1-03	48,918	38,990
Q2-03	68,495	58,867
Q3-03	102,776	65,141
Q4-03	151,578	83,900

Source: Axios analysis of data provided by the seven companies in the AAI.

Of course, the increase in access to anti-retroviral treatment in Africa did not result solely from the efforts of the AAI. But the AAI played an important role as a catalyst for the origination, continuation and expansion of initiatives both within and outside its framework. These initiatives included both expanding the availability of differentially priced drugs and establishing partnerships with other organizations and governments. The AAI helped to encourage efforts in African countries, by NGOs, by private companies and in the public sector, as government officials and other stakeholders learned from the experiences of their neighbours. In addition, the AAI companies have implemented a number of related initiatives in both the public and private sectors (e.g., supplying ARVs to employers and NGOs) and have extended their efforts to Asia and Latin Ameria and the Caribbean as well. Examples of programmes instituted individually by the AAI pharmaceutical company partners follow.

RELATED ACCESS INITIATIVES BY AAI COMPANIES

Abbott Laboratories

In 1985, soon after the virus was first identified, Abbott introduced the first licensed test to detect HIV in blood. In the years since, Abbott has continued its leadership in HIV diagnostics and expanded its scientific commitment into therapeutics, discovering and developing both Norvir® (ritonavir), one of the first HIV protease inhibitors (PIs), and Kaletra® (lopinavir/ritonavir), a second-generation PI. Abbott's commitment and involvement have expanded as the tragedy of the HIV/AIDS pandemic has deepened. Today, Abbott is not only pursuing scientific innovation, but is also working in the humanitarian arena to help those infected and affected by the virus. Abbott has implemented a range of programmes in partnership with governments, non-governmental organizations (NGOs) and industry partners, designed to help build an expanding foundation to fight HIV/AIDS in Africa and developing countries where the pandemic is most prevalent and the need for assistance is greatest.

Abbott Access, launched in 2001, is the company's direct contribution to the fight against AIDS through broadened access to Abbott's HIV-care therapies in 69 countries including all of Africa and the least developed countries (LDCs) as defined by the United Nations. Through Abbott Access, the company offers Kaletra and Norvir at a loss to Abbott. Abbott is the only pharmaceutical company to provide an HIV rapid test, Determine® HIV, at no profit, in addition to providing therapeutics as part of its access programme. Abbott Access is available to any organization or institution that provides products to patients as part of a sound and sustainable programme of care.

Prevention of mother-to-child transmission of HIV. One of the most effective anti-AIDS interventions is prevention of transmission of HIV from pregnant mothers to their babies at birth. Enabling pregnant women to know their HIV status is the first step toward prevention. In 2002, Abbott began donating its Determine HIV rapid tests to programmes for prevention of mother-to-child transmission (PMTCT) in Africa and the LDCs. The Determine HIV Donation Program complements existing PMTCT programmes by adding a testing component to their focus on the treatment of pregnant women and mothers. Abbott partners with leading organizations working in PMTCT and collaborates with Boehringer-Ingelheim, who provides free HIV treatment for PMTCT programmes.

Step Forward. Currently, there are some 14 million children orphaned by AIDS, a number projected to rise to more than 40 million by 2010. The Abbott Laboratories Fund created Step Forward to help orphans and vulnerable children who are infected and affected by HIV/AIDS, and the communities that care for them. Step Forward supports model programmes in Tanzania and Burkina Faso on the African continent, India, and Romania by contributing grant funding, donated healthcare products, and the time and skills of Abbott volunteers.

Working with international partners (Axios Foundation, International HIV/AIDS Alliance, and Baylor College of Medicine/Texas Children's Hospital in Houston), local governments, and in-country non-governmental organizations (NGOs), the initiative aims to develop and support models to address specific community needs in four interrelated areas: healthcare services and infrastructure, voluntary HIV counselling and testing, education, and basic community needs such as clean water. The long-term vision of Abbott through the Step Forward programme is to share its success in increasing the coverage and quality of care for orphans and vulnerable children by encouraging the adaptation and use of these models around the world.

Tanzania Care. Improving Access to Care. Tanzania Care is a partnership among Abbott, the Abbott Laboratories Fund and the government of Tanzania to modernize the country's public healthcare facilities and systems and to improve services and access to care for people living with HIV/AIDS and other serious illnesses. The overarching goal of Tanzania Care is to create a public/private model that can be adapted by other countries, companies and organizations working to fight HIV/AIDS in the developing world. Tanzania Care covers multiple hospitals and laboratories in Tanzania, including modernizing health-care facilities and systems, training medical workers and laboratory personnel, and expanding access to HIV counselling and testing (VCT). Tanzania Care focuses largely on renovating and modernizing Muhimbili National Hospital in Dar es Salaam, Tanzania's largest public health institution, and enhancing the hospital's role as the country's primary research, referral and teaching facility.[6]

Boehringer-Ingelheim

Boehringer-Ingelheim is contributing to the fight against HIV/AIDS in the developing world through diverse activities that all serve the ultimate goal of providing access to affordable medicines. Since July 2000, Viramune® has been made available free of charge to developing countries for the prevention of mother-to-child-transmission of HIV-1 through the Viramune Donation Programme. Boehringer-Ingelheim donates Viramune in accordance with the WHO Guide-lines for Drug Donations, based on the expressed interest of governments, NGOs, charitable organizations or other healthcare providers with comprehensive PMTCT programmes. As of July 2004, Viramune had been provided free of charge to more than 300,000 mother-child pairs in 52 developing countries. Most of the 110 programmes are in sub-Saharan Africa (e.g. South Africa, Zambia, Kenya), but also in Eastern Europe (e.g. Ukraine, Russia), Latin America (e.g. Peru, Ecuador) and Asia (e.g. China, Vietnam); many more are currently under review.

In resource-poor settings, the Viramune Donation Programme has been a catalyst for local developments of healthcare infrastructures. Therefore Boehringer-Ingelheim and the WHO recognize the potential for PMTCT sites to serve as

---

[6] For additional information on these Abbott access initiatives, see *http://www.abbott.com/ citizenship/access/global_access.shtml; http://www.accesstohivcare.org; http://www.abbott-pmtct-testing.org; http:// www.stepforwardforchildren.org;* or *www.tanzaniacare.org.*

entry points for the introduction of chronic ARV therapy.

To further increase access to treatment in Africa and encourage local production, Boehringer Ingelheim has also granted licences for nevirapine to the generic manufacturers Aspen Pharmacare and Thembalami (a joint venture of Ranbaxy and Adcock Ingram Pharmaceuticals) in South Africa, and Memphis in Egypt.

The success of these access programmes has been made possible through multiple partnerships with private and governmental organizations, both locally (e.g. with African First Ladies organizations) and internationally (e.g. with the German Society for Technological Cooperation, GTZ). On the local level, cooperation has been strengthened with many key healthcare implementers such as Axios, the International Council of Nurses (ICN), the Elisabeth Glaser Pediatric AIDS Foundation, and UNICEF.[7]

Bristol-Myers Squibb

Bristol-Myers Squibb has responded to the global HIV/AIDS epidemic in three important ways: by creating the philanthropic programme *Secure the Future: Care and Support for Women and Children with HIV/AIDS in Africa*; by expanding access to the Company's anti-HIV medicines in countries hardest hit by the epidemic; and by discovering, developing and improving anti-HIV medicines.

Secure the Future is a multi-year, $115 million initiative of Bristol-Myers Squibb and the Bristol-Myers Squibb Foundation to fight the HIV/AIDS pandemic in Africa. It is among the first significant and largest corporate commitments to support programmes in Africa to help women and children affected and infected by HIV/AIDS. To date, the initiative has provided grants totalling more than $100 million to more than 160 programmes in nine countries in southern Africa (Botswana, Lesotho, Namibia, South Africa and Swaziland) and western Africa (Burkina Faso, Côte d'Ivoire, Mali and Senegal).

After five years in Africa, Secure the Future is now applying the lessons learned by establishing new comprehensive, community-based treatment sites in five countries in southern Africa and one in west Africa. It has gone to some of the hardest-hit and most rural areas to make a difference: areas that have limited or no infrastructure, a lack of trained medical personnel and limited access to food. The goal of this round of grant-making, which totals $30 million, is to develop, implement and document sustainable models of treatment, prevention and care in resource-limited settings to help these communities increase their capacity to fight HIV/AIDS. Each of the sites will be supported with anti-retrovirals and medical care.

Bristol-Myers Squibb has committed $6 million to help fund the continent's

---

[7] For an update on Boehringer-Ingelheim's Viramune donation programme, see *http://www.boehringer-ingelheim.com/hiv/news/download/VAU7_RZ.pdf.*

first pediatric AIDS clinic in Botswana. In December 2003 its Chairman and Chief Executive Officer, Peter R. Dolan, made a commitment to fund a second centre to care for children with HIV/AIDS in Africa. The new clinic will be created in partnership with the Baylor College of Medicine in Houston, together with the government of the country selected for its site.

Bristol-Myers Squibb is committed to expanding access to its HIV/AIDS medicines. In sub-Saharan Africa, it makes its HIV/AIDS medicines available at no-profit prices, and ensures that its patents do not prevent access to inexpensive HIV/AIDS therapy in the region.[8]

Gilead Sciences

Gilead Sciences is committed to bringing advanced HIV research to the developing world. The Gilead Access Program is designed to expand sustainable global access to Truvada™ (emtricitabine and tenofovir disoproxil fumarate) and Viread® (tenofovir disoproxil fumarate) by offering the once-daily medicines at a reduced price representing no profit to Gilead in 68 countries (every country in Africa and in 15 other countries designated as 'least developed' by the United Nations). Any organization operating HIV treatment programmes in these countries can request access to reduced-price Truvada and Viread, including governments, non-governmental organizations, employers, UN agencies, hospitals and clinics. Gilead is working with Axios International to coordinate the request process. Gilead will ship Truvada and Viread directly to qualifying programmes and will also provide information and guidance to programmes seeking access to these drugs.

Gilead also supports the Uganda Cares clinic, a partnership between Uganda's Ministry of Health and AHF Global Immunity. Gilead provides its anti-retrovirals, Viread and Emtriva®, at no cost, to 1,000 patients treated at the clinic and provides support to help facilitate the expansion of the clinic and scale up the number of patients served.

Gilead participates in research to optimize HIV treatment strategies, through clinical trials that help to define the best methods for delivering anti-HIV therapy in resource-challenged settings. In collaboration with a number of government, non-governmental, and scientific organizations, the company is participating in studies to evaluate the efficacy of Viread as a potential preventive.

Gilead believes that simplification of therapy is very important in the developing world. Truvada is a fixed-dose combination pill dosed once daily and Gilead is evaluating other options to further simplify treatment.[9]

---

[8] For information on *Secure the Future*, see the newsletter and resource material at *http://www.securethefuture.com/publications/data/public.html*

[9] For more information, see *www.gileadaccess.org* or *www.accesstotreatment.org*.

GlaxoSmithKline (GSK)

In addition to participation in the AAI, GSK provides its anti-retrovirals at not-for-profit preferential prices to a wide range of customers in the LDCs and in sub-Saharan Africa – a total of 63 countries. For example, GSK's antiretroviral Combivir®, which is the backbone of WHO-recommended HIV/AIDS treatment regimens, is available at US$ 0.65 per day. Additionally, all projects that are fully funded by the Global Fund are eligible for GSK's not-for-profit prices regardless of whether they are in the LDCs or sub-Saharan Africa. In total, GSK not-for-profit prices are available in over 100 countries. GSK has concluded over 175 arrangements covering 56 countries for the supply of preferentially priced ARVs. These arrangements are with a wide range of stakeholders, including governments, NGOs, public hospitals and employers, including concluded deals with Anglo-American and De Beers in Southern Africa. As a result, during 2003, GSK shipped 11 million tablets of preferentially priced Combivir to the developing world, more than they shipped in the whole of 2002 and 2001 combined.

Sustainable preferential pricing is one element of GSK's continuing contribution to improving health care in the developing world. GSK is also a leader in the research and development of medicines and vaccines for diseases of the developing world, including the search for an AIDS vaccine and new anti-retroviral treatments. GSK is an industry leader in R&D into HIV treatment, with a broad discovery and development pipeline (16 active treatment projects). In conjunction with other partners, GSK continues to support 27 HIV clinical trials in developing countries, including 20 in Africa. The purpose of these trials is to assess the use of anti-retroviral therapy for treatment, and prevention of mother-to-child HIV transmission, in resource-poor settings. In total, some 16,500 patients form, or will form, part of GSK's HIV collaborative studies in these regions, including those due to commence in 2004.

GSK has a strong commitment to community investment activities to promote health care. *Positive Action*, GSK's international programme of HIV education, care and community support, is now entering its 11th year. Positive Action pioneered the private-sector response to HIV/AIDS. During 2003 it supported 39 international programmes in partnership with 28 community-based organizations in 34 countries.

The GSK France Foundation, set up in 1998, supports programmes that reduce the risk of vertical transmission of HIV and that provide medical care, monitoring and treatment for people living with HIV. It has supported 32 programmes in 13 African countries and aims to reach 200,000 people, providing VCT facilities and appropriate care and treatment services.

GSK seeks other innovative partnerships to improve access. For example, in October 2001, GSK granted a licence to Aspen Pharmacare for the manufacture and sale in South Africa of its ARVs: Retrovir® (AZT), Epivir® and Combivir.

This licence was extended in October 2003 to cover both the public and the private sector in all of sub-Saharan Africa. In June 2004, a second licence was granted to Thembalami Pharmaceuticals (Pty) Limited of South Africa. In May 2004, GSK announced that it had entered into discussions with Boehringer-Ingelheim to assess the development of a co-packaging of Combivir and Viramune.[10]

Merck & Co., Inc.

The Merck/Gates/Botswana partnership (known as the African Comprehensive HIV/AIDS Partnerships, or ACHAP), was established in 2000 by the government of Botswana, The Merck Company Foundation/Merck & Co., Inc. and the Bill & Melinda Gates Foundation. The partnership's goal is to support and enhance Botswana's response to the HIV/AIDS epidemic through a comprehensive approach to prevention, care, treatment and support. The Merck Company Foundation and the Gates Foundation are each contributing $50 million in cash to the initiative. In addition, Merck is donating its anti-retroviral medicines to Botswana's national ARV therapy programme – known as Masa (or 'new dawn') – for the partnership's five-year duration.

Among other things, the partnership:

- supports Botswana's National AIDS Coordinating Agency with strategic planning and epidemiological analyses;
- works to strengthen healthcare infrastructure, promote behaviour change and de-stigmatize HIV/AIDS;
- provides grants to community and faith-based organizations to support grassroots efforts to tackle HIV/AIDS at the local level.

In each project the partnership supports, efforts are made to ensure that programmes are locally owned and driven, promote local capacity and can be sustained. While reducing the impact of HIV/AIDS will not happen overnight, early results from Botswana are promising. Today, Masa is the largest national HIV/AIDS treatment programme on the African continent. As of September 2004:

- nearly 27,000 patients were enrolled;
- more than 21,000 patients were on ARV therapy;
- proportionately more women are receiving ARV treatment than men – by a 3 to 2 ratio;
- approximately 1,000 new HIV-positive patients each month are being enrolled in the programme.

[10] For a summary of GSK's access initiatives, see *Facing the Challenge – Two Years On: An Update on GSK's Contribution to Improving Healthcare in the Developing World* (2003) at *www.gsk.com/community/downloads/FTC-TwoYearsOn.pdf.*

To expand this reach, the partnership is supporting the construction of 32 regional treatment centres – of which 16 are currently operational. It also is working to prevent HIV/AIDS through de-stigmatization and disease awareness education. To date, the partnership has reached educators in nearly 70 per cent of the nation's primary and secondary-level schools. It also helps provide confidential pre- and post-HIV test counselling, disease information and support for AIDS orphans through community-based centres.

Most importantly, partnership programmes are enhancing local capacity by strengthening healthcare infrastructure and transferring technical skills. To assist *Masa*, the partnership has supported the development of laboratory capacity to test and monitor patient response to treatment. Information technology systems are being developed to track patient adherence. A didactic training course is providing all healthcare professionals in Botswana with the opportunity to enhance their knowledge in HIV/AIDS clinical care, while more than 1,900 healthcare workers have received hands-on, clinic-based training from international HIV/AIDS experts through the partnership's clinical preceptorship programme.

The strength of the Merck/Gates/Botswana partnership lies in its full integration with government strategy and its ability to harness private-sector expertise in support of national efforts to address HIV/AIDS. Success to date demonstrates the value of public–private partnerships in the fight against HIV/AIDS. As lessons are documented, the partnership's process and content will inform and guide others similarly committed to reducing the human and economic impact of HIV/AIDS.[11]

F. Hoffmann–La Roche

Roche prioritizes initiatives to increase access to its medicines towards a broad policy level, designed to have the greatest potential to benefit people in greatest need. Roche seeks to make its medicines more accessible in all the least developed countries (as defined by the United Nations) and has pioneered a clear patent policy for all its medicines in these countries; thus no patents for any of Roche's medicines, across all disease areas, will be filed in the LDCs.

To improve access to those most in need of HIV/AIDS medicines, Roche has developed a specific HIV/AIDS patent policy:

- Roche will not file patents on new HIV medicines in LDCs and sub-Saharan Africa.
- It will not take action in LDCs and sub-Saharan Africa against the sale or manufacture of generic versions of HIV medicines.

---

[11] To learn more about the Botswana partnership and its programmes, see ACHAP (2004a and 2004b), de Korte et al. (2004); and Distlerath and Macdonald (2004).

- As a result of Roche's patent policy, generic versions of saquinavir can be produced in LDCs and sub-Saharan Africa without the need for a voluntary or compulsory licence. (Roche does not hold patent rights for nelfinavir.)

Roche makes its two HIV protease inhibitors, Invirase® (saquinavir) and Viracept® (nelfinavir) available at no-profit prices to the LDCs and sub-Saharan Africa. Roche also has reduced pricing for low-income and lower-middle-income countries (as classified by the World Bank). It has thus focused its efforts to improve access to its HIV protease inhibitors where there are the greatest number of people in urgent need of HIV therapy and fewest resources. Roche patent and no-profit pricing policies apply to an estimated 26 million people and two-thirds of all people living with HIV/AIDS globally.

Additional activities implemented by Roche to increase sustainable access to health care include working in partnership with committed governments, NGOs and other parties sharing similar goals; and facilitation of education, training and sharing of experience. For example, in partnership with Pharm-Access Foundation, Roche is taking steps to widen access to HIV therapy in Africa, in a controlled and clinically sound way, by focusing on the improvement and build-up of the local medical infrastructure. The goal is to expand access to HIV health care and therapy in Côte d'Ivoire, Kenya, Senegal and Uganda.[12]

As these examples indicate, the AAI has received enthusiastiac support from its seven partner companies and has helped to create a remarkable structure of policies and programmes in the developing world. There are also many other initiatives undertaken individually by the seven AAI partner companies and other research-based pharmaceutical companies.[13]

LESSONS AND INSIGHTS FROM THE AAI

The AAI has already had an important impact on those aspects of the HIV/AIDS epidemic that it was meant to address. The experience of creating, implementing and sustaining cooperative efforts through this unique public–private partnership offers lessons to all those concerned about the epidemic and eager to learn how to respond to this worldwide crisis. Many of the lessons reflect the considerations outlined in the six principles of the Joint Statement of Intent, which remains as relevant today as when it was developed in early 2000.

---

[12] For more information on Roche's initiatives, see *Removing Barriers, Increasing Access: Roche's Commitment to Increase Access to Medicines for HIV/AIDS and Malaria* (July 2004), available at *www.roche-hiv.com*.
[13] For more information on pharmaceutical industry access initiatives, see UNAIDS (2001); IFPMA (2004); *http://www.efpia.org*; and *http://world.phrma.org/index.html*.

The AAI sparked an expansion in HIV care and support in developing countries by providing an important framework for dialogue and learning. Here are some of the lessons that have emerged from this collective experience.

Projects must be tailored to meet local needs

Programmes for addressing the epidemic successfully must be based not only on local needs and abilities but also on local values, attitudes, and social and cultural practices. Governments and civil society in the recipient countries are better placed than outside donors to understand what approaches are appropriate. The close involvement of local, private and public organizations in programme design both facilitates taking these factors into account and creates a sense of ownership important to effective implementation (Attaran and Sachs, 2001, p. 61).

Success is determined by both national and international capacity

The importance of national capacity was not a new lesson, but it was reinforced by the AAI experience. Perhaps one of the most compelling examples is that of nevirapine (Viramune®). As of July 2000, the manufacturer, Boehringer Ingelheim, had offered the drug free to 120 low- and middle-income countries for use in the prevention of mother-to-child HIV transmission. Even with the free drug, however, only a few programmes were able to take up the offer at first because supporting infrastructure was not adequately in place to benefit from the donation (Attaran and Sachs, 2001, p. 60).

At its third meeting, in May 2001, the UNAIDS Contact Group noted that 'the greater availability of medicines has to be matched by corresponding growth in health services and the necessary diagnostic technologies. At the same time, the need for treatment continues to outstrip the capacity of public and private health systems to deliver it.' (UNAIDS, 2000b) UNAIDS's July 2002 report similarly noted that 'Drug prices are only one of many obstacles to boosting access to HIV/AIDS-related medicines. Effective treatment depends on general health services being able to procure, store, diagnose, select and administer the necessary drugs and to provide related treatment, care and diagnostic services to monitor health status and treatment response.' (UNAIDS, 2002c)

The concept of 'capacity-building' has been sharpened through experience and is now applied not only to countries but also to outside support (Potter and Brough, 2004). One of the cornerstones of the AAI has been the development of national plans, with technical support provided through the UN system at the request of participating countries. The need for this assistance has been starkly demonstrated; responding to demand has stretched the human resources available at both the national and international levels. The need for technical expertise will not wane soon. In December 2002, the Executive Director of UNAIDS placed capacity development first among four actions of 'particular urgency' for maximizing the effectiveness of that programme. Capacity was described as including 'monitoring and evaluation, planning, civil society and private-sector partnerships, and resource mobilization and tracking' (Piot, 2002a). More recently, attention has focused on the critical shortage of skilled professionals at all levels of the healthcare system in those developing countries hardest hit by the HIV epidemic. In one of the cruel ironies of the epidemic, migration of trained doctors and nurses between developing countries – and from developing to developed countries in search of better opportunities – has put additional strain on already challenged public health institutions in many countries (Buchan and Sochalski, 2004; Stillwell et al., 2004).

Treatment and prevention are important for maximizing the impact of ARVs

The importance of efficient and appropriate use of ARVs, and also of other drugs to fight HIV/AIDS-related disease, has come to the fore as the AAI has made these products more readily available. Very practical issues have become prominent. At first, it was unclear whether patients with limited resources and diverse healthcare practices and beliefs would adhere to therapy. The experience of Botswana, for example, has shown that high adherence rates can be achieved. As the programme evolved they proved to be comparable to those seen in developed-country settings (Grunwald, 2002; UNAIDS, 2003c, pp. 15–27; Weiser et al., 2003; and ACHAP, 2004b).

Practical clinical issues include defining standardized regimens for ART in programmes where few physicians or laboratory facilities are available. In addition to concerns about how to treat patients today, the greater use of ARVs in these settings raises the concern of increasing viral resistance unless treatment is carefully monitored and coupled with efforts to promote adherence (Weidle and Mastro et al., 2002, pp. 2262–3; Kuritzkes, 2004; Lange and Perriens et al., 2004). Technical guidelines for the use of ART were developed through a series of consultative meetings with clinicians, scientists, government representatives, representatives of civil society and people living with HIV/AIDS. The guidelines were published by the WHO in April 2002 and updated in 2003 (WHO, 2002 and 2004e).[14] As with all such guidelines, continuous updating – and timely, effective distribution of new versions – will be essential for incorporating crucial new information, evidence and therapies.

The battle against HIV/AIDS cannot be won through treatment alone, as

[14] See also WHO (2004b and 2004d) – both available at *www.who.int/hiv/en.*

the rate of spread of HIV will soon overwhelm even the most valiant efforts to ensure access to treatment. As the UN General Assembly Special Session on HIV/AIDS (UNGASS) Declaration bluntly states, 'Prevention must be the mainstay of our response' (UNGASS, 2001).

Prevention and treatment are viewed as intertwined efforts that should be integrated into planning. The idea behind their complementarity is that the availability of treatment will provide an incentive for people who are possibly infected with HIV to seek out testing and care, while treatment programmes also provide additional opportunities to address prevention with appropriately crafted messages and interventions. Contact with care providers then offers opportunities to encourage changes in risky behaviour – not only for the patient, but also for the patient's family and other close contacts (UNAIDS, 2002a; WHO, 2002; Global HIV Prevention Working Group, 2003, 2004).

Experience to date, however, reveals a rather different story. Until the disease has progressed to its later stages, stigma and denial are stronger motivators for avoidance of treatment than the availability of treatment is for seeking it. Despite all its resources, the partnership in Botswana – involving the government, the Gates Foundation and Merck – has come up hard against this reality. The anti-retroviral project was designed to start 19,000 patients on HIV therapy in 2002; but only about 3,000 began therapy, usually the 'sickest of the sick', whose needs severely strained the infrastructure. In a country with an estimated 300,000 people currently infected, attitudes – of patients, providers and the wider community – are still the primary determinants of success or failure. An encouraging note is that ready access to treatment, coupled with broad public education efforts and the introduction early in 2004 of a routine offer of HIV testing, have begun to shift attitudes and behaviour. More people are now coming forward to avail themselves of anti-retroviral treatment (Grunwald, 2002; ACHAP 2004a, 2004b; de Korte et al., 2004).

A study on insurance coverage in South Africa suggests a similar story. Although most private insurers cover a range of care for HIV/AIDS – 90 per cent include triple-ARV therapy, for example – only 0.3 per cent of eligible beneficiaries have sought access to these benefits. Possible explanations include inadequate information about benefits, HIV stigma and discrimination, public confusion about the safety and efficacy of ART, high co-payments and the inequitable distribution of people with HIV between public- and private-sector care coverage (TAC, 2002; Stein et al., 2002).

Heineken's efforts to provide care, including free ART, to its employees in Rwanda (with expansion to other countries planned) have met with similar reluctance. Some employees have suspected that the purpose of the new approach is to discover and dismiss sick workers. Others have expressed deeper feelings. As one worker explained: 'I am not afraid of losing my job; I am afraid of losing my dignity.' (Sansoni, 2003)

These examples (and others) deserve further exploration as the international effort to fight the pandemic proceeds. Current assumptions about prevention and its link to treatment need to be re-examined, with a view to adjusting both programmes and funding estimates to take account of our experiences and new knowledge.

Pragmatic public–private partnerships are critical

The AAI demonstrates that pragmatic public–private partnerships, based on a clear understanding of goals, can be very successful. It also suggests that effectively countering the AIDS epidemic requires the involvement of all sectors of society – governments, civil society, religious and cultural institutions, and businesses – at the local, national, regional and global levels.

Lower ART prices and technical assistance to governments are critical in strengthening the response, but they are only a start. Partnerships have an important role to play, particularly when they 'add up to more than the sum of the parts', as McKinsey observed in their early work on the AAI:

> The pharmaceutical industry and the private sector more broadly have a greater role than merely discounting drugs. Many companies have expertise, beyond their specialized medical knowledge, that could help control AIDS in developing countries: the distribution capacity to reach remote areas, the mass-marketing capabilities to improve awareness and overcome the social stigma associated with prevention, and the project-management and planning skills to establish and maintain access programs. In nations wracked by AIDS, these business strengths can literally be lifesaving (Fine et al, 2001).

Broad national partnerships have already contributed to success. To take just two salient examples, Uganda, which reduced the national prevalence rate of HIV infection from a peak of about 15 per cent in 1991 to only 5 per cent in 2004, has done so through a concerted and highly inclusive effort based on the ABC approach (abstinence, be faithful and use condoms when unable to do the first two) (Green et al., 2002). Another important determinant of Uganda's success was the mobilization of all actors in society – particularly policy-makers and civil society groups such as UWESO and TASO – for a response that included both care and prevention. Similarly, Botswana is involving a broad range of public and private groups and organizations in their effort to build an effective, sustainable response to the HIV/AIDS epidemic.

Ministries of health were the primary partners at the national level for the UN agencies and the pharmaceutical companies involved at the outset of the AAI. The Contact Group provided a valuable forum for comments and input from a broad range of groups at the inception of the initiative, but was never intended to serve as a vehicle for programme development or implementation. As the AAI effort evolved, the focus of dialogue and partnership has naturally shifted to stakeholders at the national level.

Since the AAI was established, and in part as a result of the example it provided, the role of the private sector in strengthening the global response to the HIV/AIDS epidemic has come to be better appreciated. Private-sector initiatives are rapidly gaining momentum as more and more companies become mobilized. This is clear at both the policy level – in the prescriptions for action from bilateral donors and multilateral organizations – and at the practical level, in the growing number of reports and guidance from such business groups as the Global Business Coalition on HIV/AIDS, the Global Health Initiative of the World Economic Forum, and the Corporate Council on Africa.[15] The pharmaceutical companies in the AAI were among the first businesses to address the global challenge of HIV/AIDS seriously, but it is encouraging now to see a broader business-sector response developing. This includes those firms implementing workplace programmes and thus displaying awareness that fighting AIDS 'makes good business sense' (Rosen et al., 2003).[16] Robust public–private partnerships will remain a key feature in implementing effective national programmes and in developing good working relationships among all the groups involved, including communities of people living with HIV infection and civil society organizations.

Funding remains a critical challenge

The reductions in prices for ARVs for the developing world that has occurred since mid-2000 as a result of the individual actions by each of the AAI companies are well known and often cited. Less often noted are the funding difficulties faced by countries that had negotiated supply agreements. In only a third of the 19 agreements concluded by mid-2002, for instance, could the recipient country fully subsidize the implementation of ART. The other countries relied

[15] See, for example, the comments on private-sector involvement in DFID (2004), Section 5.4, pp. 34–8; US Office of the Global AIDS Coordinator (2004), pp. 74–5; UNAIDS (2004), pp. 55–7, 102–4, 141–2, and 158–61; WHO (2004c), p. 51; and European Commission (2003), pp. 14–22. For the work of the Global Business Coalition on HIV/AIDS and the Global Health Initiative, see the materials on their respective Web sites, www.businessfightsaids.org and http://www.weforum.org/site/homepublic.nsf/Content/Global+Health+Initiative. See also the background and case studies in Corporate Council on Africa (2001); USAID (2004); and Whiteside and O'Grady (2002).

[16] For early reports on how workplace programmes are beginning to make a difference, see UNAIDS (2003b), pp. 23–27; and UNAIDS (2003a), pp. 38–40, 62. For overviews of workplace programmes on HIV/AIDS, see ILO (2002, 2003 and 2004); Rau (2002); and the resources available at www.businessfightsaids.org and http://www.weforum.org/site/homepublic.nsf/Content/Global+Health+Initiative.

on a range of approaches, from out-of-pocket payment by individual patients to revolving funds, work-based schemes, private insurance, debt relief and bilateral and multilateral aid. This experience has provided an unsettling glimpse of the practical realities of scaling up HIV/AIDS care, treatment and support: available funding was usually aimed only at the cost of therapy, while care, support, prevention and the expansion of testing, clinical and laboratory facilities, as well as staff training and retention, have required additional expenditure.

In 1999, global funding resources for HIV/AIDS were $300 million; by 2002, they were $3 billion. In December 2002, UNAIDS projected that 'needs in low- and middle-income countries will be $10.5 billion by 2005, rising to $15 billion by 2007 (Piot, 2002b). Devoting an estimated $4.8 billion of this to prevention could forestall 29 million new HIV infections by 2010 (Piot, 2002a, p. A17). Some of this funding can come from domestic and regional sources, particularly in middle-income countries, but the private sector in general is also expected to play a greater role at the national and international levels. The pharmaceutical company partners in the AAI were among the leaders in this regard, as many had already supported local programmes with funding in excess of what some developed countries were providing in foreign assistance.

The AAI experience with ART showed that treatment and care can be provided effectively in resource-limited settings. This demonstration has already helped to reshape the direction and content of major international commitments, as reflected, for example, in the action plan that came out of the African Development Forum organized by the Economic Commission for Africa in Addis Ababa in December 2000; in the Abuja Declaration on HIV/AIDS, Tuberculosis and other related Infectious Diseases issued in April 2001 by the Heads of State of the Organization for African Unity; and in the Declaration of Commitment on HIV/AIDS adopted at UNGASS in June 2001. Additional evidence of the changed attitude of donors towards financing the purchase of ARVs is clear in the remit and first four rounds of grants of the Global Fund to Fight AIDS, TB and Malaria; in the availability of World Bank financing for care and treatment; and in major new bilateral programmes such as the US President's Emergency Plan for AIDS Relief, which proposes to provide $15 billion over five years to help fight the HIV/AIDS epidemic in 15 targeted countries in Africa, Asia and the Caribbean (US Office of Global AIDS Coordinator, 2004).

Still, overall funding to fight the epidemic remains insufficient. During 2003–04 the Global Fund, for example, agreed to support more than 300 programmes worth $3.1 billion in nearly 130 countries – more than half for HIV/ AIDS. But as of June 2004, the Fund estimated that, if it was going to continue at the same pace, it faced a funding gap of roughly $3 billion for 2005 (Global Fund, 2004, p. 11; Feachem, 2004). International assistance channelled through such alliances is not the only way to fund progress, but the lack of more substantial support from the donor community for this highly visible, well-respected new effort is discouraging.

The virus has its own agenda

The HIV virus and the opportunistic infections that characterize AIDS have the same simple agenda as all microbes: survival. Prevention can stop that agenda, but successful prevention is years away, even in the best of settings. Treating those infected with appropriate ART can lessen the chances of easy transmission, as well as prolonging the lives and easing the suffering of those infected. But the virus mutates rapidly; resistance to ARVs is already appearing all around the world. A vaccine that could seriously inhibit the spread of HIV, or one that could cure those infected, might tilt the scales against the virus. But progress in understanding how to design a vaccine that will provide effective immunity against this wily adversary – either through neutralizing antibodies or through a cell-mediated immune response – has been difficult. Moreover, such advances take major investment, and the incentives for that are at best weak and do not seem likely to improve appreciably in the near future. Complex rules governing new research, the potential involvement of many interests in deciding the direction of research, and unrealistic expectations about the pace of discovery all threaten to slow the progress of humankind's response – to the distinct disadvantage of the developing nations. But thanks to the continued efforts of several major pharmaceutical companies and academic and government researchers – and the tireless advocacy of organizations such as the International AIDS Vaccine Initiative – more promising HIV vaccine candidates are moving into human clinical trials to evaluate their potential.

CONCLUSION

In practice, the AAI's primary focus has been to increase access to drug therapies for HIV/AIDS-related diseases in resource-limited settings by individually reducing costs and increasing supply. As a result, the number of people reached with ART in Africa has increased by more than an order of magnitude. Although in absolute terms the numbers are still small compared to the need, the steady progress in patients receiving anti-retroviral treatment in Africa through the efforts of the AAI partners is encouraging. This is particularly true when we look at the apparent increase in the rate of growth since mid-2003, as the global community mobilized more resources for the developing world.

Working with partners among the affected communities, with others at country level in both the public sector and civil society, and also within the UN system, the companies involved in the AAI have helped to provide proper care to many individuals living with HIV/AIDS. Each of us continues to help expand affordable and equitable access to HIV care, treatment and support in developing countries (UNAIDS, 2002d). The starting point provided by the AAI suggests essential lessons for the scaling-up of access to therapy – lessons that can be applied as funding and infrastructure improvements enable developing nations to absorb what is offered. At the same time, work proceeds every day in our laboratories to develop new medicines and new combinations to treat HIV infection and to discover a safe and effective HIV vaccine that can be delivered efficiently to the countries where the need is most acute.

As UNAIDS Executive Director Peter Piot observed in his 2003 World Bank Presidential Fellows Lecture, 'AIDS demands that we do business differently. AIDS requires more than personal behavior change. It also requires institutional behavior change.' (Piot, 2003, p. 16) The Accelerating Access Initiative has been a pioneering experiment in creating just the kind of institutional behaviour change needed to rise to the HIV/AIDS challenge. The AAI has brought together complementary resources and expertise to help mount an expanded multisectoral response and shows what can be accomplished through cooperation and collaboration. Much remains to be done if we are going to stop the spread of this deadly infection. But the experience of the AAI offers guidance and hope for the future.

ANNEX 6.1
TECHNICAL NOTE

The estimated number of people on treatment was based on actual quarterly drug supply data from the six companies, individually provided on a confidential basis by each company to Axios International, a third party with experience in the area of HIV/AIDS care in the developing world, for independent analysis. The drug unit data were converted into patient-equivalent numbers by quarter, based on dosage and indications. The estimated patient numbers are a conservative estimate of the number of people actually treated with anti-retrovirals in Africa, since they do not take into account such factors as patient adherence to therapy, the number of children treated, use of other drugs, and drug wastage.

The data provided are either in packs, tablets or grams of active substances supplied each quarter. In addition, many products exist as multiple dosages or pack sizes. For the sake of consistency, a single formula relying on the weight of active drug is applied to convert the figures into an estimated patient number for each quarter. At this stage, the assumption is that all patients take the recommended daily dosages. As some patients may take lower dosages in reality, the estimated number of patients calculated is lower than the actual number of patients.

Once these data are converted into the estimated number of patients for each product per quarter, the data are pooled as follows:

- It is assumed that all patients take at least two nucleoside reverse transcriptase inhibitors (NRTIs) and that all patients follow the standard daily dosages. A proportion of the patients have in addition one non-nucleoside reverse transcriptase inhibitor (NNRTI) or one protease inhibitor (PI). As it is a common practice to combine Norvir® (ritonavir) with Crixivan® (indinavir sulfate) or with Invirase®/Fortovase® (saquinavir) the analysis took this aspect into consideration. The combination of Norvir as a booster to another PI was considered as one PI.

- All NRTI figures for data units (per product and per quarter) were added and pooled and divided by two to obtain the number of patients on at least 2 NRTIs. Countries are divided by regions. For Africa, four regions are categorized, i.e. North Africa, West Africa, South Africa and East Africa (see Table 6.1). NNRTI and PI data are then pooled and matched with the NRTI figures to constitute the calculated number of patient-equivalents on triple combinations.

- The clinical assumption is that all patients are on at least 2NRTIs. Some are on double combinations with 2 NRTIs only and the others are on triple combinations: 2 NRTIs + 1 PI or 2 NRTIs + 1 NNRTI. It is therefore logical to think that the number of patients on at least 2 NRTIs should always be higher than the number of patients on triple combinations. If the calculated number of patients on at least 2 NRTIs happens to be lower than the number of those on triple combinations, it implies that not all NRTIs used by the patients are actually supplied by the AAI companies.

- The total number of patients on ARV reached by the AAI companies is therefore calculated for each African region separately. The number of patient-equivalents used is either the number of at least 2 NRTIs or the number of triple combinations, whichever is higher. The total number of patient-equivalents for the African continent is the sum of the regional numbers mentioned above.
- The results are therefore presented per quarter and for the whole of Africa and by region as follows:
  - Total estimated number of patients on ARVs = patients on at least 2 NRTIs or patients on triple combinations, whichever is higher;
  - Estimated number of patients on double combinations of 2 NRTIs;
  - Estimated number of patients on triple combinations including 2 NRTIs + 1 NNRTI; 2 NRTIs + 1 PI .

The fact that this analysis was based on drug units supplied and converted into estimated patient numbers implies a number of advantages and limitations compared to formal country surveys. The data are collected precisely and consistently as they represent units supplied and actual sales. The analysis is therefore underpinned by reliable data. The calculated number of patients represents only an estimate of the number of patients treated by anti-retrovirals supplied by the six companies in the Accelerating Access Initiative. It does not represent an estimate of the total number of patients treated in Africa, as it does not take into account the patients treated with anti-retrovirals supplied by other companies. At the same time, owing to a number of factors noted above, the actual number of patients is likely to be higher than the reported figures.[a]

Even if the estimated numbers in this interim report do not exactly represent the total number of patients treated with anti-retrovirals in Africa, they do provide very relevant information on:

- the trends in the quality of treatment provided;
- the substantial increase in patient numbers since the Accelerating Access Initiative was launched.

[a] A further explanation of the possible limitations of the data and a fuller analysis of the reasons for thinking that the patient estimates are a lower bound are found in UNAIDS/WHO (2002), Annex 3. Given that most of the limitations imply that the actual number of patients is higher than the number calculated in this analysis, it is safe to consider that the numbers provided in this analysis constitute a very conservative estimate of the number of patients actually treated with anti-retrovirals supplied by the six companies in the Accelerating Access Initiative. A 20–50 per cent increase in the calculated number would likely be closer to the real figure.

ANNEX 6.2
ACCELERATING ACCESS TO HIV/AIDS CARE AND TREATMENT
IN DEVELOPING COUNTRIES

A Joint Statement of Intent[a]
8 May 2000

Building on the work undertaken by the Joint United Nations Programme on HIV/AIDS (UNAIDS), its co-sponsors and other partners worldwide in responding to the growing demand for care and treatment of HIV/AIDS-related illnesses in developing countries, a new effort is being undertaken to enhance progressively the capacity of countries to increase access to, and use of, sustainable, comprehensive and quality HIV/AIDS interventions across the entire spectrum of prevention, treatment, patient care and support (including prevention of perinatal transmission).

Five pharmaceutical companies – Boehringer Ingelheim, Bristol-Myers Squibb, Glaxo Wellcome,[b] Merck & Co., Inc., and F. Hoffmann-La Roche – are responding to calls from UN Secretary-General Kofi Annan (in launching the International Partnership against AIDS in Africa, in December 1999), Dr Gro Harlem Brundtland, Director-General of the World Health Organization (in her address to the WHO Executive Board in January 2000, where she invited the pharmaceutical companies to 'take a fresh and constructive look at how we can increase access to relevant drugs'), and to the invitations of Dr Peter Piot, Executive Director of UNAIDS, James D. Wolfensohn of the World Bank, Carol Bellamy, Executive Director of the United Nations Children's Fund, and Nafis Sadik, Executive Director, United Nations Population Fund, to the private sector to engage in partnerships for expanding the global response to HIV/AIDS.

The five companies have begun constructive discussions with UNAIDS, WHO, the World Bank, the United Nations Children's Fund (UNICEF), and the United Nations Population Fund (UNFPA), to explore practical and specific ways of working together more closely to accelerate access to HIV/AIDS-related care and treatment in developing countries. This endeavour is expected to expand to include other partners from all sectors.

Participants acknowledge that affordability of HIV/AIDS-related care and treatment is an issue in developing countries – though only one among many obstacles to access including social/political/structural and economic issues, healthcare financing, physical barriers, and information gaps – and are willing to work with committed governments, international organizations and other

---

[a] Abbott Laboratories joined the AAI in 2001 and Gilead Sciences joined in 2004. Both companies also agreed to the principles of the Joint Statement of Intent.
[b] Now GlaxoSmithKline.

stakeholders to find ways to broaden access while ensuring rational, affordable, safe and effective use of drugs for HIV/AIDS-related illnesses. The companies, individually, are offering to improve significantly access to and availability of a range of medicines.

Intended to benefit people in developing countries, this public–private cooperation

- is designed to accelerate their sustained access to, and increase their use of, appropriate, good quality interventions for the prevention, treatment and care of HIV/AIDS-related illnesses, and the prevention of perinatal transmission of HIV.
- strives to ensure that care and treatment reach significantly greater numbers of people in need, through new alliances involving committed governments, private industry, the UN system, development assistance agencies, non-governmental organizations and people living with HIV/AIDS.
- will be implemented in ways that respond to the specific needs and requests of individual countries, with respect for human rights, equity, transparency and accountability.

The following principles reflect a common vision of how the HIV/AIDS epidemic can more effectively be tackled in developing countries:

(i) *Unequivocal and ongoing political commitment by national governments* is essential for successful efforts to reduce the impact of HIV/AIDS in line with poverty reduction and broader development strategies.

(ii) *Strengthened national capacity,* including well-designed HIV/AIDS prevention and care strategies and a strengthened healthcare infrastructure, is crucial for delivering care and treatment to people with HIV/AIDS on an equitable basis.

(iii) *Engagement of all sectors of national society and the global community* – including governments of developing and industrialized donor countries, international NGOs, industry, other segments of civil society (particularly people living with HIV) and multilateral organizations – is essential in facilitating access to treatment of HIV/AIDS-related illnesses.

(iv) *Efficient, reliable and secure distribution systems* are necessary to ensure that medical supplies and other consumables procured by the public sector or NGOs are made available to people who need them at the appropriate contact points within health systems.

(v) *Significant additional funding from new national and international sources,* commensurate with the health challenges posed by the HIV epidemic, is necessary for long-term success, so that current health and social sector priorities can be maintained.

(vi) *Continued investment in research and development by the pharmaceutical industry* on innovative new treatments for HIV/AIDS and other diseases affecting the developing world – the best hope for new and better future medicines and vaccines – is critical to expanding the global response to HIV/AIDS and to advancing world health. Therefore intellectual property rights should be protected, in compliance with international agreements, since society depends on them to stimulate innovation.

This public–private cooperation is intended to increase the proportion of people living with HIV/AIDS in the developing world who have safe, equitable, sustained and affordable access to care and treatment. As a practical response to the call for multisectoral action in the face of this global health challenge, it is an important step in a longer-term process of increasing the access to care of women, men and children in developing countries. It aims to contribute to the International Partnership against AIDS in Africa, as well as efforts to curb the spread of HIV and mitigate its impact in other continents and, more broadly, to support the international development agenda.

Source: http://www.unaids.org/NetTools/Misc/DocInfo.aspx?LANG=en&href=http%3a%2f% fgva-doc-owl% 2fWEBcontent% 2fDocuments %2fpub%2fUNA-docs%2fIntent8May2000_en %26%2346%3bdoc (last accessed 23 July 2004).

ANNEX 6.3
COUNTRIES THAT HAVE EXPRESSED INTEREST IN
ACCELERATING ACCESS

Country	Completed/advanced planning	Agreement on prices/ national plans[a]
AFRICA	(41)	(24)
Algeria	Mission being planned	
Angola	No follow-up yet	
Benin – ECOWAS	Yes	Yes
Botswana	Yes – discussions outside AAI framework	
Burkina Faso – ECOWAS	Yes	Yes
Burundi	Yes	Yes
Cameroon	Yes	Yes
Cape Verde – ECOWAS	Yes	Yes
CAR	Yes – no supply agreement sought	
Chad	Yes	Yes
Congo	Yes	Yes
Côte d'Ivoire – ECOWAS	Yes	Yes
Ethiopia	Yes – no supply agreement sought	
Gabon	Yes	Yes
Gambia – ECOWAS	Yes	Yes
Ghana – ECOWAS	Yes	Yes
Guinea – ECOWAS	Yes	Yes
Guinea-Bissau – ECOWAS	Yes	Yes
Kenya	Yes – no supply agreement sought	
Lesotho[c]	See footnote[b]	
Liberia – ECOWAS	Yes	Yes
Malawi	Yes – discussions outside AAI framework	
Mali – ECOWAS	Yes	Yes
Mauritius	No follow up yet	
Morocco	Yes	Yes
Mozambique	See footnote[b]	
Namibia	See footnote[b]	
Niger – ECOWAS	Yes	Yes

[a] Countries which, with involvement from UNAIDS, have reached agreement with companies individually on reduced drug prices in the context of national plans. Individual companies have reached agreement with additional countries.

[b] These countries are members of the Southern African Development Community (SADC) and have so far not decided whether to start collaboration with the AAI as a group. In some of these countries there is already significant use of ARVs in the private sector.

Country	Completed/advanced planning	Agreement on prices/ national plans[a]
Nigeria – ECOWAS	Yes	Yes
Rwanda	Yes	Yes
South Africa	See footnote[b]	
Sierra Leone – ECOWAS	Yes	Yes
Senegal – ECOWAS	Yes	Yes
Seychelles	No follow-up yet	
Swaziland	Yes – no supply agreement sought	
Tanzania	See footnote[b]	
Togo – ECOWAS	Yes	Yes
Tunisia	Yes	Yes
Uganda	Yes	Yes
Zambia	See footnote[b]	
Zimbabwe	See footnote[b]	
LATIN AMERICA/CARIBBEAN	(28)	(22)
Antigua & Barbuda – CARICOM	Yes	Yes
Bahamas – CARICOM	Yes	Yes
Barbados – CARICOM	Yes	Yes
Belize – CARICOM	Yes	Yes
Bolivia – ANDEAN[c]	Plan ongoing	
Chile – ANDEAN	Yes	Yes
Colombia – ANDEAN	Plan ongoing	
Costa Rica – COMISCA	Yes	Yes
Domenica – CARICOM	Yes	Yes
Ecuador – ANDEAN	Plan ongoing	
Grenada – CARICOM	Yes	Yes
Guatemala – COMISCA	Yes	Yes
Guyana – CARICOM	Yes	Yes
El Salvador – COMISCA	Yes	Yes
Haiti – CARICOM	Yes	Yes
Honduras – COMISCA	Yes	Yes
Jamaica – CARICOM	Yes	Yes
Mexico	Yes – discussion outside AAI context pursued by individual companies	
Montserrat – CARICOM	Yes	Yes
Nicaragua – COMISCA	Yes	Yes
Panama – COMISCA	Yes	Yes
Peru – ANDEAN	Plan ongong	

[c] The Andean Pact countries have indicated that they are not interested in pursuing further discussions with AAI at this time. However, individual discussions outside the scope of AAI are ongoing.

Country	Completed/advanced planning	Agreement on prices/ national plans[a]
St Kitts & Nevis – CARICOM	Yes	Yes
St Lucia – CARICOM	Yes	Yes
St Vincent/Grenadin – CARICOM	Yes	Yes
Suriname – CARICOM	Yes	Yes
Trinidad and Tobago – CARICOM	Yes	Yes
Venezuela – ANDEAN	Yes – plans completed and discussion on supply agreements awaited	
EUROPE	(5)	(3)
Georgia	Plan ongoing	
Belarus	No follow-up yet	
Moldova	Yes	Yes
Romania	Yes	Yes
Ukraine	Yes	Yes
ASIA	(5)	(0)
China	Plan ongoing	
Indonesia	A final decision whether to pursue improving access to ARVs through the AAI framework pending	
Malaysia	A final decision whether to pursue improving access to ARVs through the AAI framework pending	
Thailand	The Thai government opted to continue its planning outside the AAI framework	
Vietnam	Yes – no supply agreements sought	
MIDDLE EAST	(5)	(0)
Jordan	Follow-up by EMRO started	
Egypt	Follow-up by EMRO started	
Lebanon	Yes	
Oman	Follow-up by EMRO started	
Syria	Follow-up by EMRO started	

Source: WHO/UNAIDS (2002), Annex 2, pp. 21–2. Updated through June 2004 with information obtained from AAI companies.

REFERENCES

ACHAP (2004a), *ACHAP Review 2004* (Gaborone, Botswana: ACHAP, July), available at *www.achap.org*.

ACHAP (2004b), *Hope: Rolling Out ARV Therapy in Botswana* (Gaborone, Botswana: ACHAP, July), available at *www.achap.org*.

Adelman, Carol, Jeremiah Norris and S. Jean Weicher (2004), *Myths and Realities on Prices of AIDS Drugs*, Hudson Institute White Paper (Washington, DC: Hudson Institute).

Attaran, Amir and Jeffrey Sachs (2001), 'Defining and refining international donor support for combating the AIDS pandemic', *The Lancet*, 357 (6 January): 57–61.

Buchan, James and Julie Sochalski (2004), 'The migration of nurses: trends and policies', *Bulletin of the World Health Organization*, 82 (August): 587–94.

Chin, James (1990), 'Global estimates of AIDS and HIV infections: 1990', in *AIDS 1990: A Year in Review: Proceedings from the 6th International Conference on AIDS. AIDS*, 4: Supplement 1.

Corporate Council on Africa (2001), *Report of the Findings of the Corporate Council on Africa's Task Force on HIV/AIDS* (Washington, DC: Corporate Council on Africa, October).

de Korte, Donald, Ernest Darkoh, Patson Mazonde et al. (2004), *Strategies for a National AIDS Treatment Program in Botswana*, ACHAP Program Series, Vol. 1, No. 1 (July).

DFID (2004), *Increasing Access to Essential Medicines in the Developing World: UK Government Policy and Plans* (London: UK Department for International Development), June.

Distlerath, Linda and Guy Macdonald (2004), 'The African Comprehensive HIV/AIDS Partnerships – A new role for multinational corporations in global health policy', *Yale Journal of Health Policy, Law and Ethics*, 4: 147–55.

European Commission, Directorate-General for Development (2003), *The European Union Confronts HIV/AIDS, Malaria and Tuberculosis: A Comprehensive Strategy for the New Millennium* (Luxembourg: European Commission), November.

Feachem, Richard (2004), 'Report from the Executive Director', Eighth Board Meeting, Global Fund, Geneva, 28 June, available at *http://www.theglobalfund.org/en/about/board/eighth/openingspeechfeachem/*.

Fine, David, Judith Hazlewood, David Hughes and Adele Sulcas (2001), 'AIDS: A Flicker of Hope in Africa', in *A New Era for Nonprofits: The McKinsey Quarterly Anthology* (New York: McKinsey & Company), pp. 100–09.

Global Fund to Fight AIDS, Tuberculosis and Malaria (2004), *A Force for Change: The Global Fund at 30 Months* (Geneva: Global Fund).

Global HIV Prevention Working Group (2003), *Access to HIV Prevention: Closing the Gap* (Seattle, WA and Menlo Park, CA: Bill & Melinda Gates Foundation and Henry J. Kaiser Family Foundation), May, available at *www.gatesfoundation.org* and *www.kaisernetwork.org*.

Global HIV Prevention Working Group (2004), *HIV Prevention in the Era of Expanded Treatment Access* (Seattle, WA and Menlo Park, CA: Bill & Melinda Gates Foundation and Henry J. Kaiser Family Foundation), June, available at *www.gatesfoundation.org* and *www.kaisernetwork.org*.

Green, Edward, Vinand Nantulya, Rand Stoneburner, and John Stover (2002), *What Happened in Uganda? Declining HIV Prevalence, Behavior Change, and the National Response* (Washington, DC: USAID), September, available at *http://www.usaid.gov/our_work/global_health/aids/countries/uganda_report.pdf*.

Grunwald, Michael (2002), 'All-out effort fails to halt AIDS spread; Botswana's program makes progress, but old attitudes persist', *Washington Post*, 2 December, p. A01.

IFPMA (2004), *Building Healthier Societies Through Partnership, May 2004 Update* (Geneva: IFPMA), available at *http://www.ifpma.org/site_docs/Health/Health_Initiatives_Brochure_May04.pdf*.

ILO (2002), *Implementing the ILO Code of Practice on HIV/AIDS and the World of Work: An Education and Training Manual* (Geneva: International Labour Office).

ILO (2003), *Workplace Action on HIV/AIDS: Identifying and Sharing Best Practice*, Tripartite Inter-regional Meeting on Best Practices in HIV/AIDS Workplace Policies and Programmes, 15–17 December (Geneva: International Labour Office).

ILO (2004), *HIV/AIDS and Work: Global Estimates, Impact and Response*, ILO Programme on HIV/AIDS and the World of Work (Geneva: International Labour Office), available at *www.ilo.org/aids*.

International HIV Treatment Access Coalition (2002), *A Commitment to Action for Expanded Access to HIV/AIDS Treatment* (Geneva: World Health Organization, December), available at *http://www.who.int/hiv/pub/prev_care/en/ITACdocE.pdf*.

Katzenstein, David, Marie Laga and Jean-Paul Moatti, eds (2003), articles evaluating Drug Access Initiative in Côte d'Ivoire, Senegal and Uganda, in *AIDS*, 17 (supplement 3), pp. S1–S111.

Kuritzkes, Daniel R. (2004), 'Extending antiretroviral therapy to resource-poor settings: implications for drug resistance', *AIDS*, 18 (Supplement 3), pp. S45–S48.

Lange, Joep M. A., Jos Perriens et al. (2004), 'What policymakers should know about drug resistance and adherence in the context of scaling-up treatment of HIV infection', *AIDS*, 18 (Supplement 3), pp. S69–S74.

McNeil, Donald G., Jr. (2000), 'Companies to cut cost of AIDS drugs for poor nations', *New York Times*, 12 May, p. A1.

Médecins Sans Frontières (2002), Campaign for Access to Essential Medicines, 'From Durban to Barcelona: Overcoming the Treatment Deficit' (July), p. 2.

Piot, Peter (2002a), 'Fighting AIDS with a sound investment', *Washington Post*, 27 November 27.

Piot, Peter (2002b), Speech to opening session of the 13th meeting of the Programme Coordinating Board, UNAIDS, 11 December, available at *http://www.unaids.org*.

Piot, Peter (2003), 'AIDS: The Need for an Exceptional Response to an Unprecedented Crisis', Presidential Fellows Lecture (Washington, DC: World Bank).

Potter, Christopher and Richard Brough (2004), 'Systemic capacity building: a hierarchy of needs', *Health Policy and Planning*, 19 (September), pp. 336–45.

Rau, Bill (2002), *Workplace HIV/AIDS Programs: An Action Guide for Managers* (Arlington, VA: Family Health International).

Rosen, Sydney, Jonathon Simon et al. (2003), 'AIDS Is Your Business', *Harvard Business Review*, 81 (February): 80–87.

Sansoni, Silvia (2003), 'Keeping alive', *Forbes Magazine*, 20 January 20; available at *www.forbes.com/forbes/2003/0203/064_print.html*.

Stein, Andrew, Heather McLeod and Zackie Achmat (2002), *The Cover Provided for HIV/AIDS Benefits in Medical Schemes in 2002*, CARE Monograph No. 10 (Cape Town: Centre for Actuarial Research, University of Cape Town), July, available at *www.commerce.net.ac/care/monographs/mono10.pdf*.

Stillwell, Barbara, Khassoum Diallo, Pascal Zurn et al. (2004), 'Migration of health-care workers from developing countries: strategic approaches to its management', *Bulletin of the World Health Organization*, 82 (August): 595–600.

Treatment Action Campaign (2002), 'TAC statement on medical schemes research conducted by TAC and CARE' (Muizenberg, South Africa: TAC), 7 June, available at *www.tac.org.sa*.

UNAIDS (2000a), 'New public/private sector effort initiated to accelerate access to HIV/AIDS care and treatment in developing countries', press release, Geneva, 11 May.

UNAIDS (2000b), *Report of the First Meeting of the Contact Group on Accelerating Access to HIV/AIDS-related Care*, 29 September, available at *http://www.unaids.org/acc_access/contact_group/index.html. 2000*.

UNAIDS (2001), *Contact Group on Accelerating Access to HIV/AIDS-related Care: Report of the Third Meeting*, 29 May 2001, available at *http://www.unaids.org/acc_access/contact_group/index.html. 2001*.

UNAIDS (2002a), *Keeping the Promise: Summary of the Declaration of Commitment on HIV/AIDS*, UNGASS, 25–27 June 2001, New York, UNAIDS/02.31E (Geneva: UNAIDS).

UNAIDS (2002b), *Report on the Global HIV/AIDS Epidemic. July 2002*, UNAIDS/02.26E (Geneva: UNAIDS).

UNAIDS (2003a), *Accelerating Action Against AIDS in Africa*, UNAIDS/03.44E (Geneva: UNAIDS).

UNAIDS (2003b), *Progress Report on the Global Response to the HIV/AIDS Epidemic, 2003*, UNAIDS/03.37E (Geneva: UNAIDS).

UNAIDS (2003c), *Stepping Back from the Edge: The Pursuit of Anti-retroviral Therapy in Botswana, South Africa and Uganda*, UNAIDS Best Practice Collection, UNAIDS/ 03.46E (Geneva: UNAIDS, November).

UNAIDS (2004), 2004 *Report on the Global AIDS Epidemic: 4th Global Report*, UNAIDS/ 04.16E (Geneva: UNAIDS).

UNAIDS/WHO (2000), *AIDS Epidemic Update: December 2000*, UNAIDS/00.44E (Geneva: UNAIDS/WHO).

UNAIDS/WHO (2002), *AIDS Epidemic Update: December 2002*, UNAIDS/02.46E (Geneva, Switzerland: UNAIDS/WHO).

UNGASS (2001), United Nations (General Assembly), Special Session on HIV/AIDS, *Declaration of Commitment on HIV/AIDS* (New York: United Nations).

UNICEF/UNAIDS/WHO/MSF (2004), *Sources and Prices of Selected Medicines and Diagnostics for People Living with HIV/AIDS* (Geneva: World Health Organization, United Nations Children's Fund, Joint United Nations Programme on HIV/AIDS, Médecins Sans Frontières), June.

USAID (2004), *HIV/AIDS and Business in Africa* (Washington, DC: US Agency for International Development).

US Office of the Global AIDS Coordinator (2004), *The President's Emergency Plan for AIDS Relief: U. S. Five-Year Global HIV/AIDS Strategy* (Washington, DC: Office of the Global AIDS Coordinator), February.

Waldholz, Michael (2000), 'Makers of AIDS drugs agree to slash prices in Third World', *Wall Street Journal*, 11 May, p. A1.

Weidle, Paul J., Timothy D. Mastro et al. (2002), 'HIV/AIDS treatment and HIV vaccines in Africa', *The Lancet*, 359 (29 June): 2261–7.

Weiser, Sheri, William Wolfe, David Bangsberg et al. (2003), 'Barriers to antiretroviral adherence for patients living with HIV infection and AIDS in Botswana', *Journal of Acquired Immune Deficiency Syndrome*, 34 (1 November): 281–8.

Whiteside, Alan and Mary O'Grady (2002), 'AIDS and the business sector: Lessons from Southern Africa', in Anne Sisask (ed.), *One Step Further: Responses to HIV/AIDS*, SIDA Studies, No. 7 (Stockholm: Swedish International Development Agency), pp. 116–37, available at h*ttp://www.sida.se/Sida/articles/12400-12499/12451/SIDA1693en_Studies_ No7.pdf.*

WHO (2002), 'Contribution of WHO to the follow up of the United Nations General Assembly special session on HIV/AIDS', Provisional Agenda item 5.2, WHO Executive Board, 111th Session, 20-28 January 2003, Document EB 111/4, 9 December; available at *http://policy.who.int.*

WHO (2004a), *3 By 5 Progress Report, December 2003 through June 2004* (Geneva: World Health Organization), available at *www.who.int/hiv/en.*

WHO (2004b), *Emergency Scale-up of Anti-retroviral Therapy in Resource-Limited Settings: Technical and Operational Recommendations to Achieve 3 by 5* (Geneva: WHO), available at *www.who.int/hiv/en.*

WHO (2004c), *Investing in a Comprehensive Health Sector Response to HIV/AIDS: Scaling Up Treatment and Accelerating Prevention.* WHO HIV/AIDS Plan, January 2004– December 2005 (Geneva: WHO).

WHO (2004d), *A Public Health Approach for Scaling Up Anti-retroviral (ARV) Treatment: A Toolkit for Programme Managers* (Geneva: WHO), available at *www.who.int/hiv/en.*

WHO (2004e), *Scaling Up Anti-retroviral Therapy in Resource-Limited Settings: Treatment Guidelines for a Public Health Approach – 2003 Revision* (Geneva: WHO), available at *www.who.int/3by5/publications/documents/arv_guidelines/en/.*

WHO/UNAIDS (2002), *Accelerating Access Initiative: Widening Access to Care and Support for People Living with HIV/AIDS: Progress Report, June 2002* (Geneva: WHO/UNAIDS), available at *http://www.who.int/hiv/pub/prev_care/en/isbn9241210125.pdf.*

7 NON-PROFIT DRUG DISTRIBUTION: THE EXPERIENCE OF THE INTERNATIONAL DISPENSARY ASSOCIATION

Henk den Besten and Joseph Gonzi

The International Dispensary Association Foundation (IDA) was established as a charitable venture by Dutch pharmacists and students in Amsterdam in 1972. Its main aim was and remains to assist people in developing countries by assuring them access to affordable essential pharmaceuticals and medical supplies. Since that time, IDA has grown into a major international operation; it sells pharmaceuticals and medical supplies with a market value of US$15 million to the public and non-profit sector in over 100 developing countries. At this writing, IDA is the world's largest non-profit distributor of essential medicines.

The core business model of IDA is based on sourcing generic medical products on a large scale and on a competitive basis. In order to ensure the quality of the products, an independent quality assurance and quality control (QA/QC) assessment of each supplier and product is undertaken. For this, IDA has its dedicated staff and laboratory facilities available. Individual orders received from buyers in developing countries are filled from its stock in Amsterdam. The value-added for buyers is that they can purchase products of known quality, in a reliable supply chain, for little more than if they were to perform the sourcing themselves. The basic IDA product line includes a large selection of generic medicines, as found in the WHO Model List of Essential Medicines, basic medical supplies and diagnostic test kits. In addition, IDA assembles field packs of mixed supplies for special medical and disaster relief settings; these facilitate the ordering and logistical process for countries with scarce management capacity. Most recently, IDA has been selected as a distribution partner for a pharmaceutical product manufactured by the research-based pharmaceutical industry, particularly in Africa, where that industry relies on IDA to manage the logistics of distributing its donated or heavily discounted products to populations in need.

HISTORY AND CORE BUSINESS

In the beginning, religious mission health facilities provided the majority of IDA's clientele. In numerous African countries, central ecumenical importing organizations acted as regional suppliers to these end-users. Among these organizations were Chanpharm in Nigeria, Chag in Ghana and Chal in Liberia, Chasl in Sierra Leone. Individual requests from the various health institutions were combined and shipments were consolidated. IDA has also long relied on the government of the Netherlands and other bilateral donors (such as Danida) to support commodity purchases for the health sector.

IDA came of age in the early 1980s, when the choice was made to concentrate only on wholesale activities. This focus enabled it to strengthen key efficiencies, which led to a reduction in overheads. Today, the typical margin that IDA adds on to a product is in the range of 10 per cent of its net value, and this is sufficient in most cases to defray the costs of sourcing, QA/QC and logistics.

IDA's business model was refined again when the WHO introduced the concept of essential medicines (formerly called essential drugs) through the WHO Drug Action Program. IDA strives to adjust its product line as much as possible in response to each periodic revision of the WHO's Model List of Essential Medicines, although the recent addition of some patented medicines to that list (notably, the anti-retrovirals) has required it to revise some of its standard operating procedures (SOPs). There are, for example, considerable logistical complications when a medicine is patented in the Netherlands, because IDA cannot then, in its usual way, source products manufactured elsewhere and tranship them via its quality control laboratories in Amsterdam. A possible solution to this problem could be found in seeking limited voluntary out-licences or waivers for these products to be transhipped via Amsterdam.

One of IDA's principal innovations has been the introduction of pre-packaged kits of essential medicines. These kits were pioneered in the Kenyan market. They are in most cases a single box containing an assortment of items (from 10 to 70) considered sufficient to help a fixed number of patients for a certain period of time. The delivery schedule of the essential medicines kits can be calibrated to the number of patients visiting the health facility; if this is matched reasonably well, the kits ensure a consistent supply of the most-needed products, with tolerable margins of oversupply or undersupply for a few products.

A second sort of kit is tailored to the needs of NGOs responding to disaster situations. These kits[1] were designed by IDA in cooperation with the World Health Organization, the International Committee of the Red Cross and

---

[1] See *www.ida.nl* for details of the New Emergency Health Kit (NEHK).

Médecins Sans Frontières, and they are now used in all major emergencies to make basic health care possible when other health systems are (temporarily) not available. On demand, the kits can be varied, with optional modules for special situations, such as cholera or meningitis outbreaks. Developing the logistics to manage the assembly of kits in Amsterdam, including assuring the just-in-time availability of all the components at IDA's automated packing facilities, has been a major accomplishment.

What characterizes IDA is its preparedness to adapt to a customer base that is exceedingly diverse and non-traditional in the sense that it is under-served by the commercial pharmaceutical industry. The challenges involved are considerable, which is why those markets are under-served in the first place. At one extreme, IDA is a 'large-scale' supplier to the major international customers, such as the World Bank, that employ standard procedures for competitive tendering and procurement of medicines in projects they finance. At the other extreme, IDA is a 'small-scale' supplier to local governments, NGOs and mission organizations, which have few established procedures, and it has sometimes collaborated with these buyers to create mechanisms that enable them to manage project cash flows and, by extension, enhance their ability to purchase. These activities, far outside the wholesaler's ordinary role, may reinforce the priorities set by major development institutions on issues such as cost recovery and charging user fees for health services as part of the 'Bamako Initiative'. But just as often, they entail IDA improvising in ways that the international development agencies have not anticipated. It is an unusual business that not only supplies medicines but also may have to share with its buyers basic aspects of how to manage funds, plan orders and deal with exchange rate variations or limitations on access to hard currency. Today, this is IDA's role.

AN EXPERIMENT IN MANUFACTURING

IDA has not only been a wholesaler, but also has intense experience in manufacturing. During the late 1980s, an insufficiency of top-quality generic suppliers interested in developing countries led IDA to invest in its own production facility; it took a majority stake in Pharmamed Ltd of Malta. Pharmamed's production facilities were upgraded and extended, and a sterile production line was added to produce parenteral medicines, making Pharmamed a small but highly flexible producer for IDA's diverse needs.

This experience in manufacturing gave IDA first-hand insight into the microeconomics of pharmaceutical production. Its manufacturing team learned that the principal driver of an oral generic pharmaceutical's price (up to 80 per cent) was the active pharmaceutical ingredient (API), so it set up branch offices in India and China in order to purchase APIs near their centres of production.

After attempts by other generic manufacturers to marginalize its buyers, IDA succeeded in establishing long-term supply agreements for APIs. Its proximity to suppliers gave IDA the leverage to resume the production of orphan medicines, such as chloramphenicol in oil, which the principal supplier (Roussel Uclaf) stopped making after its merger into Hoechst Marion Roussel (HMR) in 1995.

The vertical integration offered by the Pharmamed facility also permitted IDA to become inventive, to introduce at affordable prices generic formulations hitherto unavailable in the public sector. An example is the rifampicin-containing fixed-dose combination medicines for first-line tuberculosis treatment. These products demonstrated bioequivalence *in vivo* and were used as a reference in a number of clinical studies, including those conducted under WHO supervision.

More recently, the need for specialized production, which justified the acquisition of Pharmamed, has changed. There are more good-quality generic producers in developing or middle-tier countries than before – for example in India, South Korea, Thailand, Brazil, South Africa and Mexico. Their good manufacturing practice (GMP) certified technology is on a par with that of European producers; indeed, they are sometimes the market leaders for a specific product. Their installed production capacity is more than what is required to fulfil local and, in some cases, world requirements. For this reason, IDA recently divested its share in Pharmamed and ceased its own production, in the knowledge that it is more economical to enter into a strategic alliance with producers in the countries above.

IDA's involvement with Pharmamed should be a cautionary story for those who today advocate local production of generic pharmaceuticals in developing countries as a panacea. The financial risk of pharmaceutical manufacturing, unless properly administered, is considerable. In IDA's experience, it is normally possible to source high-quality generic medicines elsewhere, and at a lower cost.

IDA'S QUALITY PROGRAMME

The central purpose of IDA has always been to distribute at no profit but also to distribute safe and effective medicines. There are many vendors who will sell inexpensive generic medicines to developing countries, but there are few who will do so and give the assurance that they are not peddling counterfeit or substandard medicines.

Today, IDA's quality programme rests on three pillars: review of manufacturers, review of products and quality testing of batches (see Table 7.1).

IDA began its quality control efforts in the late 1980s by building a laboratory to perform chemical analysis on batches received at its central warehouse. The laboratory came to perform thermo stability studies, in simulated

Table 7.1: IDA's quality assurance and quality control programme

Review of manufacturer	• Check of manufacturing licence • GMP certificate • GMP audit by IDA pharmacist (WHO norm)
Review of product	• Verification of marketing authorization • Mutual agreement and authorization of a product specification including source/quality of API • Verification of stability data and shelf life • Verification of certificate of pharmaceutical product • Inspecting design of packing, labelling and leaflets • Verification of quality of samples by analysis • Check of additional requirements • Verification of bioequivalence (for certain products such as anti-infectives or those with narrow safety ranges)
Quality control of batches	• Inspection of label, appearance and packing and check of batch number and expiry date • Control of certificates of analysis for conformity to specification • Chemical analysis for conformity to specification (at random or 100 per cent) • If required, verification of product stability (at random)

tropical conditions. However useful these precautions were, they could not guarantee that good medicines were coming in to IDA. At best, they only prevented bad medicines from being shipped out.

Clearly, a more ambitious approach was needed. Over 15 years, IDA has developed a specific programme of quality management. The quality strategy distributes quality issues throughout the production and distribution cycle; it does not merely 'inspect in' quality at the end. An example is found in IDA's choice of partners: before the commercial department can start negotiations with a potential manufacturer, the latter must be cleared by the QA section, which performs an on-site audit of the specific production facility.

IDA uses international standards such as GMP, good distribution practice (GDP) and good laboratory practice (GLP) as the normative basis for its quality programme. These international standards each subsume a number of procedures and responsibilities that are established in standard operating procedures. The SOPs concern both the direct determinants of product quality (for example technical standards) and the ancillary determinants of 'quality' in its broadest meaning (for instance, procedures to handle product complaints or recalls). IDA requires each of its suppliers to deliver proof of GMP compliance. This is issued by the national regulatory authorities of the country where the supplier is based, and it entails a certificate in respect of the specific pharmaceutical product, and certification of the facility in which the product is made. IDA subsequently verifies these assertions in an on-site GMP audit performed by one of its own pharmacists. (Needless to say, IDA itself is GMP-, GDP- and GLP-certified by the Dutch Ministry of Health for its quality-critical processes, and it is also ISO 9001:2000 certified for its operations.)

IDA audits manufacturers' products as well as manufacturers themselves. This is automatic where a specific product both is manufactured in and has received marketing approval in a developed country (for example Canada, the EU, Switzerland, the United Sates). But for products manufactured elsewhere or lacking marketing approval, IDA imposes its own product review requirements. These are based in part on the above-mentioned certificate of GMP compliance for the specific product (misleadingly called the 'WHO Certificate'), but, more importantly, on a GMP audit. Also the product must comply with IDA's own product specification. This details the product's standard physical and chemical properties (purity, dissolution, identity, etc.). It is based on established norms in the British or US pharmacopoeias. A manufacturer's product is approved only if it can meet the IDA's product specification.

Thereafter, IDA's product specification governs each batch of any product that it sells. Each batch is sampled in its Amsterdam warehouse, and of the total number of batches per consignment a certain quantity is analysed in its laboratories for compliance to the relevant IDA product specification. About 4,500 batches are received annually, of which about 3,300 pass through the QC laboratory. A sample from each batch is retained in the archive for the duration of its shelf life.

Finally, if criteria in the product specifications are met, the batch is released for packing, packed and prepared for shipping to customers; this may also be on a monitoring base. Repackaging in strong and moisture-resistant outer packages may be required for the long journey to remote health facilities. Labelling must also meet IDA specifications: it must clearly state pack size, dosage, the generic or international non-proprietary name, storage conditions, batch number, manufacturing date, expiry date and name of the manufacturer. Depending on the product, this may be supplemented by an English-, French- or Spanish-language product leaflet detailing appropriate dosage, side-effects and contra-indications. The manufacturers often supply appropriate leaflets, but where this is not the case IDA staff can and do design them.

IDA's testing and quality assurance programme gives buyers an assurance that the products they buy are of good quality. The quality procedure alone is worth the 10 per cent mark-up that IDA imposes on medicines, particularly for markets where, through lack of adequate NDA capacity, counterfeit and substandard medicines are rife. This should serve as a warning to anyone who believes that price is the only thing that matters, because in IDA's experience, quality cannot and should not be assumed.

IDA's unique QA system and its role as a quality supplier were extensively discussed during its twenty-fifth anniversary in 1997. At that time its pharmacy team envisaged that the IDA technical dossiers that exist for each individual product-supplier combination evaluated to date could be adopted *en bloc* by developing countries, as a sufficient basis for registering a product in them. If this were done, the return on IDA's investment in QA would be greatly increased: one QA procedure would both approve the product and supplier and pave the way for the product to be used legally in-country. Such a system could greatly alleviate the burden on regulators in developing countries and could be an important means of training and technology transfer to those countries (de Goeje, 1999).

LOGISTICS

IDA also has core skills in secure delivery of medicines on a large scale throughout the developing world. Each month it handles about 700 shipments, amounting to about 600–800 tons of products delivered to customers in 800 countries. Moreover, the experience IDA has built up in supplying its own product line is attractive to other companies which may lack the ability to distribute in countries that lie outside their normal markets. An example is the agreement between Pfizer and IDA under which IDA acts as the logistical agent for Pfizer's donation of Diflucan (fluconazole) in Africa. IDA does not reject partnership with the brand-name pharmaceutical industry, but evaluates each transaction in the light of its core mission to deliver good-quality essential medicines to the non-profit and public sectors in developing countries; it is this that determines whether a partnership offers additional value for the final user.

IDA has also been selected as a preferred supplier to some key international agencies and initiatives. An example is the WHO's procurement programme for second-line tuberculosis medicines, commonly known as the 'Green Light Committee'. By agreement with the other partners of this committee, IDA is the pre-qualification and logistical agent for a range of heavily discounted medicines (up to 95 per cent) that are available only to developing countries which implement WHO's treatment guidelines for multi-drug-resistant (MDR) tuberculosis (DOTS plus). The second-line medicines are both generic, sourced through IDA's usual procedures, and brand-name, in this case from Eli Lilly. The public health advantages of this agreement could be enormous: it is hoped that by linking a country's acceptance of the WHO's MDR-TB treatment guidelines to IDA's function as the sole worldwide supplier, misuse of these medicines can be curbed, forestalling resistance to the last line of defence against incurable tuberculosis. IDA then guarantees that the required products are sourced under the best possible conditions. By pooling the demand the industry has more interest in investing in these often not easily available products.

WHAT IS IDA NOW, AND WHAT WILL IT BECOME?

Today, IDA maintains a professional staff of more than 100 persons working in Amsterdam and overseeing a stock valued at over $15 million. It has a catalogue of 800 items, 300 which are core products. In all, IDA serves over 700 customers in more than 80 countries and processes 5,000 orders annually. What started three decades ago as a vision of Dutch pharmacy students is now the world's largest non-profit wholesaler of generic and essential medicines.

Nevertheless, current trends will require IDA to grow and adapt in the coming years. One challenging area is the response to HIV/AIDS in developing countries, where access to anti-retroviral medicines is far too limited, the quality not standardized and the response of the international community too fragmented. Unlike in the case of second-line tuberculosis medicines, there is no mechanism for the anti-retrovirals to link medically sound treatment practices (such as the WHO's treatment guidelines) to a supply of good-quality anti-retrovirals at a discounted price. Others have called this 'anti-retroviral anarchy', and it could have many negative consequences: governments will procure medicines that are too costly or of poor quality; patients' therapy will fail because of substandard or counterfeit medicines; and resistance to anti-retrovirals will accelerate (Harries et al., 2001). IDA has been selected by the Global Fund to Fight AIDS, Tuberculosis and Malaria to supply anti-retrovirals for several projects, but this task is complicated by the fact that generic versions of these medicines cannot be transhipped through Amsterdam to undergo IDA's quality assurance procedures because of Dutch patent law. Accordingly, it must either develop new quality assurance procedures that bypass Amsterdam or seek a special exemption for its work. Both options are being considered.

IDA is also increasingly in demand to share its expertise with policy-makers. The Global Fund, the World Bank and other organizations have sought its help in planning or teaching pharmaceutical procurement. As a result, a new section was established in IDA to concentrate on training and consultancy from 2003, and this may eventually be turned into a new group.

Another challenge is the role of some major employers in providing health care to their employees and their families in developing countries (an example is the Dutch brewery Heineken, which is now furnishing anti-retroviral treatment at its African sites). These are private-sector companies, acting as quasi-public healthcare providers, often in countries where the formal public health sector is very weak. IDA recognizes the emerging needs of these companies and is in negotiations to see whether those needs can be reconciled with its mission, which is non-profit in nature.

These and other challenges ensure a future role for IDA, for many years to come.

REFERENCES

de Goeje, Michel (1999), '25 years of essential drugs: the quality issue: ideals, attainments and failures', *International Journal of Risk and Safety in Medicine*, 12: 59–65.

Harries, A.D. et al. (2001), 'Preventing anti-retroviral anarchy in sub-Saharan Africa', *The Lancet*, 358: 410–14.

Lewis, Rosamund F. Fabienne Dorlencourt and Jacques Pinel (1998), 'Long-acting oily chloramphenicol for meningococcal meningitis', *The Lancet*, 352: 822–3, 5 September.

8 UNDERSTANDING PATENTS AND OUT-LICENSING IN THE PROCUREMENT OF ANTI-RETROVIRAL MEDICINES

Amir Attaran

It is an often-heard indictment of patents in recent years that they make medicines too expensive for developing countries. Unfortunately, less is heard about how to assess whether patents, and not other factors, obstruct patients' access to medicines and, to the extent that they do, about what can be done in practical terms to alleviate this situation. In other words, the indictment of medicine patents has been insufficiently followed up by careful analysis and appropriate attention to solutions. This short chapter aims to stimulate thinking about both these matters, with reference to the problems faced by medicine procurement managers in developing countries, and illustrated by the examples of the anti-retroviral medicines.

THE IMPORTANCE OF KNOWING THE PATENT STATUS

Because there is a great deal of misunderstanding about medicine patents, it is helpful to describe how they work from a legal perspective. This knowledge helps medicine procurement managers in developing countries to analyse whether, in a given case, costs can be lowered by procuring medicines, including generics, under competitive tender.[1]

When faced with the need for an unusually costly brand-name medicine, a procurement manager may assume that it is expensive because the medicine is patented. But such an assumption can easily be wrong. It is not correct that a

---

[1] Managers who are procuring medicines with World Bank financing will probably be required to adhere to its rules for international competitive bidding or for its alternative, limited international bidding. The rules for both state that bidding cannot be limited to brand-name suppliers and must include generics: 'Specifications [for products] shall be based on relevant characteristics and/or performance requirements. References to brand names … shall be avoided. If it is necessary to specify a brand name … of a particular manufacturer … the words "or equivalent" shall be added after such reference. The specification shall permit the acceptance of offers for goods which have similar characteristics and which provide performance [that is] at least substantially equivalent …'. See World Bank (1999).

medicine must be patented just because it is costly, nor is it correct that a medicine patented in one country must be patented in all countries. Thus, there is often more latitude to use generic drugs than managers may be aware of; and in making incorrect assumptions about which medicines are patented, they may be denying their country options to purchase medicines from a less costly source.

The local variation in the patenting of medicines is easy to underestimate. The variation arises because the legal process of applying for and receiving a patent is normally conducted on a national (not international) basis and because in this process different pharmaceutical companies make different choices about where to patent. By way of illustration, Table 8.1 shows the number of anti-retroviral medicines that are patented in each of the named countries.

These data show extensive variation in patenting, which is often not predictable. For example, in South Africa most of the anti-retrovirals (13 of 15) are patented, but in neighbouring Mozambique and Namibia none of them are (Attaran and Gillespie-White, 2001).

The lesson for managers is *never* to assume that a medicine is patented in their country before determining that this really is the case. In making that incorrect assumption they risk believing that generic medicines are not an available option when actually they could be.

Ascertaining a medicine's patent status need not be difficult. In theory, the patent office in each national government should be able to tell the procurement manager which medicines it has patented; but in practice, most developing-country patent offices lack the data systems or knowledge to give a clear answer. If the patent office cannot help, the manager should inquire in writing to the

Table 8.1: Patented anti-retroviral medicines in 10 African countries (2003)

Country	Patented anti-retrovirals (of 15)
Botswana	6
Côte d'Ivoire	3
Gabon	4
Kenya	7
Malawi	6
Mozambique	0
Namibia	0
Nigeria	4
South Africa	13
Tanzania	5

Source: Attaran and Gillespie-White (2001).

head office of the brand-name pharmaceutical manufacturer, to ask whether the medicine is patented in his or her home country and, if so, exactly what sort of patent protection exists.[2] In the author's experience, most manufacturers will cooperate and disclose this information (Bayer is the only company that has refused to do so). Managers should avoid asking the local distributor, who has an immediate commercial interest in preserving sales and may be reluctant to disclose a medicine's patent status.

Interpreting the replies from these inquiries is straightforward. There are three possibilities:

1. If there is a patent specifically on the active pharmaceutical ingredient (sometimes called a 'product patent'), then generics normally cannot be used, *except* if an out-licence of a patent waiver is sought (this is discussed later in the chapter).
2. If there is a patent on an aspect of the medicine other than for the active pharmaceutical ingredient, such as a patented manufacturing process, then generics possibly can be used. Generic suppliers should be asked to provide an opinion as to whether their product infringes the known patents, and they should be required to provide an indemnity if they agree to sell the product in these conditions.
3. If there are no patents of any kind, then generics can definitely be used.

Ascertaining a medicine's patent status thus gives managers knowledge of when they may procure generic medicines. It also gives them knowledge of the existence of patents that lock them into a single brand-name supplier, and in doing so it advances the thought process to the next stage – of considering whether steps to gain relief from the patent through an out-licence or a waiver are desirable. The rest of this chapter discusses these two options.

IS AN OUT-LICENCE OR A PATENT WAIVER DESIRABLE?

Before a manager goes to the trouble of seeking an out-licence or a patent waiver, it is worthwhile for him or her to analyse whether this will actually help to make a medicine more affordable. Again, no assumptions should be made, and a specific inquiry should be carried out.

[2] The request has to be highly specific to be useful, but does not need to be long. Something like this is sufficient: 'I wish to inquire whether [medicine name] manufactured or sold by your company and supplied as [describe the formulation and dosage form] is currently patented or the subject of a pending patent application in [country]. If so, can you please inform me of whether the relevant patent(s) claim the active pharmaceutical ingredient, or other aspects of the medicine, as may be the case. This information is sought to determine whether a generic equivalent for [medicine] could be used in [country] without illegally infringing rights belonging to [company name].'

Table 8.2: Categories of anti-retroviral medicines: best-available prices, 2003

Class	Product (mg)	Brand-name medicine ($)	WHO-prequalified generic ($)	Unqualified generic ($)
NRTI	Zidovudine (300)	212 (GSK)	**140 (Hetero)**	140 (Aurobindo)
	Didanosine (100)	**310 (BMS)**	None	146 (Hetero)
	Stavudine (30)	48 (BMS)	**21 (Hetero)**	35 (Strides)
	Lamivudine (150)	69 (GSK)	**55 (Hetero)**	66 (Aurobindo)
	Abacavir (300)	**887 (GSK)**	None	803 (Hetero)
NtRTI	Tenofovir (300)	**475 (Gilead)**	None	None
NNRTI	Nevirapine (200)	438 (Boehringer)	**80 (Hetero)**	112 (Aurobindo)
	Efavirenz (600)	**347 (Merck)**	None	347 (Hetero)
PI	Saquinavir (200)	**956 (Roche)**	None	1022 (Hetero)
	Ritonavir (100)	**83 (Abbott)**	None	204 (Hetero)
	Indinavir (400)	400 (Merck)	**321 (Hetero)**	365 (Cipla)
	Nelfinavir (250)	**942 (Roche)**	None	1132 (Hetero)
	Lopinavir/ ritonavir (133+33)	**500 (Abbott)**	None	1971 (Hetero)

Source: Médecins Sans Frontières (2004).

Note: The best current prices for top-quality medicines where preferred by the WHO or reputable drug regulatory authorities are in bold.

Although many commentators take the simplistic view that generic medicines are always less expensive than brand-name ones, the current evidence does not support this, and there is no clear rule as to whether the brand-name product or the generic product is the cheaper. Table 8.2 presents the anti-retrovirals currently found in the World Health Organization's AIDS treatment guidelines. Using data furnished by Médecins Sans Frontières, it lists the best-available prices for brand-name products and for WHO-prequalified generics (columns 3 and 4). The medicines in these columns have satisfied either Western or WHO regulatory standards, and usually both, so they are likely to be of comparable quality. These medicines are superior to the unqualified generic medicines (column 5) which have passed neither Western nor WHO quality standards, and as a general rule medicines in this column should not be used (their prices are shown for comparison only).

A close look at these pricing data reveals two surprising facts. First, brand-name medicines often (in 8 out of 13 cases) cost *less* than WHO-prequalified generic medicines of similar quality, if there exists a WHO-prequalified alternative at all. Second, the unqualified generic medicines, whose quality is not verified by any credible authority, often (in 8 of 12 cases) cost *more* than either the brand-name or WHO-prequalified medicines. The unaware manager could therefore easily spend more money on buying an inferior product.

In practical terms, these data indicate that even in the minority of cases where a patent exists, managers should not prematurely conclude that the patent is denying access to a less expensive, good-quality generic medicine. Certainly that can happen – the extensive patents on Boehringer Ingelheim's nevirapine, and the unacceptable price it charges (five times the equivalent generic price), are a case in point – but currently it happens only as the exception and not the rule for HIV/AIDS medicines. Accordingly, it is only when there is *both* a patent *and* a top-quality generic of lower price that it is worth the effort to seek a patent waiver or an out-licence. These are discussed in the following sections.

PATENT WAIVERS

There are limited circumstances in which pharmaceutical manufacturers have been willing to waive enforcement of their patents, particularly for the poorest or most AIDS-affected countries. For example, in 2001 Bristol-Myers Squibb publicly and indefinitely waived all patents on its anti-retroviral medicines throughout Africa (Bristol-Myers Squibb, 2001).

Novartis has confirmed that it does not intend to seek or enforce patents in the 49 least developed countries for AIDS, malaria or tuberculosis medicines (Novartis, 2002). And although GlaxoSmithKline has no stated policy on the matter, as a practical fact it has taken no enforcement action against Nigeria, which acted against its own law to import generic anti-retrovirals that infringe GSK's patents (Donnelly, 2001).

These examples suggest that even when patents exist, managers may be successful in asking to have them waived. This is certainly worth attempting for the least developed or low-income countries, for which international sympathy runs high, but it is unlikely to succeed for the middle-income countries, which are widely expected to respect the ordinary workings of the patent system.

A request for a patent waiver should be made in writing by the manager and addressed to the head office of the company in question.[3] *Making this request is*

---

[3] A request can be modelled roughly along these lines: 'I wish to inquire whether [company] would please agree to waive its patent rights respecting [medicine and dosage form] within the territory of [country], for the purposes of [private/public/non-profit] use under government supervision. In particular, what is proposed is to [import/manufacture] [medicine] in its generic form, for a period of [years], in the amount of [quantity], and originating from [name of generic supplier]. In respect of this proposal, [country] seeks your company's agreement to waive enforcement of the relevant patent rights. We affirm that this remains a proposal only at this time, but as this matter concerns the public health of [country], we kindly request your written reply within [30/60/90] days.'

imperative: a reply agreeing to waive patent enforcement ensures that there will be no future legal liability for patent infringement. By contrast, unilateral action to breach a patent (such as that taken by Nigeria) leaves the prospect of being sued, which is expensive and damaging regardless of the outcome.

Finally, it is worth noting that a patent waiver can actually be financially advantageous to the patent holder. Under American tax law, it is possible to place a fair market value on a patent for donation, and this can be an allowable tax deduction as a charitable contribution.[4] Companies may therefore prefer to donate patents rather than 'waive' them informally; however, from the procurement manager's point of view these amount to the same thing.

OUT-LICENSING

Organizational aspects

For some countries which face a large number of patented medicines (e.g. South Africa), an attractive option may be to seek special permission from the brand-name company to circumvent the patent and to use generics, in exchange for a small royalty payment. In legal jargon, this permission is delivered in the form of an 'out-licence' that the brand-name company (as licensor) and the importer or manufacturing company (as licensee) negotiate and agree, much as they would any other sort of contract.

In practice, nearly all out-licences to date have been 'exclusive', meaning that they are restricted to a single manufacturer. In South Africa, both Glaxo-SmithKline and Boehringer Ingelheim have issued out-licences for their anti-retrovirals to a local manufacturer, Aspen Pharmacare (Mayor, 2001; Chegi, 2002). Aspen is in turn empowered under these licences to supply the non-profit and public sectors, at a lower price than the brand-name manufacturer. In the case of the Boehringer Ingelheim licence, and more recently for GSK, Aspen is legally authorized to sell the medicine throughout southern Africa; it is a regional, not merely a national, licence.

It would be possible for other countries to copy these examples, assuming that their public or private sectors possess the capacity to manufacture pharmaceuticals. At this writing, Nigeria and Kenya are the most likely in Africa to have that capacity. However, before they or others pursue local manufacturing as a matter of policy, the following questions must be asked:

- *Would local manufacturing really save money?* Just as generic anti-retrovirals are not always cheaper than brand-name ones, so locally produced generics are not always cheaper than generics sold on the international market. Brazil and Thailand both have a policy of manufacturing their own anti-retrovirals,

[4] Internal Revenue Service, Revenue Ruling 58–260 (1958).

but doing this costs them more than it would to import generics from India. An adult treatment course of Brazilian nevirapine, for example, recently cost $241 annually ex factory, which is 200 per cent more than the comparable product made by Hetero in India (Manguinhos, 2003; Médecins Sans Frontières, 2004). That tremendous price differential for a locally manufactured product might be defensible as industrial policy, but it is certainly indefensible as public health policy.

- *Will the local manufacturer's quality be acceptable?* Local manufacturers may experience difficulty in meeting international safety and quality standards; and if they do not meet them, aid donors (such as the World Bank) are not going to buy their products. For example, Thailand's government-owned anti-retroviral factory sought and failed to obtain WHO pre-certification for its products in 2003. The requirement to meet those standards means that new investment will be necessary, which will drive costs higher.

In the light of these questions, there are probably few countries where the appropriate conditions exist to make cost-efficient use of local manufacturing. The fact that these medicines often cost more than imported ones, as is the case in Brazil, suggests that the primary justification for local manufacturing lies in industrial policy, and not so much in health policy.

What this suggests is that out-licensing probably would work best if freed from the requirement of local manufacturing, although the two are sometimes linked, as in the two South African examples already discussed. Because the effort and expense of seeking an out-licence and meeting quality standards are fixed regardless of the supply territory, governments which want to use out-licensing are better off acting in regional groups and spreading the costs over a larger market. It would therefore be practical for regional groups in areas severely affected by HIV/AIDS, for example the Southern African Development Community (SADC) and the Economic Community of West African States (ECOWAS), to identify their members' pharmaceutical manufacturing capacity, to agree on regional licensing objectives and to negotiate as a bloc with patent holders for out-licences to supply their members. Aggregating the end-users in this way makes out-licensing more feasible both economically and practically.

However, there is no need to stop at the regional level. The optimal approach would take aggregation to its maximum and seek out-licences for the poorest and sickest countries globally. This would make the best competitive use of manufacturing capacity worldwide, by licensing multiple generic manufacturers and triggering cost-cutting among them.

A proposal on these lines was described recently by this author writing with colleagues from Pharmacia (a pharmaceutical company) and the International Dispensary Association Foundation (a non-profit charity that wholesales generic medicines) (Friedman, den Besten and Attaran, 2003). Very roughly, we envision a process whereby the patent holder issues a single master licence for a medicine to a non-profit foundation, which is then custodian of the intellectual property. That non-profit foundation in turn issues non-exclusive sub-licences to all interested generic manufacturers who demonstrate that they can meet international quality standards. Competition then ensues among these manfacturers to bring medicine prices down throughout the marketing territory, which is defined in economic and epidemiological rather than geographic terms – for example, all countries that are below a certain income level or above a certain level of HIV/AIDS infection. Legal limitations in the licence agreements ensure that none of the generic products made under licence 'leak' outside these poor or very sick markets, so the pharmaceutical company can maintain its normal profits in the rich countries while at the same time making humanitarian access possible.

Thus, with limited effort and expenditure to obtain a single master licence, a medicine can be manufactured by several top-quality generic manufacturers and priced competitively throughout the developing world. Having multiple sub-licensees and countries in turn makes the ratio of investment to return much more favourable than it would be for one-off out-licensing transactions limited to single countries or manufacturers. Further details of this approach are presented in the original proposal published in *The Lancet* in 2003 (Friedman, den Besten and Attaran, 2003).

It is therefore suggested that international organizations – principally the World Bank or the Global Fund for HIV/AIDS, Tuberculosis and Malaria – convene negotiations for multi-country, non-exclusive out-licences whose purpose would be to supply those countries for which these aid donors finance anti-retrovirals. This proposal brings the demand side (aid funding) and the supply side (manufacturing) of the anti-retroviral market into closer alignment, and fully negates any suggestion that patents stand in the way of accessing treatment. Importantly, it does this without destroying the intellectual property of pharmaceutical companies, which will be bitterly opposed to the loss of their rights; in fact it *reaffirms* the meaning of those rights in the out-licensing transaction itself. This helps to explain why the proposal to use out-licensing on a global scale was supported by one pharmaceutical company (Pharmacia), and it suggests that other companies can be persuaded to emulate it. Not doing so is certain to mean that tension over patents will remain and continue to be a source of criticism of the companies. This is the only scheme that can do away with it.

Transactional aspects

Quite apart from how out-licensing is to be organized, and the question of whether to use local, regional or global manufacturing or to use a single exclusive licensee or multiple non-exclusive licencees, legal and financial issues arise that are common to all out-licensing transactions.

The principal issue is always that of royalties and how much the intellectual property holder should be paid. Out-licences are no different from any other purchasable item, in that different varieties come at different prices, and so the answer depends on public policy, industry practice and microeconomic models.

The expectation that pharmaceutical companies will not profit from AIDS, tuberculosis or malaria medicines in the poorest countries is now an uncontroversial and accepted part of public policy. As such, the appropriate royalty rate for these diseases and countries will be low – perhaps in the range of 5 per cent of net sales, payable to the licensor (and even then the licensor may agree to donate the royalty back to charity) (Mayor, 2001). This is a significant departure from normal industry practice because it is rare to out-license a finished, ready-to-sell medicine. When it does happen, and in the context of rich rather than poor countries, royalty rates of 45 per cent are not unknown (Waters, 1999).

Where, then, should the royalty rate for an individual out-licence for antiretrovirals be established in this broad range between 5 and 45 per cent? Pragmatism and common sense are the best guides. In the low-income countries (e.g. most of Africa), public policy is obviously the most important valuation principle, and royalty rates should be minimal. But for middle-income countries such as Brazil and Mexico with a much greater ability to pay, public policy is not instructive and industry practice is almost non-existent. In their case, valuation is perhaps best based on microeconomic modelling such as a discounted cash-flow analysis (Rozek and Salisbury, 1991). A small industry of analysts and consultants exists to apply this and other valuation methods to intellectual property; guidance is available.

Another consideration is technology transfer. An enormous advantage of out-licensing over coercive patent expropriation (called 'compulsory licensing') is that out-licences are consensual, negotiated transactions, which allow other assets to change hands at the same time as the intellectual property. This can give the out-licensee vast advantages that are unobtainable under compulsory licensing: access to proprietary manufacturing technologies, validated quality-assurance methods, clinical efficacy and safety data, and the product 'dossier' that is needed to register the generic product with national drug regulatory authorities. Having access to these intangibles can save years of effort and expense in getting a generic product to market. For these reasons, technology transfer should always be discussed in the negotiations for any out-licence.

Finally, each out-licence needs to anticipate the possibility that generic medicines manufactured by licensees for the poorest countries will be diverted illicitly to pharmacies in rich countries. Although the chance of this happening on a commercially large scale is extremely remote (it hardly occurs with the thousands of generic copies of expensive patented medicines that exist today), each out-licence needs to provide for the contingency of its revocation or the imposition of lesser penalties, as appropriate. Licence agreements should also specify that medicines manufactured under licence will have a unique appearance that distinguishes them from the brand-name product (a different colour and shape, different packaging and so on), as this prevents the generic product from blending unnoticed into the supply chain.

CONCLUSION

The concern that patents impede access to medicines is fully answerable through a mixture of careful investigation of patent status and prices and judicious steps to introduce remedies such as patent waivers and out-licensing where constraints demonstrably exist. Medicine procurement managers in developing countries can probably manage the first of these tasks but, realistically speaking, they cannot manage the second. Progress in out-licensing therefore awaits overdue action at the regional and global levels, and doing this requires a consensus within international organizations, which so far have missed valuable opportunities in this regard. It is strongly recommended to the World Bank and the Global Fund for AIDS, Tuberculosis and Malaria that they assume a leadership role in bringing about further innovation in supplying inexpensive medicines.

REFERENCES

Attaran, A. and L. Gillespie-White (2001), 'Do patents for anti-retroviral drugs constrain access to AIDS treatment in Africa?', *Journal of the American Medical Association*, 86: 1886–92.

Bristol-Myers Squibb (2001), 'Bristol-Myers Squibb announces *Accelerated Program To Fight HIV/AIDS In Africa*', 14 March. Available at *http://www.securethefuture.com/program/data/031401.html* (accessed 29 June 2003).

Chegi, W. (2002), 'Boehringer allows S. African firm to make AIDS drug' (Reuters: NewMedia, 15 October 2002).

Donnelly, J. (2001), 'Nigeria reaches deal with Indian firm to buy AIDS drugs', *Boston Globe*, 26 April, p. A22.

Friedman, M., H. den Besten and A. Attaran (2003), 'Out-licensing: a practical approach to improving access to medicines in poor countries', *The Lancet*, 361: 341–4.

Manguinhos, Far (2003), Demandas e preços para o programa DST/AIDS do Ministério da Saúde 2003 (undated Excel spreadsheet provided to the author, June).

Mayor, S. (2001), 'GlaxoSmithKline licences production of generic AIDS drugs in South Africa', *British Medical Journal*, 323: 828.

Médecins Sans Frontières (2004), *Untangling the Web of Price Reductions: A Pricing Guide for the Purchase of ARVs for Developing Countries*, 19 April, 6th edn, available at *http://www.accessmed-msf.org/documents/untanglingtheweb6.pdf*.

Novartis (2002), *Annual Report 2002*.

Rozek, R. and C. Salisbury (1991), 'Using discounted cash flow analysis to determine reasonable royalty rates', *Licensing Economics Review*, 7–10.

Waters, David (1999), 'The position of the IFPMA on compulsory licensing', paper presented at conference on 'Views and Perspectives on Compulsory Licensing', Geneva, 26 March 1999, drawing on data from SKB's cimeditine litigation in the UK: [1990] RPC 203, [1990] 1 CMLR 1416.

World Bank (1999), *Guidelines: Procurement under IBRD Loans and IDA Credits* (1995 edition, revised January) (Washington, DC: World Bank).

PART IV
CONCLUSION

9 WHO NEEDS TO DO WHAT?

Amir Attaran and Brigitte Granville

INTRODUCTION

In this volume and a previous one (Granville, ed., 2002) we have reviewed the question of delivering essential medicines to poor countries and the various schemes thought to facilitate their delivery. Although the predicament can be put simply – rich people have access to 'rich-disease' medicines, but poor people lack access to 'poor-disease' medicines – more solutions than can possibly be wise or correct are circulating in the debate about policy.

This volume has shown that producing good health and accessing essential medicines necessarily involve a large array of players and actions. It has also implied different senses of perception, timing and need among the players depending on variables such as national wealth, industrial policy and the endemicity of disease. We attempt in this final chapter to transcend their various positions, aims and interests and furnish a unifying framework delineating the contributions that are needed from all parties in order to deliver public health through essential medicines.

THE PATENT QUESTION

Intellectual property rights have historically been divisive.[1] And in the case of access to essential medicines, the subject has become so contentious that it has taken on a life of its own and is discussed apart from the variables within the public sector that affect access to medicines. This happens perhaps because the transnational institutions in charge of intellectual property, the World Intellectual Property Organization (WIPO) and the World Trade Organization (WTO), are perceived as somewhat outside the control of sovereign governments. Also the WTO possesses judicial powers that can order governments to comply with

---

[1] See, for instance, Machlup and Penrose (1950) on the nineteenth-century debate on patents.

treaty law, specifically the Agreement on Trade-Related Aspects of Intellectual Property Rights (TRIPS).[2] Patents thus seem far less negotiable than they once were.

Leaving aside the thorny question of whether the intellectual property system is uniformly desirable, we can make some empirical statements about patents and medicines.[3] Patents are rarely the primary barrier to accessing medicines in low-income countries, and are only infrequently the barrier in lower- and upper-middle-income countries.[4] This is not to say that patents *never* affect access to medicines in developing countries but that this happens with a low frequency, which is overshadowed by other causes.[5] Thus although it would be wrong to think of patents as a 'non-issue', it would also be wrong to imagine that by prioritizing them, the most urgent needs of the poor and ill are being met.

This is abundantly clear from the data. Fully 306, or 94 per cent, of the 325 products on the WHO's 2002 Model List of Essential Medicines are not patent-protected anywhere in the world, and because of their vintage they cannot become patent-protected in the future (Grabowski, 2002, p. 856). In 62 developing countries around the world, fewer than 2 per cent of the same essential medicines are patented (Attaran, 2003a). The most highly patented category of medicine is currently the anti-retroviral HIV/AIDS medicines – HIV/AIDS is a new pathogen, so all the anti-retrovirals (ARVs) are new and therefore still patentable – but even among 53 African countries, they are patented under 22 per cent of the time. This is a significant figure, but not to the extent that it precludes the supply of generics for the medically most highly recommended treatment regimens (Attaran and Gillespie-White, 2001, p. 1891).

Higher rates of prevalence of patents are found in larger markets. In South Africa, for example, which accounts for 17 per cent of Africa's HIV/AIDS cases,

---

[2] Scotchmer (2003, pp. 5–6): 'The earliest large-scale intellectual property treaties were the Paris Convention of 1883 on patents and other industrial property, and the Berne convention of 1886 for literary and artistic works. ... Both established the idea of national treatment. ... A shortcoming of the Paris and Berne Conventions is that they made no provisions for enforcement. ... Better enforcement provisions were introduced in the Agreement on Trade-Related Aspects of Intellectual Property (TRIPS), as administered by the World Trade Organization.'

[3] The literature on the value of the intellectual property system is large. See, for instance, Penrose (1951), Machlup (1958), Kremer (1996), Thurow (1997), Heller and Eisenberg (1998), Stiglitz (1999), Sachs (2003).

[4] Developing countries are those classified by the World Bank as low-income, lower-middle-income and upper-middle-income. Source: *http://www.worldbank.org/data/countryclass/classgroups.htm*.

[5] These other causes include limited volume and competition, import duties and tariffs, local taxes and mark-ups for wholesaling, distribution and dispensing. See the Commission on Intellectual Property Rights (2002, pp. 38–9).

13 of the 15 ARV drugs are patented. Similarly, in Botswana, Gambia, Ghana, Kenya, Malawi, Sudan, Swaziland, Uganda, Zambia and Zimbabwe, which together account for 31 per cent of HIV/HIV/AIDS cases in sub-Saharan Africa, six to eight of those drugs are patented (Commission on Intellectual Property Right, 2002, p. 35). The more wealthy and populous a country, the more likely it has affluent consumers, who constitute a lucrative pharmaceutical market and thereby create an incentive to patent. But the rule – that essential medicines are seldom patented in developing countries – is the observable and true basis for creating policy, subject to a few (but important) exceptions (International Intellectual Property Institute, 2000).

This realization immediately frames what one should *not* do where developing countries are concerned, which is to become either too evangelical about defending patent rights on behalf of commercial interests or too optimistic about cancelling those rights on behalf of public health. Sweeping policies do not make sense for insular problems; and in developing countries, the existence of pharmaceutical patents is insular. There is too weak a factual nexus between patents and either pharmaceutical revenues or public health to make these sweeping policies wise.

Contemporary history is littered with instances in which rich and poor governments have misjudged their policy response and have been made to look foolish. The United States, for example, went to the WTO to challenge Brazil's right to license medicines compulsorily at a time when the Brazilians were threatening to do so in order to force down the price of imported HIV/AIDS medicines. But after extensive US posturing and blustering, the case had to be dropped once America was made to understand how legally meritless its case was (the prospect of Brazilian retaliatory litigation, leading to a trade war, also helped).[6] Similarly, Nigeria flamboyantly pledged before African heads of state that it would treat HIV/AIDS using the cheapest Indian generic anti-retrovirals that it could purchase – patent rights be damned. But then it so badly mismanaged the treatment programme's implementation that the medicines passed their expiry date before they were used and the money ran out for continuing the treatment of patients who needed the medicines daily (Donnelly, 2003).

---

[6] See Bermudez (2002, p. 189) for a full account of the dispute. As emphasized by the Commission on Intellectual Property Rights (2002, p. 43), Brazil was in a unique position (not open to every developing country): 'Far-Manguihos ... is the main government drug producer, developing the technology that provides the country with low-cost anti-retroviral drugs. ... Because Far-Manguihos has the technical capacity to reverse engineer patented drugs, and can estimate realistic production costs, the Health Ministry is in a strong bargaining position for negotiating price reductions with foreign producers, backed up by the credible threat of compulsory licensing. In 2001, the Health Minister used this approach with Roche and Merck for their drugs Nelfinavir and Efavirenz, eventually negotiating price reductions of 40 to 70 per cent.'

The government of Zimbabwe, which also announced that it would break patents in order to provide HIV/AIDS medicines, and which was enthusiastically supported by Médecins Sans Frontières for this, never bought the medicines and never treated the patients (Attaran, 2003b, p. 750, note 14).

These three cases illustrate that the fixation of governments and civil society on patents can be *counterproductive* for focusing limited human resources on patients, as it diverted attention from other public health variables that would have reaped bigger clinical benefits for patients. We repeat: absolutist stances, whether for or against pharmaceutical patents, are profoundly illogical and of proven detriment to public health. They should be condemned swiftly when articulated.

There is a corollary to this. If absolutism about pharmaceutical patents is illogical and bad, then encouraging pharmaceutical companies to voluntarily introduce flexibility into the patent system, which accords with the demands of civil society, is logical and good. Rather than merely objecting when countries resort to compulsory licensing or, worse, pretending that it is not an established legal right, companies would do better to be proactive in sharing their technology for legitimate reasons of international health and development. This could render compulsory licensing otiose. One proposal, supported by both the pharmaceutical industry and the non-profit sector, is to carefully structure voluntary licences: rights would be granted on a territorially restricted basis to developing countries, at a low rate of royalty (see Friedman, den Besten and Attaran, 2003). Done properly, this sort of voluntary licensing could fully reconcile philanthropy for the poor with the profitability of core markets.

This sort of voluntary licensing will succeed in de-escalating tensions over the patent system only if companies have the foresight to engage in it proactively and do not wait until they must act under duress. A recent episode, in which Boehringer Ingelheim and GlaxoSmithKline issued voluntary licences for the import or manufacture of their anti-retrovirals in sub-Saharan Africa, might have been a humanitarian and business triumph were it not for the fact that these companies 'volunteered' the licences only after HIV/AIDS activists sued them successfully before South Africa's Competition Commission for pricing their products abusively (Competition Commission, 2003). By adopting this incrementalist, defensive conduct, the pharmaceutical industry sends the self-destructive (and therefore unwise) signal that if people want access to generic medicines, they should adopt as combative and litigious a stance towards the industry as possible, because only then will it give ground. A more foolish piece of managerial judgment would be hard to find, and shareholders ought to take notice.

Finally, there is something that governments can do to alleviate future tensions over patents, and that is to cease the troublesome insistence on a 'one-size-fits-all' approach to development. It remains a fiction of touching naivety that Switzerland and Swaziland are, for the purposes of TRIPS, treated as equals when it comes to administering the law of patents and running an expert-staffed patent office. Critics of the patent system point out the depth of this fiction by noting that today's rich countries became wealthy in part through relaxing intellectual property protection and enabling copying. Similarly, they point out that current standards of intellectual property protection result in a net outflow of wealth from low-income countries to rights-holders elsewhere.

In this, the critics are right. It is an inconvenient fact of economic history for the advocates of patents, but one that cannot truthfully be denied, that economically ascendant countries have been well served by maintaining different rules about patents. For instance, even Switzerland, with a historically strong pharmaceutical industry, only introduced product patents on medicines in the 1950s (Cullet, 2003, p. 141).[7] Between 1960 and 1980 Taiwan and South Korea relied on imitation to develop their innovative capacity, and only revised their patent laws in the mid-1980s under heavy American pressure (Commission on Intellectual Property Rights, 2002, p. 20).

Rather than ignore these historical lessons and weaken their own credibility, proponents of the patent system should find the legal means to 'officialize' it within the system, perhaps through amendments to TRIPS that accelerate technology transfer to developing countries and that accelerate countries' convergence to a less differentiated patent system in the future. To be helpful, the rules on technology transfer would have to affect most or all fields of technology, not just pharmaceuticals, which have brought the issue to light. To be sure, rules alone will not suffice, as much of technology transfer is determined by extra-legal factors (e.g. access to quality education), but greater attention to technology transfer by scholars of economics, development and law is needed in order to set the rules that could help most (see Granville and Leonard, 2003).

Clearly, the global trade system is far from mature where the rules of patents and technology transfer are concerned. Does this mean that a meltdown is coming? Probably not. The poorest countries will go along with the 'one-size-fits-all' patent system as long as they can gain other advantages in trade negotiations. They know they can always subscribe to the obligation of pharmaceutical patenting, and combat it later in the court of public opinion with the language of human rights – just as Brazil did when it humbled the United States with the argument that generic anti-retrovirals were the key to saving HIV/AIDS patients' lives. As long as that is the case, whatever assurances there are for pharmaceutical patenting in bilateral and multilateral trade negotiations are nearly meaningless,

---

[7] For the history of the introduction of patents in Switzerland, see Penrose (1951, pp. 120–4), quoted in Commission on Intellectual Property Rights (2002, p. 19).

and efforts to enforce those rules will prove to be a political and ethical impossibility (Cullet, 2003, p. 160). Countries such as the United States must take that reality to heart rather than waste too much political capital in pursuit of a goal that they probably cannot attain.

EVALUATING WHAT TO PAY FOR

Public health policy must be devised in terms of wealth, health and other social inputs simultaneously, for each case and as a rule rather than an exception. This recommendation, if followed, would fill probably the single greatest lacuna in global public health policy.

Wealth, income, health and social welfare are intimately connected. Improvements in health increase productivity, especially in low-income countries, where labour is the key factor of production; ultimately, they cause income to grow.[8] And although most health economics literature denies any causal effect from income to health, income determines the quantity and quality of health interventions that can be bought.[9] The tragic scenario eloquently described by Alex Preker (in Chapter 2 of this volume), where both health and wealth are locked in a downward 'development trap', also has a corollary in the upward sense: financial investment in health augments wealth, which then augments health, and so on in a compounding and exponentially growing virtuous circle.

What does this mean for access to medicines? Principally, it signifies that with medicines as with other health interventions, traditional cost-effectiveness analysis is an insufficient decision-making tool. Measures of cost-effectiveness, such as the disability-adjusted life-year (DALY) or years of life saved (YLS), are useful to decide *which* health intervention is optimal for a given health budget – it is the one that avoids the most sickness and death per dollar – but it can never decide *whether* a particular health intervention is worthwhile. This is because even a relatively expensive intervention can boost health and cause productivity and income to rise. In other words, cost-effectiveness analysis can tell us about comparative merit but not about absolute merit.

Health policy often takes wrong decisions because this distinction is not understood. For example, there is a raging debate about whether, among the malaria medicines, clinically effective artemisinin-based combination therapies (ACT) at $1–2 per treatment are cost-effective compared to clinically

---

[8] According to Fogel (1997), the improvements in health can explain as much as one-third of the total rise in labour productivity over the past two centuries.

[9] Deaton (2002a, p. 3): 'Much of the health-economics literature does not accept the existence of any causal effect running from income to health, except possibly through the purchase of healthcare, arguing that the correlation between them is driven in part by a causality running from health to income, and in part by third factors, such as education, or rates of time preference'.

ineffective (sometimes 80 per cent ineffective) chloroquine therapy at $0.13 (see Bloland et al., 2000). The question is usually answered by comparing the probability-weighted costs of different cures (i.e. the cost of the treatment, including medicine, multiplied by the probability that the treatment will achieve a cure), but this approach neglects the fact that perhaps half of a country's aggregated death and disability may be caused by malaria. Indeed, the whole question of cost-effectiveness is wrong *ab initio*, because the cost of treatment is such a small fraction of the overall costs of malaria – to the individual in out-of-pocket expenses and long-term disability, to the worker in lost wages, to the enterprise in lost output and to the state in lost income. Were one to consider these broader costs, then financing ACT almost certainly is worthwhile. The alternative, as public health advocates such as Médecins Sans Frontières rightly warn, is to treat quite inadequately the main disease in many countries, with the result that the public loses all confidence in the health system.

Indeed, not to look at the problem in this broad way but to stick with the comparative logic of cost-effectiveness can lead to an absurd conclusion: *no malaria treatment at all* should be given, not even cheap chloroquine, because about 499 of 500 malaria cases are spontaneously 'treated' by the immune system and would not result in loss of life anyway. So why spend money on medicine when the immune system costs nothing and saves life 99.8 per cent of the time? Of course, incorporating disability into this analysis by using DALYs instead of YLS could shift the conclusion in the direction of greater sanity, but still by not very much because DALYs only measure 'disability' in the narrow sense of incapacity. They do not account for reductions of lifelong productivity or any of the macroeconomic factors.

In fact, trying to fix cost-effectiveness analysis by incorporating DALYs just makes the whole edifice much shakier. DALYs assume that the value of a human life grows and shrinks at different ages: a year of life at age 70 counts for roughly half a year at age 25 and for two years at age two (Anand and Hanson, 1997, p. 691). DALYs also assume that life is worth more now than later: saving one life today is 'better' than saving five lives 55 years from now, even if the cost is just the same. The arbitrary and ethically questionable value judgment that makes a 25-year-old the pinnacle of humanity or that makes our descendants 55 years from now count for only 20 per cent of ourselves is almost never remembered when people use DALYs and cost-effectiveness analysis to define which medicines poor people ought to have (see Arnesan and Nord, 1999).

Given the shortcomings of human capital valuation and cost-effectiveness analysis, one may wonder what motivates donor organizations (i.e. DFID, the WHO, the World Bank and USAID) to rely persistently on these methods to allocate resources (see World Bank, 1993 and World Health Organization, 2000). A cynic might say that, actually, the aid donors understand the limitations of cost-effectiveness very well and choose to ignore them because labelling something 'not cost-effective' is a solid façade behind which to refuse to spend money on medicines for poor people. Perhaps the cynics are right. Certainly, the same interventions which aid donors shake their heads at and confine to small-scale 'pilot projects' because they are not yet proved to be cost-effective in poor countries – anti-retroviral therapy for HIV/AIDS is an example – were made available to nearly all patients in the rich countries for several years before cost-effectiveness studies there validated that action. In contrast, even with at least eight cost-effectiveness studies for anti-retroviral therapy reported in developing countries, HIV/AIDS treatment unjustly remains off the agenda of policy discussion (Freedberg and Yazdanpanah, 2003). As a result, cost-effectiveness seems to have become 'yet another tool for misallocating resources' (Jayasinghe, Mendis et al., 2002, p. 62) or a casuistic, quasi-intellectual tool to deny the poor access to medicines which, we believe, they very clearly should have.

Our recommendation is that in every instance where the cost-effectiveness question is posed about an intervention, this question should be asked too: *what is the long-run health and macroeconomic benefit of the proposed intervention?* We concede this is not an easy question to answer; and although some attempts have used multivariate regression to model the aggregate income loss caused by tropical disease, better and more widely accepted techniques are needed. It remains a tremendous intellectual challenge, and one that is very much under-researched, to acknowledge the limitations of cost-effectiveness analysis and then to devise a paradigm shift in which the broader costs of poor health are studied, monetized and therefore made economically cognizable.

Not only will this furnish a powerful new justification for spending more on medicines for poor people but it will also make clearer how a well-rounded view of development is logical and how investment in multiple social sectors is synergistic. For example, one of the best 'medicines' is actually an extra year of education. The evidence in rich countries shows that this can reduce mortality rates by about eight per cent (at all ages), through both increasing earnings and fostering health directly (Elo and Preston, 1996, quoted in Deaton, 2002a, p. 29 and Deaton, 2002b, p. 21). Rather than force trade-offs between different interventions, as cost-effectiveness invariably does, better analytical tools are needed to accumulate lessons so that *all* interventions which boost aggregate well-being, productivity and wealth are recognized as synergistic and encouraged.

PAYING FOR MEDICINES

Making medicines accessible to the poor means that someone with money has to buy them. On this front, there is not much positive to report. As recently as 2002, the Director General of the WHO commented that 'One third of the people in developing countries still have no access whatsoever to essential medicines' (Brundtland, 2002, p. 3102). This means that about two billion people have no essential medicines at all or perhaps access to a few medicines that the WHO has overlooked. This number includes nearly all the inhabitants of Africa, many of the Asia-Pacific and some of Latin America.

So what is the problem? Certainly it is not often the fault of patents, which seldom exist in the very poorest countries, where access to essential medicines is least, and it cannot all be the fault of health economists, for whom cost-effectiveness studies are legitimate even if others frequently misuse or misunderstand them. Finger-pointing at either of these simply diverts attention from the larger problem – the neglect of financing health generally and medicines specifically. In many countries, annual expenditure on pharmaceuticals may be $2 per person or less (World Bank, 1994).

But the question is, who should pay? There are two views about this. One is that poor and sick countries must spend more of their own money on development and that they do not deserve foreign aid from the rich countries, which amounts (in the memorable words of several American politicians) to throwing money into 'a foreign rat hole'. The other is that even the best-run poor countries lack sufficient wealth to develop, and so, for reason of their poverty alone, large increases in foreign aid (a doubling or more) are deserved.

Neither of these views is so correct as to be useful. In truth, even the best-run low-income country is very fiscally constrained. A quick back-of-the-envelope calculation helps to explain why the 2.4 billion people living in low-income countries cannot meet their health needs from domestic resources. An average sub-Saharan country starts out with about $350 in wealth per capita. If the government does the unheard of and captures 30 per cent of that wealth as tax (a taxation rate higher than that of the United States, and very much higher than most developing countries), this yields state revenue of $105 per capita. Assuming the health ministry then receives 12 per cent of that revenue (the same as the Netherlands, with its famous welfare state) and does not lose one penny down the 'rat hole' of corruption, this yields *under $13 per capita for health*. It is an impossibly small sum for the health-care needs that arise at all ages – and not least when, as in Africa, some countries have 30 per cent or more of adults infected with HIV/AIDS. By comparison, the United States spends over $4,000 per capita on health.[10] Foreign aid, therefore, is an undeniable necessity.

However, it is also true that aid donors lamentably throw money down rat holes too, both by purchasing the wrong medicines (as in the above-mentioned chloroquine example) and by being indiscriminate in choosing the countries which receive the money. To say that foreign aid donors often invest their

[10] For statistics, see *OECD in Figures* (2003).

money without giving adequate thought to whether it will achieve a 'return on investment' is putting it very politely. In this, the aid system is fundamentally flawed. Even for the most urgent health priorities, the allocation of money is more haphazard than strategic, with the result that no sum of money is given a chance to succeed. An example is the European Commission: in 2002, it budgeted a total of €31 million for HIV/AIDS in Africa, split among 19 countries and 39 sites. This was a commitment of less than €2 million per project or €1 million per site – sums that are so insignificant in relation to the size of the HIV/AIDS pandemic that they will surely be ineffective and therefore be wasted.[11]

We therefore propose reorienting aid-giving around a more rational model in which the fundamental tactic is analogous to a venture capitalist's: do not be indiscriminate; bet on the winning countries. In this model, low-income countries get foreign aid money, which they indisputably need, but it is wisely allocated among their number on a competitive basis with respect to a country's poverty, the quality of its democratic governance and lack of corruption, and the extent to which it will leverage the foreign aid against its own budgetary allocations. Such countries are where the odds of achieving a health return on foreign aid investment are highest. We explain here.

Some well-governed low-income countries are more sincere than others in addressing their health needs. A good indication of sincerity is how much of their government budget, independent of aid, is allocated for and actually spent on public health. For example, in 2001 nearly all African countries pledged adherence to the *Abuja Declaration on HIV/AIDS, Tuberculosis and Other Related Infectious Diseases*, which promises that each country will 'set a target of allocating at least 15 per cent of its annual [public sector] budget to the improvement of the health sector'. Three years later, it is time to review their performance and to reward those countries which have adhered to the Abuja Declaration and to move to suspend aid to those which have not (excepting those where extenuating factors, such as natural disaster, are to blame). The same should be done for countries such as Uganda which, instead of making health sector aid additional to domestic resources, actually deduct it from the health ministry's core budget (Wendow, 2004, p. 222). Countries which have remained on a consistent upward trajectory for domestic health budgets relative to the overall budget should be rewarded with additional foreign aid, at the expense of countries which have not done this.

The WHO, which has not audited compliance with the Abuja Declaration's 15 per cent pledge, must do so now, and it should clearly come out on the side of countries which are taking their investment in health seriously. As the figures

[11] 'European Community Support to HIV/AIDS activities in the context of Development, Health, HIV/AIDS and Population Policies' (2002), unpublished mimeo on file with the editors of this book.

pertinent to compliance are not available, we present a proxy for them: Table 9.1 illustrates the percentage of total national income (GDP) spent on the public-sector health system (from 1990 to 2000). Looking at 2000, the closest date to the 2001 Abuja Declaration available, one sees that some developing countries are strongly pro-health while others are indifferent. India, which possesses a costly nuclear weapons programme, spends under 0.9 per cent of its GDP on health, compared with 3.6 per cent and 2.6 per cent for Malawi and Senegal respectively – and Malawi is poorer by any measure. The lesson from this is clear: given that in human rights terms an Indian's life is worth exactly the

Table 9.1: Public health expenditure (% of GDP)

Country	1990	1991	1992	1993	1994	1995	1996	1997	1998	1999	2000
Brazil	3.01	1.87	1.61	3.04	3.42	3.07	2.99	3.26	3.30	3.38	3.39
Burundi	1.13	1.20	1.17	1.32	1.25	1.68	1.70	1.29	1.47	1.37	1.65
Cameroon	0.88	0.92	0.90	0.77	0.70	0.85	0.84	0.86	0.92	1.02	1.06
Congo, Dem. Rep.	–	–	–	–	–	1.16	1.19	1.19	1.26	1.18	1.11
Côte d'Ivoire	1.47	1.47	1.80	1.54	1.45	1.27	1.19	1.15	1.13	0.94	1.00
Ethiopia	0.88	0.71	0.92	0.97	1.23	1.42	1.49	1.67	2.10	1.83	1.81
Gabon	2.01	2.20	2.10	2.10	2.10	2.05	1.99	1.93	2.03	2.02	2.06
Ghana	1.34	1.18	1.41	1.46	1.53	1.82	1.80	1.75	2.11	2.18	2.25
Guinea-Bissau	1.10	1.17	0.75	1.07	1.12	2.24	2.75	2.50	2.60	2.57	2.55
India	0.90	0.87	0.85	0.87	0.83	0.81	0.81	0.83	0.92	0.91	0.87
Malawi	–	1.46	–	1.66	5.00	3.01	2.94	3.69	3.42	3.44	3.63
Mexico	1.79	2.21	2.59	2.53	2.63	2.32	2.25	2.29	2.54	2.55	2.51
Senegal	0.66	2.50	2.50	2.42	2.46	2.49	2.61	2.62	2.63	2.64	2.60
Uganda	–	–	–	2.31	1.76	1.38	1.47	1.54	1.41	1.68	1.48
Sub-Saharan Africa	2.18	–	–	2.34	2.45	2.89	2.85	2.82	2.61	2.59	2.53
Low income	1.10	1.23	1.16	1.13	1.08	1.05	1.05	1.05	1.18	1.12	1.07
Lower middle income	2.34	2.11	2.10	2.61	2.99	2.79	2.82	2.88	2.80	2.71	2.74
Middle income	2.45	2.46	2.54	2.89	3.19	3.04	3.03	3.04	3.07	3.04	3.02
Upper middle income	2.90	3.34	3.47	3.55	3.63	3.65	3.53	3.42	3.65	3.65	3.52
United States	4.71	5.19	5.50	5.71	5.90	6.02	6.01	5.88	5.74	5.76	5.76

Source: World Bank, *World Development Indicators On Line*, January 2004.

same as a Malawian's life, any aid dollar spent on public health in India (or a similarly indifferent country) accounts for a greater share of spending but contributes less to comprehensive health system development than in a more strongly pro-health country. It is thus indefensible.

Reallocating health-sector aid in this way is both rational and just: it allocates scarce resources to those countries that have demonstrated their sincerity in prioritizing health needs. Also, it sends a clear signal to the laggards that their indifference has been noticed and admits the reality that the international community cannot (except in short-lived crises) save lives that governments themselves do not appear to care about. Other measures, some of which are being tested in the United States' innovative Millennium Challenge Account, will have merit too in separating deserving from undeserving countries; and in ten years or so it will be time to evaluate what impact this scheme has had (Radelet, 2003). In short, more aid money is indeed needed, but so is greater intellectual application to achieving the objective of betting on the winning horses instead of throwing money down rat holes.

THE FUTURE: RESEARCH AND DEVELOPMENT

In all the contention about access to medicines, one fact is agreed by all: there is too little research and development done to create pharmaceuticals for the diseases of the poorest. The difficulty of the research and/or the lack of a profitable (or even non-loss) market for these treatments remains the reason why private-sector investment is, by universal acknowledgment, small (Kremer, 2002).

There are essentially two types of disease relevant to this analysis. Type 1, HIV/AIDS, tuberculosis, hypertension, cancer, etc., is found in all countries regardless of income; Type 2, malaria, schistosomiasis, leishmaniasis, etc., is generally found in the poorest countries. The market in rich and middle-income countries is normally sufficient to drive commercial R&D on the Type 1 diseases, but it never provides a satisfactory incentive for the R&D on Type 2 diseases. Most investment in the latter has been made by the public sector, but even this is negligible: '0.8 per cent of the 1999 US National Institutes of Health Budget', it is said, 'went to tropical diseases' (Lanjouw, 2001, p. 27). Unless there were to be a malaria epidemic in the OECD countries, the stinginess of public R&D spending on Type 2 diseases is probably here to stay, and so it becomes important to ask how one might more seriously encourage the private sector to invest in this kind of R&D.

Various ways to achieve this have been proposed. They run the gamut from the reasonable to the naive. Our purpose here is to identify them briefly and to propose those which ought to be taken up.

Probably the worst idea is to negotiate an international treaty for research and development of neglected diseases.[12] The reasons why this idea would never get off the ground are numerous – treaties are slow to negotiate, they codify the lowest common denominator and they often fail to be ratified – but, above all, *international treaties are not legally enforceable*. Few treaties can be truly enforced against governments (the WTO treaties are an exception); and leaving aside the few treaties which deal with horrible things such as crimes against humanity, there are no treaties which can be enforced against private persons or companies. Therefore, anyone enthusiastic for an R&D treaty to coerce the large pharmaceutical companies into researching cures for malaria or other Type 2 diseases is quite mistaken. The very attempt will sour the public discourse as it strives to impose something mandatory, and in the end nothing mandatory will be achieved anyway. Before the public health movement goes down this blind alley, it should take a cautionary look at the experience of the environmental movement: the latter was involved in the negotiating of half a dozen major treaties in the 1980s and 1990s; and not one of them has ever been enforced against a company, because they were never intended to be.

Carrots are needed rather than sticks. There is abundant agreement that public–private partnerships can successfully tackle otherwise uneconomical R&D problems for Type 2 diseases. The Initiative on Public–Private Partnerships for Health catalogues dozens of such PPPs (see www.ippph.org). There is one for nearly every Type 2 disease, and, unsurprisingly, almost all of them are underfunded. Perhaps the problem is as simple as getting the rich countries to finance the PPPs that already exist.

Doing this will require creativity. Although theoretically it is possible to subsidize the pharmaceutical industry to do R&D on Type 2 diseases, this would entail moral hazard (i.e. an incentive to propose projects with a slender chance of success just to reap the subsidy) and it would be even more politically unpalatable than increasing public sector R&D spending, which so far has been impossible (see Kremer, 2002, pp. 82–6). A better approach would be to use tax deductions, linking them in some way to success in developing a successful product for Type 2 diseases. Incentives such as tax deductions are usually easier to legislate than appropriations, in particular because parliamentary procedure for tax laws may be less stringent than for spending laws. There is also the precedent of using tax incentives to augment research on 'orphan diseases' in the USA (Haffner et al., 2003). A similar sort of legislation, created specifically with the Type 2 diseases in mind, is needed now, principally in the United States, where the major innovative and generic pharmaceutical companies have tax liabilities and can be brought under the government's jurisdiction. The proposal

---

[12] See Trouiller, Torreele et al. (2001, p. 949) for a positive view on the treaty. Love (2003), from the Consumer Project on Technology, has proposed such a treaty.

to give the private sector tax deductions may smack of corporate welfare to some, and perhaps it is. But to oppose it for that reason would be to consign the needs of poor patients to oblivion because the alternative of increasing public sector R&D appropriations for Type 2 diseases has been tried steadily for years, has failed and is demonstrably forlorn. From the government's perspective, tax incentives and appropriations are just two sides of the same coin, and it makes sense to use both.

Of course, there is no reason why tax measures should be used only as incentives for R&D on Type 2 diseases. If the political will exists, they could be designed with a second purpose in mind – as incentives for greater collaboration between laboratories and scientists in the North and the South. The two goals can be concurrent, and in view of the broader considerations about how development is achieved, perhaps they should be. If one assumes that 'development' as a concept equals one part of human development (health and education), plus another part of economic development (endogenous growth largely fuelled by technological advancement), then a policy of offering tax incentives for R&D on Type 2 diseases conducted in cooperation with developing countries has much appeal. Even better, it may be politically saleable.

Nobody doubts that increasing research collaboration between the North and the South would be a good thing for the South, which would benefit from technological spillovers from the sharing of ideas and skills. Universities and national research councils do collaborate across borders, but none have encouraged the formation of groups of sufficient size and interdisciplinarity to constitute an entire functional R&D team. But transnational companies do this all the time, and, increasingly, Northern pharmaceutical companies are entering into collaborative agreements with pharmaceutical firms in the South. GlaxoSmithKline's link-up with Ranbaxy is an example (see Ranbaxy, 2003). Technology industries in developing countries are also frequently ardent lobbyists for education – they need to be, as skilled labour is in short supply – and ultimately their intervention strengthens governments' respect for home-grown academia. Far from being anti-competitive, giving a tax incentive to this sort of North–South technological collaboration inevitably spreads information and know-how, which leads to more inventiveness in the South. This can eventually lead to greater competition, if inventiveness is matched with capital, and that too is more likely as Northern companies gain confidence in working with Southern ones and re-evaluate their objections to foreign direct investment (FDI). All these advantages can result even if an R&D project for a Type 2 disease is a total failure, as most R&D projects are; and there is the comfort that at least the money was not totally wasted since it built know-how in the South.

This scenario presents a very attractive picture, but research is needed in order to better understand its possible downsides. For example, if we assume (as is probably true) that OECD pharmaceutical companies will invest little in India's pharmaceutical sector unless India imposes and defends patent law fully, is the utility loss to India from paying foreign patentees greater or less than the utility gain from spillovers such as FDI, advocacy for education and technological transfer? At the moment, the evidence to hand about this question is so poor that it remains unanswered. The evidence that FDI generates positive spillovers for host economies is mixed, and thus subsidies to FDI or any preferential treatment of FDI relative to domestic investment are not consistently warranted (Hanson, 2001, p. 23). In addition, there is, according to Nicholson, no evidence that stronger intellectual property rights will lead to increased productivity in the host country (Nicholson, 2002, p. 20). If the most pessimistic view of these studies is the accurate one, then our enthusiasm for technological spillovers and using tax incentives to foster North–South R&D collaboration is definitely not justified as policy. But there simply is not enough evidence to be sure of that. The need for greater economic research on these questions is as urgent as the scenario we present is tantalizing.

CONCLUSION

We have seen in this book that the issue of improving the delivery of essential medicines and producing good health is part of the more general agenda of development policy. The focus on both health and wealth calls for greater coherence in development policy. This in turn means reviewing development policy both at the bilateral and the multilateral levels. Far more money should be spent on delivering medicines to the poor, but it should also be better directed to the most deserving countries. In many countries of the South, governments themselves must spend more on health and education, as a litmus test of whether they deserve much larger sums as aid from the North. A very imaginative, ambitious and fresh look at how to foster R&D on neglected diseases is overdue. It would create alternatives to approaches that have not succeeded in a very long time and to proposals that do not deserve to succeed. This is enough to keep a good many of our colleagues and readers of this book busy for a long time.

REFERENCES

Acharya, R. (1999), 'Bio-pharmaceuticals in China, Taipei and India', in L. K. Mytelka (ed.), *Competition, Innovation and Competitiveness in Developing Countries* (Paris: OECD) 77–114.

Anand, S. and K. Hanson (1997), 'Disability-adjusted life years: a critical review', *Journal of Health Economics,* 16: 685–702.

Arnesan, T. and E. Nord (1999), 'The value of DALY life: problem with ethics and validity of disability adjusted life years', *British Medical Journal,* 319: 1423–5.

Attaran, A. (2003a), 'A Quantitative Analysis of Patents and Access to Essential Medicines in Developing Countries', *The 2nd IAS Conference on HIV/AIDS Pathogenesis and Treatment* (Paris: International AIDS Socieyy), 13–16 July.

Attaran, A. (2003b), 'Assessing and answering paragraph 6 of the Doha Declaration on the TRIPs Agreement and public health: the case for greater flexibility and a non-justiciability solution', *Emory International Law Review*, 17: 743–80.

Attaran, A. and L. Gillespie-White (2001), 'Do patents for anti-retroviral drugs constrain access to HIV/AIDS treatment in Africa?', *Journal of the American Medical Association*, 286(15): 1886–92.

Bermudez, J. (2002), 'Expanding Access to Essential Medicines in Brazil: Recent Economic Regulation, Policy-Making and Lessons Learnt', in B. Granville (ed.), *The Economics of Essential Medicines* (London: Royal Institute of International Affairs).

Bloland P., M. Ettling and S. Meek (2000) 'Combination therapy for malaria in Africa: hype or hope?', *Bulletin of the World Health Organization*, 78: 1378–88.

Brundtland, G.H. (2002), 'Essential medicines: 25 years of better health', *Journal of the American Medical Association*, 288(24): 3102.

Collier, P. and D. Dollar (2000), *Aid Allocation and Poverty Reduction* (Washington, DC: World Bank).

Commission on Intellectual Property Rights (2002), *Integrating Intellectual Property Rights and Development Policy* (London: Commission on Intellectual Property Rights).

Competition Commission (2003), 'Competition Commission concludes an agreement with pharmaceutical firm', *Media Release*, no. 33, 10 December.

Cullet, P. (2003) 'Patents and medicines: the relationship between TRIPs and the human right to health', *International Affairs*, 79(1): 139–60.

Deaton, A. (2002a), *Health, Inequality and Economic Development* (Princeton, NJ: Center for Health and Wellbeing and Research Program in Development Studies, Princeton University).

Deaton, A. (2002b), 'Policy implications of the gradient of health and wealth', *Health Affairs*, 21(2): 13–30.

Donnelly, John (2003), 'HIV fight comes up short in Nigeria', *Boston Globe*, 1 December.

Easterly, W. (2001), *The Elusive Quest for Growth. Economists' Adventures and Misadventures in the Tropics* (Cambridge, MA/ London: MIT Press).

Elo, I. and S. H. Preston (1996), 'Educational differentials in mortality: United States, 1979–1985', *Social Science and Medicine*, January: 47–57.

Fogel, R. W. (1997), 'New Findings on Secular Trends in Nutrition and Mortality: Some Implications for Population Theory', in M. Rosenzweig and O. Stark (eds), *Handbook of Population and Family Economics* (Amsterdam: Elsevier).

Freedberg, K. and Y. Yazdanpanah (2003), 'Cost-effectiveness of HIV/AIDS Therapies in Resource-poor Countries', in J.-P. Moatti, B. Coriat, Y. Souteyrand, T. Barnett, J. Dumoulin and Y.-A. Flori (eds), *Economics of HIV/AIDS and Access to HIV/AIDS Care in Developing Countries. Issues and Challenges*, (Paris: Agence Nationale de Recherche sur le SIDA, pp. 267–92.

Friedman, M.A., H. den Besten and A. Attaran (2003), 'Out-licensing: a practical approach for improvement of access to medicines in poor countries', *The Lancet*, 361: 341–44.

Galambos, L. and J. L. Sturchio (1997), 'The Transformation of the Pharmaceutical Industry in the Twentieth Century', in J. Krige and D. Pestre (eds), *Science in the Twentieth Century*, (Paris: Harwood Academic Publishers), pp. 227–52.

Government of the UK (2001), *Tackling the Diseases of Poverty: Meeting the Okinawa Millenium Targets for HIV/AIDS, Tuberculosis amd Malaria* (London: Cabinet Office, Performance and Innovation Unit).

Grabowski, H. (2002), 'Patents, innovation and access to new pharmaceuticals', *Journal of International Economic Law*, 5(4): 849–60.

Granville, B. (ed.) (2002), *The Economics of Essential Medicines* (London: Royal Institute of